D1546229

New Patterns of Power and Profit

Eric K. Clemons

New Patterns of Power and Profit

A Strategist's Guide to Competitive Advantage in the Age of Digital Transformation

Eric K. Clemons
University of Pennsylvania
Philadelphia, PA, USA

ISBN 978-3-030-00442-2   ISBN 978-3-030-00443-9   (eBook)
https://doi.org/10.1007/978-3-030-00443-9

Library of Congress Control Number: 2018954967

Cover credit: © Hiroshi Watanabe/Digital Vision/Getty Images
Cover design by Fatima Jamadar

This Palgrave Macmillan imprint is published by the registered company Springer Nature Switzerland AG
The registered company address is: Gewerbestrasse 11, 6330 Cham, Switzerland

Preface

This is About How You Can Understand the New Rules of the Information Age

This book could not have been written five years ago. Too many of the patterns that are emerging now, like the full economic power of Google, the value of platforms like Uber and Airbnb, or the risks to our personal privacy from social networks, were not yet fully clear. It was not yet clear that privacy violations could be used to determine the prices we are each charged, or for outright manipulation of our elections. The possible use of a platform like Android for unfair and even illegal competition had not yet been debated in the courts.

Additionally, this book could not have been written without the unique access to corporate and military leaders that I enjoyed as a result of my position as a senior faculty member at the Wharton School. For the past 40 years, I have served as a *consulting paranoid*, helping executives, politicians, and entrepreneurs avoid dangers and seize opportunities in a world of unfamiliar information-based strategy, and this book is based on this access and this experience.

This book is a guide to functioning, even prospering, in the twenty-first century. It's about understanding the future of shopping, manufacturing, social networks, employment, or investment. It's about seeing the future of almost any aspect of modern life that is being altered by information. That is, it's about the future of *everything*.

This book is almost about *clairvoyance*. It's about seeing things first, and sometimes knowing things before others think it is possible to know them. It's about using new patterns and mental maps to show you what you *will* want, rather than using old patterns and mental maps to guide you where you *previously wanted* to go. To do that we need to explore new patterns, with the necessary predictive power, and we need to understand how to use them.

This book is for everyone who wants to understand our information age. This book is written for CEOs and entrepreneurs considering online start-ups, since both will need to understand how information changes competition and their prospects for commercial success. It's for undergraduates and MBAs still trying to pick a career, because they will need to understand the future economy and need to anticipate what jobs will be in demand and which will be personally and professionally rewarding. It's for regulators, lobbyists, lawmakers, and voters, trying to figure out what it means to be fair to everyone, when privacy, political power, and profitability are changed by information. Fairness to citizen taxpayers, individuals paying for health care, and giant corporations everywhere, will be changed. The old implicit social contract that holds society together is coming undone, everywhere.

So, this book is for anyone willing to take the time to understand how information changes consumer behavior, corporate strategy, competition, and law. It's for everyone who knows that he or she is going to have to participate in a workplace transformed by information. It's for everyone who knows that he or she needs to understand changes in education, shopping, and life itself, and wants to know how to plan, to participate, and even to lead the transformations that are going to continue for decades to come.

You don't need to be an economics professor to read this book, or a computer scientist.

To complete the book I had to get past two different sources of skepticism, prevalent in two different populations. First, it's easy to assume that if you understand how to use an iPad to do everything you want online, then you understand the net and its impact on business and society. Many readers, especially young readers, can use an iPad to translate Chinese street signs, and to order dinner online in Singapore or Toronto, or to hail an Uber, send a text, or make a free Internet phone call. That does not ensure that they understand the *digital transformation of everything*.

My students consider themselves *digital natives* because they know how to use the net, would rather text than use e-mail, and carry smartphones instead of cameras. Initially, trying to talk to my students about *information* was like trying to talk to a fish about *water*. They couldn't imagine a world without search, without smartphones, or without a net to connect everything and everyone. Which means that they could not understand the transformations that these devices were producing and would continue to produce, because they couldn't imagine things having been done differently in the past, or things being done differently in the future. They couldn't see or anticipate the change, any more than those of us who grew up with automobiles and central heating could imagine that they were new, represented change, and could affect the climate of the planet. This book is about information, and about seeing the impacts of information, in ways that using search, owning an iPad, and surfing the net do not make fully clear.

Paradoxically, there was a second group of readers that assumed that full understanding was impossible to present in a book for masses of readers with normal interests, no matter how intelligent they were. If the book wasn't going to be intensely technical, then they believed it was going to be superficial. This group of readers expected lots of buzzy stuff, like *employment after the AI Singularity* and *immortality through a digital representation of our essential souls*. But there is so much to explain about the companies around us. *Why* did Facebook win and *why* did MySpace lose? Capital One was certainly a winner, leaping from new entrant to a position as a top-5 credit card issuer. But why did they succeed in entering a market in which they faced dozens of existing competitors? New retailers of traditional products sometimes win, sure; think about Amazon. And sometimes new retailers fail; think about Pets.com.

This book presents tested theories that explain a lot. You don't need an economics degree or a computer science degree to read this book. If you have studied both economics and computer science this book won't annoy you, talk down to you, or introduce errors through oversimplification. It just won't use your professional jargon much, and won't ever use jargon without explanation.

Additionally, there is some really cool stuff that I left out. Will people become immortal and be able to load their true essence into the cloud? Will people become redundant after the Singularity, when computers represent greater intelligence than any single human mind, or, worse yet, more intelligence than the entire human species? Will our life become paradise, as depicted in the New York World's Fair view of the future, as seen from 1964, with almost everything automated and almost everything done for us? Will we be both immortal *and* redundant, as described by Arthur C. Clarke in *The City and The Stars* in 1956? Those are great questions, and they have been handled better than I could, by people who write science fiction and speculative science better than I can.

The Role of Experience and Simplifying Experience into Patterns

It's Easier to Understand Something If You've Already Seen It Before!

The modern world is a risky place, with unknown alternatives facing all of us, every day. But these alternatives are not *unknowable!* For different clients, at different times, my team has included anthropologists and marriage counselors, historians and negotiators, computer scientists, and even poets and historians.

- As consultants to the travel industry, we examined the impact of an act of terrorism involving using a commercial aircraft as a suicide weapon, years before 9/11.
- As consultants to 3-Star and 4-Star admirals, we studied the evolution of social networks and their impacts for regime change in the Islamic World, long before they had emerged as a problem for US diplomacy or for the US military.
- As consultants to a major consumer packaged goods company, we discussed the implications of eCommerce. We focused on the increased power of online retailers, relative to manufacturers. We concluded that manufacturers would be unable to compete with these online retailers, and that manufacturers would be unable to sell their own low margin consumer goods directly to consumers. Producers of goods like canned foods, paper products, or soft drinks would have to avoid offending their critical retailers.
- In contrast, when working with companies in the travel industry we concluded that airlines would quickly be able to bypass traditional agencies. Traditional agencies would quickly lose importance, and airline ticket sales would quickly move online.

Each experience led to a strategic insight. More importantly, each experience led to a *reusable insight*, since each resulted in the team's understanding a pattern that could be used to develop strategy quickly and systematically in similar settings.

We all need strategies, and to formulate strategies we need accurate mental maps, or models, of the emerging world. These mental maps enable us to make decisions and plan our actions. The ocean of information has changed our world. And our new world requires new mental models and new mental maps to guide us.

Survival in a complex and competitive environment has always required the right models of the world. These are templates, based on observation of patterns that occur frequently. The earliest humans developed patterns that were strikingly simple:

1. *It's best to eat ripe sweet fruit.* You need to know where the fruit ripens first or something else will eat it before you do.
2. *If an animal is slow, or dead, it is safe to approach and see if it is food.* If an animal is big and fast, it is best to leave it alone, or even run away from it. It is not food. It may even think you are food.

The early humans who observed these patterns ate and did not get eaten. Of course, the invention of language, society, and simple tools changed the world and changed its patterns. These changes resulted in the need for new patterns, which replaced the previous, simpler ones.

1. *Agriculture lets us grow the fruit we want.* We can have a sequence of ripe fruits and vegetables, each in their season.
2. *Anything we want is food.* Organized hunting lets us hunt even the largest animals, like the woolly mammoth and American buffalo, as food. And we are no longer food ourselves!

The bands of humans that mastered these new patterns prospered and dominated their environment and their neighbors.

But technology is changing the patterns we need to recognize. Indeed, technology has *always* changed the patterns of life. The most powerful men in Tombstone or Abilene in the 1870s looked very different from their counterparts half a century earlier. The fastest gun and the richest banker might not have been very impressive physically, but every survivor in Tombstone and Abilene knew when to bow, when to apologize, when to step aside, and when to leave the saloon.

This book presents the six new patterns that we need to know, whether we are voters or the candidates who want their votes, investors or entrepreneurs who need their funds, brewers or their customers, retailers or consumer packaged goods producers. As importantly, we don't just need to know these patterns, we need to know how to use them to gain control of our information-based world. This book presents my three rules for seeing, selecting, and using the appropriate pattern for every situation you need to master. Surprisingly, there are indeed only six new patterns to learn, and only three rules you need to master them.

My First Rule—Learn to See the Patterns

Seeing Clearly Enables Recognition and Response

Information changes everything, from the behavior of your customers to the actions of your competitors, from the behavior of your voters to the behavior of competing candidates, and from the power of dominant brands to the power of high-price high-margin new products. Perhaps most importantly, it changes the balance between previously dominant organizations and nimble new competitors, in everything from brewing, to banking, to political parties.

Everything looks new, altered, and apparently unfamiliar. Your response requires three steps to make the world look familiar again. These three steps are easy to understand, easy to learn, and easy to apply. These three steps enable you to master the patterns of information-based strategy and the patterns of power that were created by changes in information-based strategy.

Reframe: I start by acknowledging that there are problems I cannot solve as they are initially presented to me, and by acknowledging that I can often *transform* the problem into a similar problem that I can solve. You can do this too. Start by *reframing* the problem you face in different ways, until it becomes something you know you can work with. If you don't understand the problem you are trying to solve and you can't answer the questions you are trying to answer, change them. Problems in digital strategy often appear new and unfamiliar, but they are seldom unique or unprecedented. Google's business model was used by United Airlines and American Airlines in the 1980s to control other airlines' access to customers. Controlling access, and charging for access, was a profitable business model even two decades ago; until regulators intervened, controlling other airlines' access to passengers was more profitable than operating an airline. Uber's business model, targeting the most profitable customers of existing taxi companies, is not so different from the business model of Capital One, which was based on targeting the most profitable customers of existing banks and credit card issuers. Rather than trying to look at Uber as a company that provides rides to people in a hurry, try thinking of Uber as a company that serves the most profitable customers of an entire existing industry. Reframing takes a problem you've never seen before and turns it into something you recognize, which allows you to reframe your critical strategic questions in a form you can now answer. When you do, the information-based world no longer seems so mysterious.

Recognize: Once I realize that I need to reframe a problem, I try different patterns and different ways of looking at the problem, until I find one that I recognize, and that enables me to solve the original problem I was given. For example, Uber's business model and Google's business model both initially appear novel, even unique, but I was able to recognize both of them as business models that are actually decades old. Once you recognize that the problem you are facing has been solved before, it is much easier to move forward. When you have the right transformations you will recognize the problem and you will have your *"aha moment."* That's when you say, *"Oh, yeah! Now I get it."* You see the *new patterns of power and profit in an information age.* This is so critical to the solution of digital problems that it was the original working title of this book.

Respond: Once you reframe your problem and recognize the underlying pattern, you can respond to the situation you need to master. Now you know what to do. Responding is the easy part.

- Maybe you need to reclaim control over your distribution channel. Are the customers loyal to you or to your distributors? Can you safely attempt to reach out to your customers, move them online, and get them to adopt you fast enough to avoid punishment? Or will slow transition to online channels allow your current retailers to punish you while you still need them?
- Maybe you need a strategy for defending your own most profitable customers. Has someone found a way to locate your best customers and make them an offer that is better than what you are offering them now? Can you match the offer? Can you provide a better offer? Can you counter-attack and offer something to the attacker's customers?
- Maybe you need to reduce the variation in service quality so that you can eliminate bad reviews that are killing you online. You can't control what people write, but you can control what they want to write. Properly managing service experiences ensures that your customers never want to write anything that would damage your image online or damage future customers' perception of you.
- Maybe you want to win a national primary campaign without the backing of a major political party. *Word of Mouth* and persuasive oratory have been effective since the time of the Greeks and the Romans, but they were voting over small geographic regions. Does that scale up? Maybe you don't need ads or a large grassroots political organization to win the primaries; maybe you can reach out through social media, or by winning coverage from traditional mainstream media. Nobody wins a primary election by appealing to the massive number of moderates, who usually do not vote in primaries or participate in caucuses; you win a primary by appealing to the

most passionate voters, just like you sell a $15 bottle of beer by appealing to the most passionate consumers. 2016 marked the election of the first word of mouth candidate in American history, the first candidate without a ground game or the backing of his party organization. Is this a permanent change? Are we going to see the evolution of political campaigns that look more and more like using Word of Mouth to sell craft beer, and less and less like using traditional advertising to sell industrial lager?

- Maybe you need to vote in a referendum about the sharing economy and the implications of Airbnb or Uber for your community. What is best for you, your neighbors, and your community? What is fair to everyone?
- Maybe you need to tell your kid whether or not it is safe to use a particular social networking tool, or maybe you need to decide for yourself whether or not it is safe to click on a link in an e-mail that truly is from a trusted sender.

Once you recognize the problem as something that has been faced before and solved before you will know what to do. You need to evaluate your options, perhaps dealing with significant levels of uncertainty. You need to make your decisions, and if you are part of a large organization you need to build consensus, evaluate costs and plan the necessary investments, and allocate responsibility for each of the changes that need to be implemented. Still, your way forward is now something you understand.

We review how to reframe and recognize problems in Chapter 3.

Using an Information-Based Pattern to Solve a Problem in Information-Based Strategy

From *What's in Your Wallet* to *Who's in Your Taxi*

An example will help explain how to use an information-based pattern to solve a problem in information-based strategy. Imagine you're looking at Uber for the first time, and trying to understand the company. Uber allows those of us who need transportation right now to get it *right now*, even during rush hour or in the middle of a torrential thunderstorm or in the middle of blizzard. It's faster than waiting for a taxi. It's much cheaper than arranging a limo and driver. And it allows us to get a car right now, even if we did not anticipate the need earlier. It's a great way to deal with meetings that end at an unexpected time, or that end during unanticipated and really nasty weather.

Suppose you're looking at Uber as an investor, or as the owner of a center city taxi fleet. Can Uber succeed? Should you invest? Should you worry about the survival of your own taxi business?

How should we examine this problem? Is Uber a just a new entrant into a crowded market? Is it just another new competitor for taxis, or for limo services, or for car rental agencies? Is it just another competitor for spot market providers of cars like Zipcar but with drivers? If Uber is a competitor for some or all of them, how does this help us predict their success? If it is something entirely different, and if it is something different from any other transportation company, can we predict their success at all? What can we find that looks similar to the launch of Uber?

Surprisingly, Uber's business model is a common pattern in information-based strategy. It is the entry of a small new competitor into an established market that for one or more reasons has become newly vulnerable to attack by outsiders. Perhaps the best-known example is the successful, even triumphant, launch of Capital One's credit card, decades ago. Uber doesn't look like a bank! But then Capital One never thought of itself as a bank, any more than Uber thinks of itself as a taxi company. Both are companies with an information-based strategy, and both attacked a newly vulnerable market.

Let's look at Capital One first. Every creditworthy American household already had two or three credit cards when Capital One entered the market. Citibank was blanketing the country with ads for their own Visa and MasterCard offerings. AT&T Universal Bank was competing as well, offering cards with lower interest rates on finance charges, and without an annual fee. Why did America need another credit card issuer? And what can the launch of yet another credit card issuer tell us about the future of a transportation services company?

Using the story of a non-traditional credit card company to explain the success of a non-traditional ride service company initially seems unintuitive. Learning to reframe a problem means learning to find the right information-based pattern, even if it is not in the most obvious industry. Every airline's standard safety announcement before takeoff includes reminding you that the closest available emergency exit may not be the one in front of you. Similarly, the closest available pattern may not be the one in your industry.

My Second Rule: Once You have a Pattern, Use It!

Understanding Capital One, and Using That to Understand Uber

Capital One's history truly is the closest available pattern for predicting the future of Uber and its portfolio of businesses. The launch of Capital One's credit card was targeted at consumers who did not and indeed could not pay off their monthly credit card balances. The launch of Uber Black was targeted at consumers who wanted a ride *now* and almost did not care what the ride cost. What could the two launches possibly have in common?

All examples of newly vulnerable markets have the same three things in common.

First, these markets were both ***newly easy to enter***. Changes in consumer behavior and in financial instruments opened the way for Capital One to enter the credit card market. Consumers were starting to understand that they could get their credit cards from any issuer. Likewise, the nearly universal adoption of smartphones made it newly possible for consumers to reserve a car, track its location as it came to pick them up, and pay for their ride effortlessly; this made the market for on-demand car services newly easy to enter. Neither Capital One nor Uber would have succeeded if their markets had not been newly easy to enter.

These markets were also both ***attractive to attack***. They were characterized by extreme differences in customer profitability for their service providers. Capital One targeted only customers of existing banks who paid slowly, incurring finance charges and generating profits.

Similarly, Uber does not target all taxi customers. Uber targets the most profitable segment. Sometimes, profitable customers are those who need a taxi *now* and who are willing to pay more than standard taxi prices to get one immediately, when taxis are not available. Sometimes, profitable customers are those who are not in a hurry, are willing to share a car, and allow the driver to earn more than 100% of the fare associated with the distance of the rides. Uber targets customers who request a car online, and do not require drivers to cruise around looking for or waiting for fares. These customers are the basis of Uber's success, just as customers who pay finance charges every month are for Capital One.

Finally, these markets were both also ***difficult to defend***. Attackers enter newly vulnerable markets because their competitors' simplistic pricing strategies created opportunities, and they wanted to profit, not to teach their competitors more effective pricing. For an attack on a newly vulnerable market to succeed there must be some reason why competitors cannot respond simply by duplicating the attacker's strategy and eliminating the attacker's business opportunity.

For a variety of reasons, Citibank and AT&T Universal were not able to fire their existing customers and replicate Capital One's strategy.

Likewise, taxi companies cannot easily replicate or counter Uber's strategy. Uber is not a taxi company and is not regulated by taxi commissions or public utility commissions. As a result, Uber can raise their rates through surge pricing to serve the most profitable segment of the taxi market, while taxi companies cannot. Indeed, all that taxi companies could do was continue to pick up the customers they were able to serve, while losing large numbers of extremely profitable customers during periods of peak demand.

We describe factors that inhibit firms under attack in detail in Chapter 3. These factors make markets difficult to defend.

History Is the Source of Our Patterns

We Use History as a Source of Competitive Advantage

We care about history only because it gives us the ability to predict future outcomes. Patterns of behavior occur over and over. When we see a pattern we recognize in an otherwise unfamiliar setting, we have a very good idea of what will happen next. When the conditions for a pattern are absent, the pattern is unlikely to recur. While Uber remains attractive to its consumers, similar services for the delivery of food and laundry are progressing much more slowly. Let's see why.

Are these markets newly easy to enter? Not really. Most big city laundries already will pick up and deliver without charge, at least from large apartment buildings. Most big cities already have delivery services for takeout restaurant food. The same smartphone technology used by Uber could be used to launch a surge pricing system for food delivery or laundry services, which might be attractive to customers if they could ensure significantly faster service. But could Uber Laundry or Uber Eats use new technology to ensure faster delivery than existing competitors? If not, then the market is not newly easy to enter, even if it might initially appear to be. If food is prepared in response to each customer's order then preparation time will remain significant, as will drive time needed to deliver the product from the restaurant to the customer. If my suit is going to be cleaned and pressed, this will also take a significant amount of time, plus the time to pick the suit up from me and to deliver it back when cleaned. Uber's car services work as fast as they do because there are usually cars available only three to ten minutes away from me, even before I request a car. Uber Eats can't pre-position vehicles with my food ready to deliver, before I order it. Moreover, since I actually want my own suit returned, rather than one like it that has been cleaned in advance and pre-positioned for delivery, Uber really can't get me my laundry any faster than anyone else.

Are these markets attractive to attack? Is there a huge difference in customers' willingness to pay for food delivery or for laundry delivery, as there was in willingness to pay for taxi service? This is unlikely.

Are these markets difficult to defend? Is there any reason why existing delivery services, from Grub Hub to Caviar, would be unable to respond to new services introduced by Uber Eats or Uber Laundry?

Almost instant expedited delivery services are not yet available because they are not really attacks on newly vulnerable markets. The problem is not that existing courier services have not figured out how to provide something that would be effortless for Uber to add to their existing platform; the problem is that there is no easy way to create these new markets. That doesn't mean Uber Eats will fail; it's just not poised to be transformational.

My Third Rule: Learn the Entire Set of New Patterns

We Need to Master More Than One Pattern—But Not Too Many!

We have already established the power of the *newly vulnerable markets* pattern for spotting opportunities. We quickly review five additional new information-based patterns for information-based strategies.

- Likewise, we explore how a related pattern, **newly vulnerable eMarkets**, explains the evolution of online markets for products as different as securities trading, insurance, air travel, and groceries.
- Many markets have been transformed by the power of social media and online word of mouth marketing, frequently called *Word of Mouse*. Information changes consumer behavior. Information reduces consumers' uncertainty about new product offerings. New ways of informing consumers that do not require advertising have led to an explosion of small new brands, each catering to the preferences of small groups of passionate consumers. We call this **Resonance Marketing**, in which new products are introduced that delight small niches of consumers for whom these products are perfect.

- *Platform Envelopment* occurs when the developer of a system thinks of additional capabilities, each of which interacts with prior capabilities, and each of which now becomes more valuable as a result of the interactions. Platform envelopment is the term applied by computer scientists to what engineers call "super-additive value creation," historically also known as the whole being more than the sum of its parts. The Apple ecosystem, including laptops, iPads and iPhones, iTunes, and the App Store together, is worth much more than each of them separately. Microsoft's Windows operating system and Office Suite are more valuable to customers together than each of them would be individually, because of how easily users can move content across Microsoft's applications.
- *Online Gateway Systems* control which businesses have access to customers, and in many cases can use this power to determine which businesses succeed and which fail because they cannot access customers. Gateway system operators have almost unlimited power to set fees for providing access to customers. The gateway's power comes from deciding who can be found and who cannot be found. Sellers are not paying simply *to be found*, which of course is useful to them; sellers are paying *to not be not found*, which can be a matter of survival. Gateway operators also have the ability to integrate into and to take over entire, previously unrelated markets for products and services, as Google is doing around the world.
- There is a new category of online system, which we call *Mandatory Participation Third Party Payer Systems*, or *MP3PPs*. These systems are especially interesting because competition does not cause operators of these systems to lower prices. Indeed, competition can often *increase* prices. Perhaps the best-known example of an MP3PP is Google search and its keyword auctions. Companies can choose to purchase key words in Bing if they wish, but participating in Bing is not a substitute for participating in Google keyword auctions.

These Patterns Have Been Proven Over Time, in Many Industries

Trust Me—But Verify!

These six patterns have occurred over and over, in different locations and in different industries, and as a result they have been useful to planners many, many times. Likewise, the rules of **Reframe, Recognize, Respond** have been proven many very different situations, in many industries.

They have worked in traditional business settings. I have successfully used one of the patterns, newly vulnerable electronic markets, to examine the risks of attempting to bypass traditional account executives and replace them with online trading systems at a prominent investment management firm, and the risks of attempting to replace existing insurance agents with online insurance sales at a major insurance company.

Almost all of the companies I describe in the book are American. That is not because I do not know about Baidu, 360buy, Alibaba, Yihaodian, and Tencent in China, or about Daum and Naver in Korea, or about Softbank in Japan. I have visited most of them and written about all of them. I use mostly American companies because in most cases they were the earliest examples in their industries. They are the best known. I can make a point about platform envelopment as easily using Google as Tencent, but the example will be more effective and will reach more readers if I use companies the readers already understand.

Moreover, these patterns are truly robust and have been as effective in predicting the development of craft brewing in the USA as in China, and as effective in understanding politics in France as in the USA. You can use the *new rules of power and profit* to master the ongoing digital transformation of your world.

The winners and losers will change, but the patterns will continue to be universal.

Philadelphia, USA   Eric K. Clemons

Acknowledgements

I'd like to acknowledge the role that my mentors have played in shaping my own life, both personally and professionally.

Bob Rose, my undergraduate advisor for most of my time at MIT, taught me how to learn. To say he engaged in tough love sounds like a cliché, but it seems to fit. One day, while I was working on my car in his garage, he requested that I stop for a few minutes so that he could remove everything that would be damaged by an explosion. He did not exactly tell me what to do next, but he certainly communicated the need for me to think about what I had planned to do next! He also taught me a great deal about appropriate interactions between faculty and students, as mentor and as friend. He and his wife Martha continued to be my closest advisors and friends over the decades, through changes in academic direction and the vagaries of life in a complex and uncertain world.

Howard Raiffa, Dick Meyer, and Steve Bradley were my colleagues during a gap year between MIT and graduate school. I was without a doubt the most junior researcher at the Harvard Business School, and they welcomed me as a full collaborator, rather than as the naïve kid I knew I was. From them I learned the joys of the fellowship among faculty members, the joys of research and knowing something first, and the joys of teaching and communicating what you have learned. I learned that being a student is interesting, but that being a scholar is a source of endless joy.

Bill Maxwell was my advisor at Cornell University while I was getting my Masters and Ph.D. in Operations Research and Computer Science. Bill taught me about the importance of friendship between faculty and doctoral students. Bill taught me the many roles that an advisor plays and the many responsibilities that an advisor has for the well-being of his students. Bill did everything from making sure I met the deadlines associated with applying for jobs to making sure that I remembered to eat during particularly stressful times. He taught me to garden. He taught me to bake bread. And me made sure that I did not drown, no matter how theatrical my sailing style might have been.

Paul Kleindorfer was my colleague at Wharton. He was the wisest, smartest, kindest man I've been privileged to have as a department chair, which is the closest thing that a professor has to having a boss. He taught me lessons I'm still trying to master, like true strength can be gentle, and true brilliance can be humble. He always knew the right thing to say, from topics in regulatory economics to comparing the operas of Wagner (not his favorite) to Verdi.

My research director for years, Josh Wilson, has read drafts of the book, over and over, checking for clarity, for consistency, for serious errors, and for the most minor of typos. All remaining errors are my responsibility, of course.

My graduate students over the years have been colleagues and friends, not distant subordinates, a behavior I learned from Bob Rose. Michael Row contributed so many ideas over the years that I don't always know what is mine and what is his. Ravi Waran has been out for decades, but he continues to be a useful member of my team. He has been the best copy editor anyone could hope to find, correcting typos and thought-os, and engaging me in endless debates about what we could include if the book were allowed to be 20% longer.

Steve Barnett and Liz Gray taught me different ways of thinking. Steve is a cultural anthropologist and a frequent coauthor, with a completely different way of understanding complexity. Liz Gray is a poet and a negotiator, who truly does bring virtuoso skills to every negotiation.

I dedicated my doctoral dissertation to Jeff Rosenstock, who was my best friend in high school. Jeff was sure he was going to be a better computer scientist than I could ever be. Jeff died before he completed his undergraduate degree. My choice of computer science as a profession was probably motivated in part to continue the work that he never got to complete.

Of course, no acknowledgments would be complete without acknowledging my daughter Julia, who taught me more than anyone else about life.

And a special cryptic shout-out for some very special years, 1966, 1970, 1976, 1981, 1989, and 2012.

Contents

Part III   I Got It! Learning to Work with These Patterns?

List of Figures

Part I

Patterns for Efficiency, Value Creation, and Competitive Advantage

1

Introduction: You Get Control When You Recognize the Patterns

This book is for everyone who wants to understand our information age. This book is written for CEOs, entrepreneurs considering online start-ups, and undergraduates still trying to pick a career. This book is for regulators, lobbyists, lawmakers, and voters who need to make informed decisions about the future direction of our society. This book is for anyone willing to take the time to understand how information changes consumer behavior, corporate strategy, competition, and law. This book is for everyone who knows that he or she is going to have to participate in the digital transformation of work, education, shopping, and life itself and wants to know how to plan, to participate, even to lead the transformation.

We are immersed in a sea of information, provided by cheap and powerful information technology. For the first time in human history, most of us no longer think of information as an asset or a liability, or think of information as a source of power or of weakness. Instead, we think of iPads and smartphones, Google and Apple and Amazon. Mostly, we no longer think about *information* at all, any more than fish think about the water that surrounds them. But information tides, information currents, and information tsunami affect us in our information oceans as profoundly as tides, currents, and tsunami affect the fish in their oceans.

We need to understand our information oceans, not just understand how to operate our devices.

This book describes the *digital transformation of everything*. It describes the new patterns of power in this transformed world and provides a survivor's guide to the information age.

© The Author(s) 2019
E. K. Clemons, *New Patterns of Power and Profit*,
https://doi.org/10.1007/978-3-030-00443-9_1

We're going to start by learning about all of the changes produced by information. These are the individual pieces that, when taken together, create the digital transformation of everything. We're going to see how information changes the behavior of individuals, the strategy of firms, and the structure of organizations. We're going to learn to see new patterns as they start to emerge, before their impact on behavior, strategy, or structure is readily visible. This will not only enable us to understand the changes that have occurred, early, before others see them. It will also enable us to *predict* the changes that are going to occur, even before it is possible to see them. It will give us competitive advantage.

This book is about patterns, developing a set of patterns by observing history, and using those patterns to make predictions. A *pattern* is just a shortcut that we use over and over again for solving problems.

Patterns are essential when trying to understand and solve complex problems. You focus on the elements that occur over and over, that truly matter, and ignore everything else. You look for a set of general principles that apply to large collections of problems like the one you have just tried to solve. The more problems a pattern lets you solve, the more you trust the pattern, the more you value it, and the more you use it. Physicists, engineers, and economists use patterns all the time. The field of business strategy is starting to develop its own patterns.

However, information changes everything in our modern world. Changing business strategy changes everything, from the goods and services available in the market to how and where we shop, what we wear and what we eat, how we learn, and how we vote. This book reviews a set of patterns that have proved their worth in explaining our modern world, in a wide range of industries, over the past decade. For executives, the book is about rapidly recognizing a pattern, rapidly diagnosing a problem, and rapidly finding the best ways to reach a solution. But for all of us, it is intended to be a field guide to understanding and prospering in the information age. Fortunately, there are only six patterns that we need to learn.

As importantly, this book is about how to solve complex problems by turning them into related problems that are easier to understand. This book is about learning to *think* in the information age. It's conversational and informal, because I want you to enjoy it. It was written to sound like my favorite conversations with my students, my clients, and my colleagues.

The book could be shorter, if all I wanted was for you to remember a few critical patterns. But I want more, because you need more. I want you to understand how we *found* the patterns, and how and when to *use* them. I want you to know how to *develop* your own patterns in the future, when none of the existing patterns precisely fit the problem you are trying to solve. And I want you to *trust* this book, and sometimes, for some readers, trust requires *proof*. I want you to remember more than the results. When absolutely necessary, I have provided the supporting mathematics, but always hidden in footnotes and in appendices. Feel free to skip anything that sounds less like learning to surf in the information ocean and more like learning to study the physics of how waves form, travel, and crash ashore.

This chapter introduces the book's first pattern, *Newly Vulnerable Markets*.

> **Newly Vulnerable Markets:** Newly vulnerable markets are markets that appear mature, with all potential customers served, and which appear to be dominated by a set of powerful firms. There appears to be no need for new entrants and little possibility for new entrants to succeed. And yet, newly vulnerable markets are characterized by a combination of factors that shift competitive advantage away from apparently dominant existing companies, and towards new entrants, which places these previously dominant firms at risk. All newly vulnerable markets share the same three elements, which together create an advantage for new entrants: (1) They are *Newly Easy to Enter*, (2) They are *Attractive to Attack*, and (3) The established firms in the industry find it *Difficult to Defend* their current dominant positions against the new strategies of their attackers.

Firms that attack newly vulnerable markets can weaken or even destroy the advantage of established firms, even established firms that enjoy larger market share, better brand recognition, and lower operating expenses. Newly vulnerable markets offer *the competitive advantage of new entrants*. This is not because new entrants are more nimble or more creative, although they may be. This is because new entrants are following a digital strategy that was not available to the established firms when they entered the market years or even decades earlier.

1.1   The Structure of This Book

This book is based on my decades of experience with computing, communications, and strategic consulting around the globe, in industries ranging from Wall Street to the E-Ring of the Pentagon, and from craft brewing at a small start-up to detergent marketing at one of the world's largest consumer packaged goods companies. It's based on an understanding of historical patterns. This way the complexity of the information ocean can be understood in terms of familiar patterns, rather than seen as incomprehensible and unpredictable because of the overwhelming number of constantly changing small details.

The book has three parts. Part I, consisting of this chapters through 5, is about understanding problems. It's about recognizing if the problem is something you have seen before. It is about transforming an unfamiliar or difficult problem into something easier to solve. It is about diagnosing a problem, setting up a problem, and solving it. It's about economics, and strategy, but it's about more than that. It's about learning to solve almost any problem, if the problem can be solved at all. In Part I, we introduce four patterns, all of which provide advantages to both businesses and consumers by making businesses more efficient. These patterns are not about the form of efficiency that most of us have experienced as a result of automation, which involve making things faster, or making them cost less, or allowing them to use less energy. Rather, these patterns involve changing the firms' basic business model. Pricing more efficiently gives the firm an advantage over competitors following outdated pricing strategies. Providing goods and services to customers who are easiest to serve and offering them lower prices will allow the firm to capture customers that their competitors do not want to lose; this represents *price efficiency*. Similarly, when goods are in scarce supply, *allocative efficiency* gives a firm competitive advantage. Taxis try to serve all customers equally, while Uber's surge pricing allows them to allocate cars to those who most value a ride immediately. In general, efficiency is a good thing. These patterns, which encourage efficiency, are widely deployed in information-based strategies.

Part II, consisting of Chapters 6 through 9, is about a very different set of patterns in information-based strategy. These patterns are less about producing gains through efficiency. They are more about gaining and exploiting power in information-based businesses. These patterns are less benign. Sometimes they do create value for their users. Often they confer so much power to the companies that deploy them that we can consider these companies in the business of harvesting value, or taking wealth away from others, more than in the business of creating value for anyone else. These patterns, which can make some companies very, very profitable, are frequently seen in online gateway businesses like Google, Hotels.com, and a limited number of others.

Part III, containing Chapters 10 through 12, explores some of the implications of the strategic changes described in this chapter through Chapter 9. It explores working with the patterns to manage strategic uncertainty about the firm's operating environment. It explores making the decisions regarding which information-based strategies to implement, based on the uncertainty of the firm's future competitive environment. It explores how information-based strategy can change the structure of the firm and the options available to regulators. The last chapter puts all of the pieces together and provides a terse summary of the process of digital transformation.

All of the chapters in this book contain several short, related sections. The structure of this chapter illustrates the structure that will be followed throughout the book. Section 1.2 introduces the important role of patterns, models, and model-based learning in rapidly diagnosing the problems that you face; it's about *thinking about thinking about* our new online world. That is, it is more about how to think about our new world than about analyzing any specific problem, issue, or transformation that has already occurred. Section 1.3 motivates our first pattern, the *Theory of Newly Vulnerable Markets*, and describes how the pattern was actually developed. Section 1.4 presents the complete theory of newly vulnerable markets and describes its applications.

I have two reasons for carefully laying out *how* I developed the theory of newly vulnerable markets in Sect. 1.3, instead of simply stating it as I do in Sect. 1.4. First, and most importantly, it is far too easy to see an interesting and puzzling event and make up an explanation that fits that single observation. These explanations may have little or no value when making predictions about future events. These stories may be interesting. They may even sound plausible. But how do you know if they are correct? If you know how a theory was developed, and how many different examples it can explain, you know when you can trust it. Next, technology continues to evolve and continues to change *what we know about any situation*. Likewise, changing information endowment continues to change all aspects of our world. We may need new patterns over time. Understanding how I developed the patterns that I use will help you develop your own ways of seeing, your own ways of thinking, and your own patterns.

This insistence on theories that make testable predictions is important and will be followed throughout the rest of the book. It is not only of interest to academics fighting over theories. It is essential that strategic management be based on sound, tested, reliable theories. Understanding how a theory is developed allows you to assess its value as a predictor of future behavior and allows you to understand when it can be used as the basis of planning your strategy.

1.2 Patterns, Pattern Recognition, and Thinking Strategically About Thinking Strategically

The best way to learn from experience is to learn the new patterns and learn how to recognize which ones fit

Before we can solve any problem, we need to know exactly what problem we are solving. When we are about to act, we need to understand the situation facing us before we can possibly know what to do. We need to recognize problems quickly, so that we can anticipate what we will encounter, quickly, in time to develop an effective response.

This book specifically addresses the fact that the most challenging problems we face every day are complex. Every academic course has a syllabus, and you can look at the entry for each date in the syllabus to know which problem you will encounter in class and what technique to use to solve it. Unlike classrooms and courses, life does not offer *syllabusization*, and problems never arrive fully labeled or fully specified. Sometimes problems are simple enough that we can respond almost by habit; indeed, this is what makes our everyday tasks effortless, like driving the car or making a cup of coffee. But some problems are more complicated, especially if we are encountering them for the first time and do not immediately recognize how to approach them. How do you anticipate the ways that social networks will become agents of change, affecting Western elections, destabilizing regimes in the Middle East and accelerating the rise of extremist jihadist movements? How do you anticipate the impact of changing consumer behavior on craft brewing, designer jeans, traditional journalism, or music and book publishing? How do you anticipate the power of manipulation of search on retailers who now need to pay for access to consumers? How do you anticipate the ability to tailor fake news to the ideas that each reader will find most convincing, and how do you anticipate the impact that this will have on elections and on voters around the world? When you know what will happen, before it happens, you have enough time to respond.

Information changes everything, and we need a new set of patterns as a result. Fortunately, the number of new patterns we will need is actually quite small; we will need to learn six new patterns. The rest of this chapter addresses one pattern, newly vulnerable markets, in detail.

1.3 Developing the Theory of Newly Vulnerable Markets

How I developed my first pattern for thinking about information-based strategy

One of the most interesting recurring patterns in modern business is the vulnerability of historically dominant players, even in mature industries with little apparent room for growth or for new competitors, and even in the presence of strong economies of scale. I am not referring to losing out to new and superior products. Kodak and Polaroid were crushed by other players in their industry who exploited digital photography while Kodak and Polaroid did not. There was no reason, other than lack of strategic vision, why Kodak and Polaroid could not have made digital cameras.

In contrast, what we see constantly today is an industry that is being destroyed more by a new strategy than by new products. In every major city in the USA, passengers can hail a traditional taxi with the taxi company's new app. And yet Uber, especially Uber Black initially, transformed the industry and captured a huge portion of the taxi industry's passenger base. Why? Why do I use the Uber app rather than using the taxi company's app when I desperately need to get to the airport at rush hour or when I desperately need to pick up a visiting colleague during a blizzard?

Uber is simply the latest example of a clash of business models that I have observed dozens of times now, over several decades. Uber may be very new, but the clash of business models is not. I find it very helpful to explain the historical precedents for Uber, not because executives like history lessons, but because executives like to know how to figure things out for themselves. It is extremely useful to understand the precedents and the experiences of companies that had to endure the sort of attack that taxi companies are now suffering from Uber. It is helpful to know what responses are possible. Unfortunately, sometimes no response can succeed, and it is helpful to know that too.

When Capital One attacked the credit card industry it did so when virtually every credit-worthy American household had one or more credit cards, just as every major American city had taxi service when Uber began its attack. Capital One did not introduce a new form of credit card; its initial offerings did not have a rewards program like frequent flyer mileage credit or cash back refunds on purchases. The cards were not offered through a merchant or through a university as an affinity card. Indeed, Capital One initially offered cards that were the most basic available in every way. In some ways, the Capital One card offered less service than its competitors, since Capital One had no other products or services, and therefore could not create a bundle of interrelated offerings for their customers. The firm was definitely a new entrant, and it did not even exist before 1995. And yet, somehow, it became a dominant player while bringing a basic me-too card to a mature market. It is now the fourth largest bank credit card issuer in the USA, behind Chase, Bank of America, and Citibank.

Clearly, Capital One found a way to compete without being torn to pieces by existing banks, with their great operating efficiencies. Capital One's initial entry strategy was to compete by poaching the best existing accounts from competitors, so that competitors' advantages became irrelevant. It was an *information-based strategy*, since Capital One used information to identify customers to target and to determine what prices to charge each.

This is not a unique event, or it would not warrant the development of a pattern to describe similar occurrences. Let's explore the pattern, by exploring my encounters with numerous examples of newly vulnerable markets. This pattern represents a recurring source of opportunities to new entrants, as well as a recurring threat to dominant players in many industries. Finally, let's explore how my encounter with examples of the pattern helped me codify my description of it and enabled me to convert a set of similar experiences into a unifying theory.

My first experience in developing the theory of newly vulnerable markets occurred when the Chairman of AT&T, Charles Brown, addressed a Wharton audience and explained why he had agreed to the breakup of AT&T as a means of ending the regulation of his company in a market that was changing rapidly. He described the way that MCI had become a threat to AT&T. He described MCI's opportunistic pickoff of the first AT&T customers, in markets like Chicago. These markets were easy for MCI to attack since they had high population densities and had high levels of traffic to a few cities that MCI wanted to target.

MCI did not have to be a full-service provider. MCI did not have to provide local service to all customers; indeed, since AT&T did not earn much on local service to consumers, MCI did not provide any local service at all. Long-distance service was profitable, so MCI focused there. But again, MCI did not have to offer long-distance service for all customers; MCI only had to offer service for those AT&T customers who it thought it would be profitable. MCI could choose the city pairs it wanted to attack. The choice of city pairs was critical. MCI targeted pairs that had *enough* volume, but *not so much* volume that AT&T's scale would offer an enormous advantage. MCI was able to charge lower prices because it was serving only the customers it wanted and providing only the services it wanted. Note that MCI was able to charge lower prices to these customers, even though, in general, AT&T enjoyed greater economies of scale and could have beaten MCI's prices for any service provided to specific customer. AT&T's problem was that as a regulated company AT&T could not make choices with the freedom that MCI enjoyed.

Mr. Brown described the initial response of AT&T, which was to raise prices to restore profitability in the presence of declining revenues. He described the pricing umbrella that this created for MCI and the dangerous beginnings of *Death Spiral* that resulted.[1] If AT&T raised its prices, this would create additional cities where AT&T's prices were higher than necessary, and MCI would attack those cities as well. If AT&T raised its prices again, this would create still more cities where AT&T's prices were too high, and it would create still more cities where MCI could attack.

As Brown described the problem, it was due to the fact that some customers were easier and cheaper to serve than others, but AT&T's pricing did not fully reflect the differences in customers' profitability to AT&T. Partly, this simplistic pricing may have been due to AT&T's philosophy of overcharging some customers, like long-distance customers in big cities, to subsidize other customers, like rural users of local telephone service. Partly, this simplistic pricing may have been due to regulation, which limited AT&T's ability to apply more complex pricing algorithms. But it was clear to Brown and to his audience where this would end if AT&T could not achieve the same pricing freedom as its unregulated competi-tors. AT&T would continue to raise prices, continue to lose customers, continue to reduce its profitability, and would need to raise prices still further. Ultimately, it would lose all but the worst customers, the most difficult to serve, and the most expensive to serve.

It's useful to understand AT&T's business model. They were committed to providing service to all residential customers, many of whom could not be served easily. This meant overcharging its best customers, which were urban businesses that were easy to serve and that made extensive use of long dis-

---

[1]This phenomenon has been intuitively understood for centuries. The Nobel Laureate Akerlof noticed that over time bad used cars drive better ones out of the market. Gresham's Law, named after a sixteenth-century financier, states that bad money drives good money out of circulation; if you had two shillings, one containing more than a shilling's worth of silver and the other containing less, which would you spend and which would you hold on to? And if your competitor had two types of customers, which would you target and which would you let him keep?

tance and other phone services. This enabled them to subsidize their worst customers, rural users in communities that were hard to serve. These rural users required fixed landlines and equipment, just like urban users, but the landlines were longer and more expensive to install. These customers also made less use of profitable services, like long-distance calls. These truly were the worst customers, customers who were expensive to serve but who produced only limited revenue. We now refer to the best customers as *love 'ems* and the worst as *kill yous*. AT&T was operating a *"money pump,"* collecting money from the *love 'ems*, who paid too much, and transferring it to the *kill yous*, who paid too little. MCI was stealing the *love 'ems*, while leaving AT&T to subsidize the *kill yous* alone.

After AT&T raised its prices, it became possible for MCI to target more of AT&T's *almost best* customers. AT&T lost more customers. Its profits were reduced. The initial temptation was to raise prices still further. However, if AT&T had responded by raising prices again, it would have been well on its way to *Death Spiral*. If each time it lost customers it responded by raising prices and creating new opportunities for its competitors, it would have ended up with no good customers.

My next experience with newly vulnerable markets occurred when meeting officers from Hong Kong Shanghai Bank, which made it clear that AT&T's experience was not unique. The bank officers described their own experience with *love 'ems* and *kill yous*. *Love 'em* customers had large balances and banked electronically, or with limited teller interactions, while *kill you* customers kept small balances, interacted with the bank frequently, and always needed to see a teller rather than interact online or with kiosks or ATMS. Indeed, sometimes these customers would make a withdrawal just to see that their small accounts were still in the bank and then would immediately redeposit them.

The bank was suffering, because foreign banks were targeting their *love 'em* customers and leaving them with the *kill yous*. The *kill yous* were destroying profitability and the officers could see no simple solution. I asked why the bank could not just *'fire'* the *kill yous* and was told that it was politically impossible. Hong Kong was about to be returned to the Mainland, and 'firing' vast numbers of low net worth ethnic Chinese customers was politically impossible at that time. I asked why the bank could not just raise the fees to the *kill yous* alone and was told that too was politically impossible for the same reason. I asked why the bank could not simply raise the prices it charged to all customers and was told that this would merely accelerate the movement of their best customers to other banks.

Indeed, they believed that there was no solution. Everything they wanted to do was blocked for one reason or another. The bank had extreme differences among their customers, but could not respond by differential pricing. They were indeed going to lose their best customers or have their profitability destroyed by bad customers, unless they could get relief from the rules that limited their responses.

It was only when I encountered Capital One and saw the same problem a third time that I really understood how newly vulnerable markets operate. By chance, I received two solicitations from Capital One in the same day. One solicitation came to my office and was addressed to 'Dear Professor Clemons.' This solicitation offered me a card that provided 'the respect I deserved.' At that point, I was already tenured. I had a secure job, and I had a strong credit rating. The card they offered me allowed me to skip payments during the summer, when I would not be teaching. I might want to travel, away from my office, away from my home, and possibly out of the country and away from my checkbook; this was before easy access to online banking and online credit card payments. The offer assured me that there would be no penalty for missing payments; however, regular finance charges would accrue while I was traveling, although at a special, very low rate. Note that a low credit card rate might be 5.9 or 6.9%, significantly lower than the standard credit card rate of 19.8% that most banks were offering, but still significantly higher than Capital One's cost of funds at the time. This offer might be attractive to faculty members who traveled. It was certainly attractive to Capital One, since it was virtually risk free, and allowed them to acquire what I later learned were the ideal customers they were seeking. Faculty members who acquired this card would pay them back, would pay them back in full, and would do so ... slowly.

The other solicitation from Capital One came to my home and was addressed simply to 'Current Resident.' Not much warmth here, and no offer of 'respect.' The card's terms were simple. If I responded to the offer I would receive a secured credit card, no questions asked. I would post bond, and I could then use the card to make purchases up to but not exceeding the amount of my bond. There was only one catch: This card had no grace period after purchases in which finance charges were not accrued. I would be charged the maximum legal annual percentage rate interest on all purchases, and these finance charges would accrue from the time I made the purchase until the time my payment was received by Capital One. This card entailed no risk for Capital One, since it was fully secured. This card was clearly also attractive to Capital One, because they would earn the highest legally permitted rate of return on risk-free loans. But it would also be attractive to any customer who could not get any other card. Try renting a car at an airport without a credit card and see how many companies will trust you with a $30,000 vehicle if you are not considered safe enough to have a credit card. Try paying for air travel with cash at the airport and see how many questions you have to answer before being allowed to board a plane. If you needed a credit card, and if you had no other alternatives, you would accept this card no matter how expensive it was to you.

So now, after AT&T and Hong Kong Shanghai Bank and Capital One I saw a consistent pattern. A new entrant attacker, in this case Capital One, was entering a mature market and was doing so with a strategy based on offering customers at least two prices. Every other bank I knew of had one price. Citi was charging all customers 19.8%. AT&T Universal was charging all customers 14.9%. Capital One had more than one price. And they were using pricing to attract customers away from other banks.

But was it working? There was one more piece I needed to learn. It was easy for MCI to figure out how to target the customers that AT&T could not afford to lose; geography and the customer's location were all that MCI needed to know. Since Capital One did not know the history or the profitability of its competitors' customers, it needed a way to get the best customers to identify themselves. I only learned this piece when I started working with Capital One; this will be described in Chapter 2.

1.4   The Complete Theory of Newly Vulnerable Markets

One theory, so many companies!

We now have our first pattern, the theory of newly vulnerable markets. All newly vulnerable markets exhibit the following three characteristics.

- **They are *newly easy to enter*.** Markets become newly easy to enter after any discontinuous change, but the usual drivers are (i) deregulation, which makes it *legal* to enter the market, (ii) technological change, which makes it *possible* and even *inexpensive* to replicate the functions of the dominant players at much lower cost, or (iii) changes in consumer preferences, which reduce the value of the established products and strategies of the previously dominant players.
- **They are *attractive to attack*.** Markets are attractive to attack when there are extreme differences in profitability across different groups of customers. This occurs when some customers are far more expensive to serve,

or some generate far more revenue, but the firm treats them all equally. Equal treatment could involve equal pricing, or equal levels of service, for customers with very different value to the firm. There are many reasons why markets may have become attractive to attack, but the most common are regulations, which legally blocked firms from using a more rational pricing structure, and technological limitations, which made it too difficult to implement a more rational pricing structure.

- **They are *difficult to defend*.** Markets are difficult to defend when there are barriers that prevent incumbents from immediately replicating the strategy of the attacker. The most common causes are regulatory asymmetry, which restricts incumbents but not new entrants, and legacy infrastructure, where the incumbents' outdated information architecture obscures their ability to separate their *love 'ems* from their *kill yous*.

We discuss the importance of all three in more detail, below. We also explain how Capital One's experience allowed me to understand each of the three.

1.4.1 Newly Easy to Enter

Markets that are newly easy to enter may be vulnerable to attack by new entrants, even if the market's incumbents appear to be firmly entrenched, with significant market share, and thus with significant economies of scale, cost advantages, and brand recognition. This is a necessary first condition; you can't compete if you can't enter. Other conditions must be met as well, if you are going to succeed against established competitors that enjoy numerous advantages. But first you have to be able to enter.

Markets can be newly easy to enter for a variety of reasons, including deregulation, new technology, and changes in consumer preferences and in consumer behavior. Deregulation of air travel and telecommunications are examples of the first cause. After deregulation, it became legal for new entrants to compete in these industries for the first time in decades. Without deregulation, we would not have companies like Comcast in telecommunications or JetBlue and Southwest in air travel. New telecommunications technology and widespread access to the Internet provide examples of the second cause of markets that are newly easy to enter. They enabled online travel sales to compete with travel agencies and online discount brokers to compete with traditional full-service brokers. With these new technologies, it was now possible and even inexpensive to establish online alternatives to existing travel agencies. Finally, consumer preferences and behavior can shift rapidly and dramatically, making established competitors less attractive or making new entrants more attractive. The gasoline price shock of the late 1970s made large, fuel-hungry American cars less attractive, opening the market for smaller and more fuel-efficient Japanese competitors. Consumers now wanted a different kind of automobile than the Big Three car companies were producing.

The word 'newly' is critical here. If a market has been easy to enter for a long time and no one has bothered to attack it, that tells you that probably there are hidden problems you have not seen yet. You may not know what these problems are, but you should assume that there are some significant problems that will block your attack.

1.4.2 Attractive to Attack

If a market that is newly easy to enter is *also* attractive to attack, it is starting to look very vulnerable to new entrants. A market is attractive to attack when there are extreme differences among customers but the industry is charging simple, uniform prices to very different consumer groups. Important differences among customers include differences in the cost to serve and differences in customers' willingness to engage in activities that are profitable for the firm. The presence of great differences in cost to serve creates what Capital One called a *customer profitability gradient* (or CPG). Similar customer profitability gradients can exist in insurance, in travel, and in any industry where there are extreme differences in customers' willingness to pay or in the cost to serve them.

Again, both of these factors were present in our previous examples.

1.4.3 Difficult to Defend

If a market that is newly easy to enter *and* attractive to attack is *also* difficult to defend, it truly *is* very vulnerable to new entrants. The first two conditions suggest that a new entrant can succeed with a strategy that targets the *love 'em* end of the market's customer profitability gradient. The final condition suggests that incumbents are in some way blocked from replicating the attacker's strategy. If incumbents cannot respond and cannot nullify the attacker's advantage, then the attacker's initial success will not be reversed by established players successfully copying the attacker's strategy.

Why are newly vulnerable markets so difficult to defend? Anything that the new entrant attacker knows, defenders should also know, and defenders should have much better economies of scale and much lower operating expenses. Any of several factors can block defenders and create opportunities for attackers.

- Defenders may be unable to recognize totally unfamiliar patterns. GM and Ford were unable to counter the initial onslaught of imports from Nissan and Toyota and Honda because they did not believe that customers would now want smaller, more fuel-efficient cars or that customers would be willing to sacrifice speed, acceleration, and space.
- Firms may have problems with technological learning curves, as when GM and Ford were unable to solve problems with fit and finish fast enough to compete with foreign imports.
- Sometimes existing firms have to deal with continuation of the regulations that created their customer profitability gradients, while new entrants may not have the same regulations. This asymmetric regulation often exists when industries are making the transition to a deregulated environment. Often new entrants are more free to set their own prices and select their own customers.
- And sometimes defenders have existing contracts that they cannot cancel, forcing them to provide inexpensive subsidized service to *kill you* customers that the new entrants will refuse to serve.

And again, these factors explain our previous examples. AT&T could not defend itself against MCI's opportunistic pickoff of its most profitable customers during the earliest stages of attack by MCI because of asymmetric regulation. AT&T was still regulated, but MCI was not. Hong Kong Shanghai Bank Corp could not defend itself from the same form of opportunistic pickoff because of the fear of offending officials in Beijing.

These examples are all profitable for the firms that exploited newly vulnerable markets. They reduce the prices paid by the most profitable credit card customers, or by air travelers who don't need complex services that are expensive to provide, while increasing prices for less attractive customers. This is price efficiency.

We have seen similar examples of newly vulnerable markets in banking, insurance, securities trading, air travel, and a host of other industries.

Chapter 2 will address learning more about vendors, customers, or applicants, in order to gain an information advantage and find your most attractive customers and partners.

1.5   Summary

Information changes everything. Some of the changes looked small and inconsequential at the time they occurred and were easily overlooked. But together the small changes have contributed to the digital transformation of everything.

That does not mean that vast amounts of information are needed for understanding digital strategies, or that vastly complex technology must be mastered. Changes in information access and availability demand new patterns for recognizing and understanding new business problems. Patterns matter. Patterns can be used to develop and test theories. Valid theories can then be used to make accurate predictions and can be used as the basis for successful strategies. With the right patterns you know what is going to happen first, before anyone else does. You recognize what will happen initially, and how the situation will unfold; you know what to do first, and what to do over time. This knowledge can be a great source of sustainable competitive advantage. We will continue to explore this in the chapters that follow.

2

Information Changes Everything:
It's Not What You Know,
It's What You Know Before Everyone Else!

This chapter is about information and the power of information. Any discussion of competitive advantage in the information age must begin with an exploration of the *power of information*, which is quite separate from the roles of technology and strategy. First, we need to understand the *value of information*, the power that comes from having more information, or more accurate or more recent information, than your competitors and knowing how to use it. We need to understand the weakness that comes from having less information than they do. Only then can we begin to address the impact of information on consumer behavior, the strategy of firms, or the structure of organizations. And even then, we can leave the technology of obtaining and managing information in the hands of technical experts. Our interest here is in *what* information to obtain and *how* to use it, not on the underlying technology.

This chapter introduces our second pattern, *Information Asymmetry*.

> **Information Asymmetry:** Information asymmetry occurs any time that one party in a relationship, in business, military conflict, or elsewhere, knows more than the other party. When you buy a used car, or accept an invitation to join as the fourth on a blind double date, you can assume that the others know more than you do. Should you buy the car, have it inspected, or just walk away? Dealing with information asymmetry is so important that animals have found mechanisms to deal with it when choosing mates, insurance companies have found ways to deal with it when pricing policies, and we all have developed mechanisms to cope with information asymmetry in our social and professional interactions. The most common mechanisms are (1) *Signaling*, or taking actions that *reveal your true quality* as a potential partner;

© The Author(s) 2019
E. K. Clemons, *New Patterns of Power and Profit*,
https://doi.org/10.1007/978-3-030-00443-9_2

> (2) *Screening*, or designing sets of actions that *cause the other party to reveal its true quality* to you; (3) *Data Mining*, which is a form of your going through the other side's history, transactions, and debris, so that *you can assess their true quality*; and (4) *Versioning* is a close cousin of screening, which will be discussed after screening.

Information changes everything, and we must all adapt our actions to respond to changes in information availability. The basic design of technology changes constantly, but its capability moves in only one direction. Information availability and information access have consistently increased. We have more websites, more storage, faster telecommunications speeds, faster processing speeds, smarter algorithms, and better image quality, and all at lower cost. As a result, firms have more control over what they make, how they price it, and how they distribute it. Firms can learn more about their customers. How does all of that change business? How does that change society and government? How, indeed, does that change life?

Information has power. Increasing what you know increases your power. Yeah, we all know that. As I write this chapter, search for the string <<"Knowledge is power">> produces about 23 million results. That's a lot, and almost four times as many as the search for <<"In God we trust">>. But what does it mean to say that information has power? Learning to understand information asymmetry is the first step toward harnessing the power of information. This chapter will discuss firms that have used the power of information to increase market share and profit margins.

2.1   Information Asymmetry and Market Collapse

You don't want to be the last one in the game to know what the game is!

What do we mean when we say that information changes everything?

For example, life insurance is based on *symmetric ignorance*. The customer "bets" that he is going to die, while the insurance company "bets" that the customer is going to live. Neither party really knows what is going to happen, of course. And both parties use similar estimates of probabilities of living or dying. These estimates are based on information that is usually available to both sides, like the applicant's age, health, and good behavior (regular exercise) or bad behavior (smoking cigarettes), so both parties can assess the probabilities of life or death with almost equal accuracy. Indeed, symmetric ignorance is necessary for all betting, not just for insurance, and betting is unwise when the other party has information that is superior to yours.

But what happens if customers somehow know their true riskiness and insurance companies do not? Suppose you knew you had much *lower* risk than the average person your age and you knew that the price of insurance reflected the risk of the average person? Would you still buy the insurance if it were offered to you at the same price that everyone else had to pay? Possibly not, since the price of the insurance is based on the expected cost of people with average risk, and since you have lower risk, the price you are offered is higher than it should be for you. Suppose you knew that you had much *worse* risk than the average customer? Would you still buy the insurance if it were offered to you at the same price that everyone else had to pay? Of course you would, since the price is now lower than it should be for you. And what would happen to insurance companies in the presence of extreme information asymmetry, where all customers knew their riskiness much better than the insurance companies did? In this case, all customers would decide whether or not to buy insurance based on whether it was priced advantageously for them. Those for whom the insurance was priced too low would buy it, and those for whom it was priced too high would not. The insurance company would end up with a very skewed portfolio and would lose money more often than they would earn money.

To be even more concrete, assume that you have a *personal guardian angel* (PGA) watching over you, and even looking into your future. Assume that your PGA always lets you know if you are going to have an expensive insurance claim, tells you the size of claim, and does so in time for you to increase your coverage. You would only buy coverage if you knew you needed it, and would buy it just in time to be eligible to file your claim. The insurance company would certainly lose money selling insurance to you.

Could any insurance company survive if all of its customers had similarly helpful and similarly accurate personal guardian angels? Customers would only buy insurance when they knew with certainty that they were going to need it. Now insurance companies would be certain to lose money on all of their customers.

Is there any way for insurance companies to respond to this extreme form of information asymmetry? Companies might try to respond by dramatically increasing their prices, which would drive away the customers who had not been briefed by their guardian angels; that is, policies would now be priced too high for normal drivers with normal risks. But this would not help drive away customers who had been briefed by their PGAs. Any price lower than a million dollars on a million dollar policy would be acceptable to customers who knew with certainty they were going to file million dollar claims. Even this can't work, since prices would be set so high that they would drive away all customers from whom the firm could expect to make any profits.

When customers have perfect information on their expected risk, raising prices for everyone would drive away the customers the company wanted to keep and retain the customers the company hoped to drive away. The company would need some way of increasing prices only for customers who were going to have claims soon, while leaving rates unchanged for customers who were not going to be abnormally expensive to serve. To deal with customers with nearly perfect information, the insurance company would need to have nearly perfect information as well.

Information asymmetry can alter markets. Indeed, information asymmetry can destroy entire markets. George Akerlof shared the Nobel Prize in economics for showing how information asymmetry can lead to market collapse, by studying a highly stylized and simplified market for used cars. Basically, Akerlof described market collapse as follows:

- If you are *buying* a used car of any specific type, all you know is its model, age, mileage, and the most obvious aspects of its appearance. You know that you don't know much about its quality, its condition, or its maintenance history. As a result, you are not willing to pay more than the average for cars of that type.
- However, if you are *selling* a used car of any specific type, you do know a great deal about its quality and its condition and maintenance history. You know what your car is worth. If your car is in better condition than the average car of its type, you know that it is worth more than average, and thus you know that your car is worth more than the market is going to pay you. You would decide to keep the car a little longer, until its value drops closer to the amount you would be paid for it.
- If the owners of all of the best cars start holding onto them, then only cars worth less than average become available in the market. The average value of cars in the market decreases as the average quality decreases, and the average price the market pays for cars decreases as well.
- Now buyers pay less than they did for the same model and age of cars, and sellers withhold more high-quality cars, which lowers the average quality in the market and the average price still further.

- This continues until only the worst cars, the true *lemons*, are available through the market.

Akerlof named this form of market collapse the *Market for Lemons*. Information asymmetry is an increasing strategic problem, as more online information can be used in different ways, and both regulators and corporations need to figure out how this information should best be used.

2.2 Dealing with Information Asymmetry Through Signaling

If you've got it, flaunt it!

There are three principal mechanisms that are available for dealing with information asymmetry. In general, things come in a range of qualities. Some customers pay you slowly and owe you finance charges on their credit cards, some workers are industrious and productive, and some patients get sick more often than others. Sometimes it is not always obvious which types should be considered good; a customer who pays you slowly is good for a credit card issuer but bad for a merchant, and a patient who gets sick more often may be profitable for a physician but unprofitable for an insurance company. In the material that follows, we assume that individuals usually know their types, and that the party they are communicating with usually knows which types they want to attract.

Mechanisms have evolved for dealing with information asymmetry and learning about the other party's type:

- *Signaling*—actions you take to communicate your true type and your quality to the other side.
- *Screening*—actions you take to induce the other side to reveal its true type and quality to you by offering them alternatives and having them make explicit choices.
- *Data mining*—going through the other side's history to figure out its true type and quality.

We will review each in more detail.

Information is critically important to all three. *Information advantage* is critically important as well. Signaling and screening do not explicitly require *information technology.* The role of information technology has been to accelerate changes in the way information is obtained and used, and to create new opportunities to gain information advantage or to compensate for information disadvantage. It is information that matters, and information will be the subject of this book.

As noted, signaling refers to actions you take to signal your type and your quality to the other side. Michael Spence received the Nobel Prize in economics in part for his most unsentimental assessment of the market value of a Harvard liberal arts degree. Paraphrasing, he argued that the degree conferred much higher starting salaries on Harvard graduates than the actual value of the skills the graduates learned in their four years of study. One possibility is that the markets were wrong, and the markets were simply offering Harvard A.B. graduates too much money. An alternative explanation is that the value of the degree came from something other than the skills that the student learned at Harvard. But what could that be?

Suppose students came in two types, those for whom Harvard was easy and those for whom Harvard was difficult. And suppose good students are those who can quickly understand what they read, can quickly write term papers, and can work in intense bursts when necessary to meet deadlines. That is, assume that good students make good junior employees. Attending Harvard provides useful information to potential employers, even if we assume that the Harvard education did not provide students with directly useful skills.

- **Easy for good students**: If Harvard is easy for high-quality students, then it should not take much to induce them to attend Harvard. Suppose they got to spend four enjoyable years hanging out with really smart, really interesting people, with their party time occasionally interrupted by an assignment or two. Those students might be willing to attend Harvard if they knew that their starting salaries might be 20% higher than those of their high school classmates who did not go to Harvard. Suppose moreover that they would be able to perform well in their new jobs, and that they would retain them for as long as they wanted.
- **Hard for poor students**: If Harvard is hard for low-quality students, it should take a great deal more to induce them to attend Harvard. Suppose they had to spend four hellish years hanging out with people who were much smarter than they were and who knew it, and with people who were not at all interested in them. Suppose every available moment had to be spent struggling through assignments they could barely complete. Suppose those students also knew that if they could somehow obtain the

same employment as the better students could, they would soon be discovered to be less talented and less productive employees and dismissed. Those students would be unwilling to attend Harvard.

So good students go to Harvard because the four years there will be easy for them, and because they expect to harvest the rewards of getting a better job. Bad students do not go to Harvard, because they know that the four years there will be extremely painful for them, and that they will not be able to retain a good job long enough to recover the true cost of their painful experience. Rationally, students choose to go to Harvard or not to go to Harvard based on ways that are consistent with what employers want to know about students. Students send a reliable signal to potential future employers, based on their decisions.

This gives us what economists call a *separating equilibrium*. That's a fancy way of saying that if firms offer salaries that are high enough to justify good students going to Harvard, but not so high that bad students are tempted to fake *goodness* by going to Harvard as well, then going to Harvard works as a signal of students' underlying quality. Two conditions are needed to create a plausible signal:

- *Faking the signal* must be expensive for individuals of the lower type.
- The reward for faking it must not be so high that lower quality individuals believe that it is still worth the cost of faking the signal.

Interestingly, signals can be used by non-verbal, non-human individuals, and have evolved in animals as well.

Skunks have a unique appearance, which makes them easy to see and thus makes them obvious targets for predators. The appearance of a skunk is not good for hiding. Any prey animal that is so easy to see must be telling us something, and indeed, skunks' appearance does tell us all we need to know. Any human, any dog, any predator of any type that attacks a skunk very quickly learns what the skunk is signaling. Faking the signal would be expensive, in that animals that were that easy to see, but were not spectacularly unpleasant to attack, would soon go extinct.

Thomson's Gazelles take great leaps, *stotting* leaps, when chased by a lion. These leaps make the individual gazelles quite obvious and quite visible, which also is not good for hiding. Can we also see this as a signal? Stotting is expensive. It converts a great deal of energy, which should be used for running horizontally away from the lion, into a vertical leap that is of no use for escaping the lion. Suppose the gazelle is communicating, *"I have energy that I can safely waste. This is as easy for me, a high quality gazelle, as attending Harvard is for a high quality high school graduate."* Lions might be tempted to ignore gazelles capable of sending such a signal and might prefer to chase gazelles that cannot stot. Is this signal expensive to fake? A gazelle that jumps and cannot resume running will surely be caught and eaten. So, yes, again we have a separating equilibrium. However bizarre stotting may seem to us, it appears to work for gazelles, since it is employed by more than one species of gazelles. High-quality gazelles stot. Lower quality gazelles do not.

If faking a signal is expensive, and if faking a signal gets you eaten, then attempting to fake the signal is rare. If faking a signal is easy, and the rewards are great enough, then faking is more common.

The technical term for faking a signal is *masquerading*, and it is relatively easy to see why. Monarchs are the familiar, beautiful, black, white, and orange butterflies, perhaps best known for migrating in their millions to Mexico every fall. They eat only the sap of milkweed, which in concentrated form is poisonous. Any bird that eats a monarch will be violently ill and will quickly learn not to eat the easily recognized noxious black, white, and orange butterflies. Viceroy butterflies have evolved to look almost identical to monarchs. But Viceroys eat whatever they want, which is easier than eating only milkweed. Since they look as much like monarchs as possible, they can piggyback on the monarch's signaling strategy. They can eat whatever they want, and they can still avoid being eaten just by looking like the much fussier monarch. Of course, this kind of masquerading must be self-limiting, or birds would learn to ignore the monarch's signal. That is, the ratio of Viceroys to monarchs must somehow remain low, or birds would once again begin to eat black and orange butterflies since they would only rarely become ill after eating one.

Sometimes signals are difficult to interpret, because the recipient of the signal can never be fully certain what an action meant to the individual who took that action, or what it cost, or how difficult it was to perform. Thus, the recipient of a signal can never be fully certain what the action should mean to him. We assume that if someone drives a Ferrari he is rich, and wants potential partners to know that he is rich. But perhaps someone is being driven in a Ferrari simply to move quickly. Even the signal in Spence's Nobel Prize winning example is ambiguous. What about the value of a Harvard physics degree? What about the value of an undergraduate degree in electrical engineering? How much of the value of these degrees comes from their use as signals, and how much of the value comes from their actual content? Signals are hard to calibrate.

2.3 Dealing with Information Asymmetry Through Screening: The Theory and an Explanation for Capital One's Success

If you don't already know, find a way to get them to tell you!

Screening refers to actions you take to get the other side to reveal its true type and quality to you. This is in contrast to signaling, which involves actions you take to reveal your true type, hoping that the other side will interpret your actions correctly. Screening mechanisms usually involve giving customers an explicit choice, where the choices are designed to get the other parties to reveal critical information about themselves. A perfectly designed screen can provide a great deal of precise and accurate information.

Capital One used a well-designed screen as an essential part of its initial foray into the newly vulnerable credit card market. It's an early example of a strategy to exploit *newly vulnerable markets*, a strategy that we have seen numerous times since, in a range of industries.

Sometimes the choices in a screening mechanism can be designed so that both sides want to answer truthfully. Imagine an insurance company that offers its customers two distinct products. The Smoker's Friend™ policy provides full coverage for all medical insurance, regardless of the cause of the illness and regardless of the reason for the claim. In contrast, the Healthy Choice™ policy is much less expensive, but it has a massive deductible for any claims provably due to smoking, and for any claims associated with lung cancer, heart attack, or other smoking-related illnesses. A smoker who could assess his own risks would purchase Smoker's Friend™ insurance, because he would understand that there was a good chance that he would need the coverage for illnesses related to smoking. Smoker's Friend™ makes good economic sense for smokers.

In contrast, a non-smoker would purchase Healthy Choice™, because it was much less expensive and the principal difference was that it provided coverage only for conditions he expected to encounter. Healthy Choice makes good economic sense for non-smokers. If the policies' attributes and prices were properly calibrated, there would be no reason for any customer to lie. A non-smoker would buy Healthy Choice™, because his lower probability of smoking-related illness made the lower coverage acceptable and made the lower price policy more attractive than the one with higher coverage. In contrast, a smoker would not buy Healthy Choice™, despite its lower price. A smoker would value the higher coverage policy because of its greater relevance to him or her, and the greater coverage would more than offset the higher price. Indeed, a non-smoker who began to smoke might rationally consider switching policies, despite the higher price associated with switching.[1]

With well-designed screening mechanisms, everyone's decision reveals his true type and no one benefits from lying. We have what economists call a *separating equilibrium*, with parties of all types choosing the policy we want them to choose, because it is best for them as well.

Sometimes screening mechanisms can be less benign, especially when the designer of the screening mechanism is able to lie about himself. The designer of a screening mechanism uses it to learn about the other party, not to reveal things about himself to the other party. During the Peloponnesian War, ancient Sparta faced a significant dilemma. Spartan men all served in the army and dedicated their lives to combat and to training for combat. All of the work of actually running their city-state, building infrastructure, and raising crops and livestock was done by Helot slaves. When the Spartan army was about to march off to attack Athens they could choose to bring all able-bodied Spartan men, leaving their women and their possessions defenseless while they were away. Alternatively, they could leave a significant force at home, which would protect their homes from a Helot uprising but reduce the forces they brought to Athens and weaken their offensive power. What the Spartan leaders chose to do was offer their Helot slaves a choice. Each adult Helot male was offered the opportunity to attempt to qualify as an auxiliary member of the Spartan army. They were promised that those men who qualified as potential recruits—the bravest, strongest, most industrious, and most independent—would become soldiers in the Spartans' war with Athens and would be made full citizens. The rest would remain at home as slaves. What actually happened was that those Helots who made the decision to volunteer and showed up for testing had indeed signaled themselves as brave, strong, industrious, and independent. They had therefore unintentionally signaled themselves as potential fighters, and as the most dangerous of the Helots. They were seen as too dangerous to be left

---

[1]Of course, life is more complicated, and people have a spectrum of risk exposures. If I worked in an asbestos factory or if I grew up in a house of smokers and was exposed to second hand smoke I might choose Smoker's Friend even if did not smoke. The basic idea here is that individuals rationally choose to buy the policy that is best for themselves, with no need for verification by the sellers.

behind, and they were promptly executed before the Spartan army left for Athens. In contrast, the remaining men, whose behavior indicated that they were slaves at heart, were allowed to live, since they clearly represented no threat.

This deceptive screening mechanism could not be used again, because no Helot would ever trust this promise from a Spartan again, but the long-term stability of their screening mechanism was not a major design consideration for Sparta. Obviously, something far more complicated than a simple screen is required when *both* parties need to learn about each other, and obviously, the Helots were in no position to design mechanisms that allowed them to demand information from their Spartan masters.[2]

Screening mechanisms are often the fastest way of exploiting a customer profitability gradient when attacking a newly vulnerable market. (Remember, as described in Chapter 1, a customer profitability gradient exists when there are large differences in customers' value to the company, but much smaller differences in the prices that customers are charged by the company.)

We still have not fully explained *how* Capital One identified its *love 'em* customers when they were stealing them away from other banks. Capital One executives knew that the average credit card customer generated only $12 a year in profits, while the best 20% generated annual profits of $1500–$1800. Not surprisingly, Capital One wanted to attract the most profitable ones, and their strategy relied upon a screening mechanism.

1. Capital One sent solicitations to millions of creditworthy individuals, inviting them to transfer their existing credit card debt to a new Capital One credit card with a much lower interest rate than the APR they were already paying at most banks. This APR might be half the 14.9% APR they were paying at AT&T Universal. It was even more attractive when compared to the rates charged by Citibank and others, usually 19.8%. This might appeal to all customers of course, and thus would not just attract *love 'ems*.
2. Capital One's balance transfer process was not fully automated and was not fast. Customers who wanted to complete the balance transfer process might be required to stay on the phone for 45 minutes or more. That was

---

[2]This occurred approximately 431 BC, making it the earliest recorded example of deceptive screening I have been able to locate. See Thucydides, Book 4, Chapter 80, for additional detail.

a *good* use of time for customers who were paying $1200 a year in finance charges, $1800 a year in finance charges, or even more. It was a *very bad* use of time for customers who were not paying significant amounts in finance charges.

Thus:

1. The customers who *eventually accepted* the balance transfer offer were those who paid finance charges that were 100–150 times the average of those paid by all credit card customers. Customers who did not pay significant finance charges found the process of applying for a balance transfer both time-consuming and offensive.
2. The customers who Capital One *wanted* to accept the balance transfer offer were those who paid finance charges that were 100–150 times the average of those paid by all credit card customers.

The potential new customers who accepted Capital One's offer, and the potential new customers whom Capital wanted, were precisely the same group. It should be no surprise that this screening mechanism quickly made Capital One's launch the most successful new launch of a bank credit card in history.

2.4   Dealing with Information Asymmetry Through Data Mining

If they won't tell you, maybe you figure it out going through their trash?

Data Mining entails going through the other party's history to figure out its true type and quality. This information can be used to set higher prices for good customers and lower prices for bad customers. It is yet another way of dealing with information asymmetry.

Data mining does not depend upon actions that one party intentionally took specifically to inform the other about itself. We don't drink bourbon so the empty bottles can be found, suggesting we have a drinking problem. Most of us don't avoid traffic accidents simply to get lower auto insurance rates and lower medical insurance rates. We don't buy great California Cabernets so the bottles can be found, suggesting that we might be appropriate targets for promotional programs at great local restaurants. Data mining is different from signaling. Likewise, data mining is not about choices that companies offer to us to learn about us. No restaurant offers us a choice of gourmet entrees simply so that someone else can analyze our credit card receipts. Data mining is not the same as screening.

I don't want to suggest that data mining is always bad for the customers. Capital One discovered patterns in the data stream of their credit card users and found ways to use them that were very helpful to their customers. Some customers clearly had cars that needed to be replaced, as evidenced by a sequence of payments for costly automobile repairs. Capital One then offered these customers attractive loans for the purchase of used cars. These loans were made available to the customer so they could be used to buy used cars from any used car dealer. They were guaranteed, so dealers would accept them. The loans were at interest rates that were much lower than those traditionally available to fund used car purchases, making them attractive to customers. Customers developed a sense of security negotiating for used cars when they knew that they would be able to pay for them. This business became so large that Capital One executives jokingly refer to auto financing as Capital Two.

Capital One has used data mining in other ways that are extremely valuable for the bank. *Retention specialists* ensure that when competing banks attempt to take customers away from Capital One, Capital One is able to respond intelligently. Suppose a bank tries to steal a customer away from Capital One. Capital One's retention specialists are equipped with software that immediately lets them know the interest rate at which a customer becomes unprofitable. Capital One is able to improve on any reasonable offer that any other bank makes to one of Capital One's customers. Indeed, the only time that Capital One would expect to lose a customer to a competitor would be if the competitor offered far too attractive an interest rate. This is technically called *Winner's Curse*, and it occurs any time the winner is the party with worse information, or worse luck, and experiences post-victory regret.

2.5   Versioning as a Form of Screening

If you don't know what they're willing to pay, you can still get them to tell you!

The term screening usually applies to offering choices in contracts, using different contracts to appeal to different types of applicant. When customers are offered different choices in products rather than different choices in services, this is usually called versioning. Versioning works because we all have slightly different values for the attributes that go into a product, and different willingness to pay for different products as a result. We can often agree on what is better: A sleeper seat in first class on a 17-hour trans-Pacific flight is *better* than a crowded seat in coach on the same flight, even though both get you to the same city at the same time. But we don't all agree on *how much better* one is than the other, resulting in customers having very different willingness to pay for the different types of seats. If we all agreed on how much better one class of service is than the other, than we would all choose the same class of service.

For example, we all agree that accurate and timely information is *more* valuable than older information, but we don't all agree *how much* more valuable the more current information actually is. Suppose I'm a *high frequency securities trader*, using computers to execute hundreds of thousands of trades daily, trying to use perfect timing to capture profit of a penny per share on hundreds of thousands of shares. I need information as quickly as possible, showing the current price on the exchange. In contrast, if I am trying to estimate the value of my portfolio, I might be happy with information that has been delayed by 20 minutes. The price for the two data feeds is very different. Why not charge everyone the higher price? Because most people don't need the real-time data and won't pay for it; there is a great deal to be earned by providing real-time data feeds to computer-based traders. Why provide delayed data at all to people who don't value it *enough* to pay for the real-time feeds? Because they value it enough to pay *something* for it, and it really costs almost nothing to produce a delayed feed.

Indeed, this is the basic idea behind versioning:

- *There is a population that values the product enough to pay a high price for it.* High frequency traders value real-time data feeds.
- *There is at least one other population that is willing to pay* **something** *for a reduced, altered or damaged version of the product, and indeed willing to pay more than the product costs to produce.* Other investors are willing to pay a low price for the data feeds after they have been *damaged* by a 20-minutes delay. This is acceptable to the sellers, because the feeds cost almost nothing to provide and even this lower price is profitable for them.
- *The two populations disagree on how much the different versions are worth.* High frequency traders would not pay anything for the delayed data, so offering delayed data at a lower price creates a new market for the slower service but does not destroy the market for real-time data feeds or reduce its profitability.

Software vendors often employ versioning, offering full capacity systems for hundreds of thousands of dollars or more, and offering student versions for hundreds of dollars or less. The student versions might have fewer commands, or might only process smaller records, or only allow smaller databases with fewer record types. Once again, we all agree that the full version is better, but we do not agree on how much more valuable it is. A firm's CIO will need a fully functional database management system to run operations, personnel, sales, and marketing. The student version is worthless to corporate officers; as long as the student version is damaged *enough* it will not reduce demand for the full version of the product. However, a much smaller version of the same software system will be quite sufficient for a class homework assignment that attempts to illustrate key concepts but does not need to support the daily operations of a corporation. Students would not have bought the full price version anyway, so sale of the discounted version represents new revenue from the new student customers. When versioning is implemented perfectly, customers who would have bought the full version still do buy it. Customers who now buy the stripped down version previously would not have bought anything. Buyers and sellers—everyone—are better off than they were without versioning.

Versioning is much less common with physical products than it is with information goods. The creation of an entire family of products to support versioning is easier with digital products than with physical products. Reducing the size of data structures the software can handle is an effortless way to *damage* the software so it can be used in the classroom but not for payroll or other commercial applications. Making copies of the installation discs for the damaged software costs almost nothing to produce. In contrast, making an actual full-size copy of an SUV, filling the back two seats of the car with an epoxy foam so they cannot be used, and reducing the horsepower by ensuring that half of the engine cannot be used, is not a profitable way to produce a low cost, fuel efficient, subcompact for city driving. There is nothing a car manufacturer can do to effortlessly create a lower priced version of a car, with capability 50% lower than the undamaged version. As importantly, there is no way to produce the damaged version with manufacturing cost that would justify a price 95% lower than the fully functional version.

So, in brief, versioning works when the producer of a physical good, an information good, or a service benefits from all of the following conditions:

- Versioning works when firms know that they have different sets of potential customers with different valuations for their product, and they know the reasons their customers have different valuations. The firm does not need to know individual customers' valuations, merely that different valuations exist and why they exist.
- Versioning works when firms can "damage" their products in ways that matter to some consumers much more than to others.
- Versioning works when consumers with high willingness to pay will not buy the damaged product.
- Versioning works when the firm can produce the damaged, low-price versions of their goods or services very cheaply.

2.6 Working with Signaling, Screening, and Data Mining: Specific Examples Where We Need to Address Information Asymmetry

There are so many ways to use this! How many will you adopt for your own life?

Look at the following attempts to resolve problems in information asymmetry and decide whether the solution is based on signaling, screening, or data mining. Remember the important differences among the three all involve intent.

- In signaling, the high-quality party designs and takes an action intended to communicate his own quality to the other party.
- In screening, one party designs a set of choices intended to learn about the other party's quality. If the other party chooses rationally, even the low-quality individuals will be communicating their low quality, but signaling their low quality is seldom their intent.
- In data mining, the party who is acting is going through transactions, history, even trash cans, and garbage heaps, trying to learn something about the other party, whereas the other party is not intentionally doing anything to signal his quality.

1. **Problem**: I'm a concerned father of a prince and I need to identify the real princesses among many potential suitors vying for my son.
   Proposed solution: I stick a pea under a stack of seven mattresses. If the young woman sleeps through the night, she is not a princess. If she tosses and turns in agony, she is a princess.

Assessment: This is *data mining*. She is not intentionally responding to a choice—sleep or don't sleep—so it is not screening.

2. **Problem**: I'm a concerned father of a princess and I need to identify a qualified husband from among all the arrogant but handsome princes who come vying for her hand and my kingdom.

   Proposed solution: I offer the young men a choice. They can read *"Hunting Lyfe Illustrated Comics"* and spend a day hunting with me. Or they can read *"Ye Moderne Judicial Kingdom Management"* and participate in a day of court decisions.

   Assessment: This is *screening*, since it involves setting up a choice. If the young princes know what I am doing, even the unqualified ones may try to masquerade and pretend to be interested in court decisions, but it will be very difficult for them to fake interest.

3. **Problem**: I'm an insurance company trying to survive in a brutally competitive industry and I don't have a gecko working for me. I need to have the lowest possible prices and I need to assess risk correctly.

   Proposed solution: I examine all the information I can get on my applicants, including accident history, speeding history, even drinking history. I offer the lowest rates to drivers without accidents, speeding tickets, or known drinking history.

   Assessment: This is clearly *data mining*. No one avoids traffic accidents, or avoids drinking, just to look good to an insurance company.

4. **Problem**: I'm a consulting firm looking for the highest quality applicants. All of my applicants have gone to great undergraduate schools, and all have gone to great MBA programs. Clearly, they are all smart and they've all worked hard. I only want the ones who expect to continue to work very hard.

   Proposed solution: I offer the applicants a contract that has very low annual base compensation and very high annual bonuses based on clearly defined performance criteria.

   Assessment: This is *screening*, even though the choice I am offering applicants is simply *"take the offer or refuse it."* Applicants know more about themselves than I do, of course. Those who don't think they will have adequate performance select to refuse my offer and go someplace else.

5. **Problem**: I'm a university looking for the highest quality new faculty members. All of my applicants have gone to great undergraduate schools, and all have gone to great doctoral programs. Clearly, they are all smart. I know that all good applicants will eventually want some security.

   Proposed solution: I promise that after a maximum of seven years all new hires will either be given tenure or asked to leave the university.

Assessment: This is *signaling* mechanism. I am telling applicants that I will not be able to abuse them forever. I will work them very hard for a while, but eventually I will reward their hard work.

6. **Problem:** I'm a thoroughly modern health insurance company. I don't want to overcharge my healthy customers. I don't want to overcharge customers who are acting to protect their health, by exercise or by other positive behaviors. And I know that other companies are attempting to offer lower prices to healthy customers, and charging higher prices to customers who don't exercise. But how can I tell who is healthy and who exercises? I can't just ask them!

   Proposed solution: I offer my customers the choice of wearing a biometric watch that reports customers' speed of motion, heart rate, and blood pressure. I can completely assess the behavior of my customers and determine who works out. I can also completely assess their health through biometric monitoring while they work out. I adjust their annual premiums to reflect what I learn about both.

   Assessment: This is complicated. Is it *data mining*, since I learn about their health by observing their behavior? Is it *signaling*, if they begin to exercise simply to inform me about their good behavior? Or is it *screening*, if the healthiest customers choose to wear the watches to tell me about themselves, and the rest choose not to wear the watches?

7. **Problem:** I'm an adult male peacock and I want to convince some peahens that I am genetically desirable.

   Proposed solution: I will carry around 36 inches of beautiful but useless tail feathers. If I can do that and still move around well enough to eat, and to escape foxes, I must have great genes.

   Assessment: This is within-species *signaling*. No conscious choice is involved on the part of the peacock; either he has a great tail or he does not. Likewise, the hens are not actually analyzing their choices; although they pick the males with the best tails, they probably have no idea *why* the choice is a good one. They're choosing tails, not general genetic endowment. Hens choose great looking tails, peacocks grow great looking tails to attract them, and as long as it takes a great set of genes to survive with this tail, rather than just great tail genes, it's not a bad thing for peacocks.[3]

8. **Problem:** I'm an adult March Hare trying to eat grass and mind my own business, and I see a fox sneaking up on me. I can stop eating and run

---

[3]Think of the peacock's tail as an expensive investment in advertising to potential mates. Only a strong peacock can afford the tail.

now, which wastes time and energy but will ensure my safety. No fox can outrun me to my rabbit hole. Of course, I would rather stay and eat grass. But I can't let the fox get any closer.

Proposed solution: I can stand up and stare right at the fox. He now knows that I see him. If he comes any closer or starts a chase I will certainly escape and he will certainly waste his time and energy as much as he wastes mine.

Assessment: This is cross-species *signaling*. And, yes, this really happens. The British were astounded by the bizarre sight of a large wild rabbit staring at a fox until the fox backed off. They made the rational assessment that the hare must be mad, as in, must have rabies, and the fox must know that only a rabid rabbit would be mad enough to stand up and try to stare down a fox. Only studies of rabbits that stood up and then got shot demonstrated that they did not indeed have rabies. This also demonstrated that signals that warn off foxes may be less effective against human hunters.

Interestingly, animals tend to communicate within and across species using signaling. Drafting agreements with clearly defined alternatives and explicit contractual terms is not a strong point of non-humans. In contrast, humans prefer screening mechanisms, because they can design them and fine-tune them. Increasingly, modern institutions use data mining, or use data mining in conjunction with screening.

2.7 Summary

Information changes everything. Some customers are expensive to serve, while others are not. Some customers value a product more than other customers, while others do not. By combining knowledge of individual customers' cost to serve and willingness to pay, firms can get a pretty good idea of each customer's profitability. As importantly, firms can get an estimate of each *potential* customer's *future* profitability. Firms use this information to decide which customers to go after, which to try to avoid, and what to charge each. Individuals can use their own sources of information to determine which firms to deal with, which firms to avoid, and what they should be willing to pay to each.

If superior information provides an advantage, then lack of information provides a significant disadvantage. No company wants to be the last one to learn that a credit card customer is about to declare bankruptcy. No individual wants to be the last one to learn that a company makes inferior products, provides inferior service, or is about to declare bankruptcy.

Although superior information provides an advantage, no one actually wants to tell you that they are going to be a bad customer or that they are going to be a bad merchant, or bad service provider. The desire for accurate information—on good and bad potential customers, good and bad merchants, and good and bad partners—motivates the use of techniques to obtain an information advantage or deal with an information disadvantage. Gaining information and information advantage can be based on technology, but it is the information itself that matters.

Firms have found numerous ways to exploit changes in information availability and to address information asymmetry. Signaling and screening are mechanisms that allow the firm to learn about individuals through their deliberate behavior. Data mining allows the firm to learn about individuals through the history of their actions. All allow the firm to provide tailored and different offerings to each customer or potential customer. Versioning is a form of screening where the customer is asked to select one version of a product out of a set, in which each version has been slightly damaged, and where each version has a different price based on how severely it has been damaged. All allow the firm to provide tailored and different prices for each individual as well.

In brief, information changes everything. Knowing this, and knowing how to use information, can be a source of sustainable competitive advantage.

3

The Power of Framing: If You Can't Answer the Question, Turn It into a Question You Can Answer

Understanding the transformation of anything is complicated. Understanding the simultaneous transformation of *everything* is even harder. By changing the way we pose problems, we can essentially transform unanswerable questions and unsolvable problems in digital transformation in ways that allow us to get the answers we need. This chapter returns to one of our rules introduced in the Prolog, the *Power of Reframing* to reduce problem complexity.

> **The Power of Reframing:** Some problems are much easier to solve than they initially appear, and a simple restatement of the problem can simplify it and make the solution obvious.

This chapter also introduces our second pattern, newly vulnerable online markets, or *Newly Vulnerable eMarkets.* This is the start of understanding the transformation of sales and distribution channels, as online channels transform competition between manufacturers and service providers and their traditional retailers and resellers.

> **Newly Vulnerable eMarkets:** Newly Vulnerable eMarkets are online markets that appear mature, with all customers served, and which appear to be dominated by a set of powerful firms. Newly Vulnerable eMarkets are vulnerable to channel encroachment, where the creator of the goods or services takes over the role previously occupied by the retailer or intermediary. Like

© The Author(s) 2019
E. K. Clemons, *New Patterns of Power and Profit*,
https://doi.org/10.1007/978-3-030-00443-9_3

> newly vulnerable markets, all newly vulnerable online markets share three elements, which together lead to the advantage of new entrants: (1) They are *Newly Easy to Enter*. (2) They are *Attractive to Attack*. and (3) the established sellers in the industry find it *Difficult to Defend* their current dominant positions against attack from the producers of their goods or services when these producers choose to take over the roles previously performed by intermediaries.

In this chapter, we explore how *Reframing* and transforming a problem can convert it from a form that is intractable and impossible to solve into one that is easier to solve and may indeed be solved by inspection. This is *really* important when trying to answer questions that no one has ever answered before, and understanding the digital transformation of everything involves asking a lot of questions that no one has ever even *asked* before.

The second pattern, newly vulnerable eMarkets, is about newly vulnerable online markets. It specifically addresses when manufacturers, airlines, insurance companies, and other service providers can safely seize control of their distribution channels and learn to bypass their traditional retailers and sales agents. As importantly, it addresses when they cannot. This is another essential element of the digital transformation of corporate strategy. It's driven by the underlying digital transformation of consumer behavior enabled by an increase in information available to everyone. Just as the introduction of businesses based on Newly Vulnerable Markets increased efficiency by allowing each customer to pay an appropriate price, businesses based on Newly Vulnerable eMarkets increase efficiency by reducing or eliminating the need for expensive intermediaries in the distribution channel. This can work in both directions, as airlines reduce their dependency on agencies, and as retailers like Amazon increasingly sell their own products.

We introduce five concepts for reframing. For the first, we start with a problem outside of business, to establish the power of the concept, and then move on to a business problem to demonstrate the concept's value. We use the technique of reframing to examine a problem in channel conflict, and then to generate our second pattern, *Channel Competition and Newly Vulnerable eMarkets*.

3.1 Introduction to Reframing for Easier Solution

Change the question! Asking the right question can, quite literally, save your life!

Years ago, I used to enjoy wading upstream of Taughannock Falls, the highest waterfall east of the Rockies. This is not an especially bad idea in August, when the creek is almost dry and the water moves very slowly. When you get as close to the edge of the cliff as you dare, you just stand up and walk out of the creek. However, this can be a spectacularly bad idea in May. The water levels are high, the creek moves quickly, and everything is covered with a slick algae slime. You can't swim. You can't walk. You are swept rapidly toward a 200-foot drop, and you can't stop.

When this happened to me, I was certain I was going to go over the falls, and I was certain I was going to die. I had maybe 60 feet before the falls, and I could not think of an answer to the question "*How do I get out of here?*" Fortunately, I thought of an alternative question, "*How do I buy some time to figure this out?*" I saw an irregularity in the surface of the water in front of me. That suggested an irregularity in the rock below it, which might give me something to grab onto. There was actually a large pothole in the rock, which gave me a place to stand and think. The stream was actually less than 30 feet across, which meant that I was perhaps a dozen feet from the closer bank of the stream. I positioned myself in the pothole, got into a sprinter's crouch, and launched myself at the shore. Obviously, I survived. Problem reframed, leading to problem solved.

3.2   Learn the Useful Forms of Reframing

Working with a fixed set of transformations makes reframing a whole lot easier!

It's useful to know that transformations exist that can make a problem easier to solve. It's much more useful to know *how* to find the right transformation. I have found the following small set of transformations extremely useful in my own consulting, teaching, and research. I frequently use one or more of them when I need to reframe a hard problem to make it easier to solve, or to make the solution easier to explain in the classroom, a boardroom, or a deposition before trial. I hope that the following list will enable you to quickly determine which transformation to use to reframe any particular problem you encounter.

- *Change the boundary conditions*. Sometimes instead of answering the question exactly as given, I can change the boundary conditions to make it easier to solve. For example, it is sometimes very difficult to answer the question, "*Will this strategy be more profitable in the new environment created by deregulation than our current strategy is now in our current environment?*" It is often easier to answer the question, "*Is this the best choice that will be available to us in the environment we are going to face?*" rather than trying to compare the choice to where we are now. Instead of comparing a new strategy in the *future* to the old strategy *now*, I compare a new strategy in the *future* to alternative strategies in the *future*. My boundary conditions are the time at which I evaluate the strategies, and sometimes changing boundary conditions create a problem that is more realistic and easier to solve.

- ***Reframe the problem so it looks like something you have already analyzed.*** Google's business model looks almost identical to the business model of Sabre and Apollo, the airlines' computer reservations systems (CRSs) from the 1980s. Engineers try not to design a bridge, or shock absorbers for aircraft landing gears, or computer programs by starting at the very beginning. Professionals try to reuse as much of their expertise and experience as possible and reuse an existing technique, and even reuse an existing solution. Perhaps the most useful skill any of us can acquire is not merely knowing *how* to use a particular problem-solving technique, but *when* to use each one. Problems very seldom identify their solution techniques for us; if we can reframe an unstructured puzzle into a solvable problem, ideally one we've already solved before, that's the best possible way to begin.

- ***Push the problem to the limit to make it easier to understand.*** When I was trying to analyze the new balance of power in different industries that were facing the introduction of online sales channels, it was very useful to look at extremes. It is very difficult for a consumer products company to sell their grocery products online. There is a complex portfolio of items to describe, freshness and speed of delivery are important, personal preferences on the perfect piece of fish or the perfect chocolate chip cookie vary, and large chains like Walmart and Carrefour exercise enormous power over manufacturers. In contrast, airline tickets are simple to describe and there is no physical delivery necessary. With eTicketing passengers no longer need any paper to confirm their reservations, and with online check-in passengers can get their boarding cards at home. Online sale of air travel was easy for me to understand—it's easy to do well and would be easy to launch successfully, even in the early days of eCommerce. eGrocery was also easy for me to understand—it's hard to do well and would be difficult to launch. It might also be dangerous for manufacturers of consumer products to attempt in the early days of eCommerce, if powerful retailers were able to punish them. By comparing these two extremes, it was easy for me to understand the factors that were important to the creation of online industries. This in turn made it easy for me to understand the future of online sales in a wide range of industries, and not just these two.

- *Reframe the question as a sequence of simpler questions that lead you to the same solution.* I call this "*The Art of Inquiry.*" It is often the most important skill of a great problem solver. Sometimes a difficult arithmetic problem can be divided into a sequence of simpler arithmetic problems. Sometimes a difficult problem in any other aspect of your life can also be divided into a collection of simpler problems.
- *Remember that there are often different ways to describe the same solution.* When I was working with a securities firm, I needed to defend an executive's decision to make an investment in an online capability that the firm *might not* need; however, if the firm ultimately did need the capability, they would need it *really, really fast.* I described the investment as purchasing an option that would enable them to initiate a strategy if they wanted to pursue it. That is, I described the investment as a hedging strategy, and everyone on the team understood it immediately because options and hedging were natural ways to describe a problem in the securities industry. On another occasion, when I was working for a senior team in an insurance company, I had to defend a similarly contingent investment, one that the firm might *not* need, but again, one that if the firm *did* need it, they would need it *really, really fast.* This time I asked for a show of hands; I asked how many of the executives had purchased life insurance. Every hand went up. I then asked how many of the executives were angry that they had wasted money on life insurance but had not gotten to collect on it yet. Every hand went back down. This time, I described the investment as a form of life insurance for the firm. Again, everyone on the team understood immediately; the investment they were analyzing could be seen as purchasing an insurance policy to protect the future of the firm. It's the same concept in both examples, of course, but the same concept is seen differently in different industries. Match your solution to context and environment in which you are working, and to the skill sets and mental models of the team working with you.

The next eight sections will examine the first four of the reframings described above. We will start with an example from outside business, which helps to set up the problem. We will then present a business example, to show how the reframing technique can be applied in a commercial setting. A later section will provide another example of matching your presentation to your audience.

3.3 Transforming a Problem for an Easy Solution

Change the boundary conditions to solve a problem that appears much too difficult!

We'll start with the problem of the village watchmaker's first clock, a variant of a problem posed by Lewis Carroll in a book called "Pillow Problems." The idea of the book is to present the reader with problems that can be solved in a matter of minutes just before falling asleep, without pencil or paper, just by properly reframing the question. I think that this problem is particularly sweet because unlike the others in the book, I did eventually solve it the way Lewis Carroll wanted; however, it took me several years before I could find the framing that allowed me to solve it in a few seconds. It illustrates perfectly the power of reframing. Here's my version of the problem:

> A quaint Swiss village lamented the fact that unlike all of its neighboring villages it did not have a clock in the tower of its town hall. It did not have a clock-maker, but it enlisted the village watchmaker to make a clock. At 9:17 one morning the clock was finished, the watchmaker started the clock ticking, and he walked down the hill to his home. Shortly after the watchmaker left, the villagers noticed a terrible problem — the watchmaker had placed the hour hand on the pinion that should have moved the minute hand, and he had placed the minute hand on the pinion that should have moved the hour hand. The hour hand was racing 12 times too fast so that it would go all the way around the dial every hour; the minute hand was crawling at $1/12$ its correct speed and would only go around the dial twice a day. A messenger was sent down the hill to get the watchmaker, who returned as fast as he could. And yet — by some wonderful coincidence — the clock showed the correct time when the watchmaker returned. This was the first time the clock showed the correct time since the watchmaker had started it.
>
> What time did the clock show when the watchmaker got back up the hill?

So what am I really asking? I want *both* hands to *appear* to rotate the *same angular distance*, so that it won't matter that *both* of the hands are going the *wrong speed*. That is, I want the rotation traveled by the fast hand and the rotation traveled by the slow hand to *look* the same, so that they will still both be in their correct positions, and it won't matter that they were on the wrong pinions and traveled the wrong distance to get there.

This problem can be solved by brute force, but the brute force solution is not pretty. Let's try the easy way instead. Let's ask the problem in a slightly different way. Let's shift the problem to a different starting condition or a different boundary condition. Let's have the village watchmaker start the clock at a more reasonable time, noon. Let's leave everything else the same. Once again, he walks down the hill, then he walks back up the hill, and when he gets to the top of the hill, the clock again shows the correct time.

At noon, both hands are in the same position. They are vertical, pointing straight up. When will the clock again show the correct time? The clock will show the correct time when both hands *look like* they've gone the same distance, even if the hour hand has gone all the way around when it should not have, and the minute hand has gone only a tiny distance when it should have gone that distance plus a full circle around the clock dial. Both hands will look like they have gone the same distance when they are on top of each other again. That's about 1:05 or 1:06 p.m. It's that easy to solve the new form of the problem (see Fig. 3.1 a and b).

But I need to solve the original problem, and that's now easy as well. I just need to add 1 hour and 5½ minutes to the time specified in the original problem, because that's the amount of time it takes for both hands to *seem* to go the same distance around the circle of the clock. If the watchmaker originally started up the clock at 9:17, then it was about 10:22 or 10:23 when he got back to the top of the hill.

In decades of teaching thousands of MBA students, almost all were able to solve the problem after reframing, that is, when I asked the problem with the watchmaker starting the clock at noon. And of my thousands of MBA students, none was able to solve the problem as originally stated, though one came very close. Clearly, framing the problem statement matters.

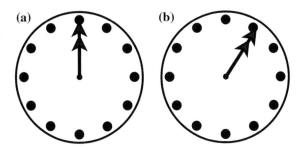

Fig. 3.1   a and b—The first and second time that hands cross on a clock, out of the 11 times each day that this occurs

3.4   Transforming a Problem for an Easy Solution

Change the boundary conditions to simplify Merrill Lynch's analysis of Bloomberg

Sometimes reframing can be especially helpful in commercial settings. This is especially true when you have been asked to answer a question that is very difficult, even impossible to answer, when what you really need to know is actually much simpler. We often find that when we analyze an entirely new opportunity in information systems, we ask questions based on the current situation, rather than on the business conditions that will exist in the future, after our system is deployed. Novel uses of information often require carefully choosing the questions needed for their analysis.

When Mike Bloomberg had just founded his company and was just starting to market his terminals and his information services, Merrill Lynch was a significant partner for Bloomberg. Merrill Lynch provided him with data feeds, without which his bond trading information services could not function. Merrill Lynch also owned a 30% share of the company and had veto rights over Bloomberg's ability to sell services to Merrill's largest competitors, which were, of course, also Bloomberg's largest potential customers. There was a list of about a dozen big banks that Merrill viewed as competitors, and Merrill had the right to block Bloomberg's sale to those banks. The Board of Merrill Lynch had been deadlocked for over a year trying to decide whether or not to limit Bloomberg's sales. Should they allow Mike to sell his services to these banks, so that Merrill Lynch could earn a 30% share of the resulting profits and a 30% share of the increase in Bloomberg's market value? Or should they block the sale of Bloomberg's services to Merrill Lynch's biggest competitors and protect the trading advantage that might accrue when they, and they alone among the world's largest securities firms, had Bloomberg's technology? The most contentious aspect of the sale was that Bloomberg provided technology that would fundamentally alter the market for corporate and municipal debt (bonds). Doing so would allow securities firms to monitor and manage their positions more accurately. It would allow all firms to price bonds and to assess risk more accurately, and trade more intelligently. This would affect both the firms that provided trading services and the large customers who managed portfolios and purchased services from them.

The Board wanted a number: *What is the true value of allowing Bloomberg unrestricted sales?* And they could not get one. They wanted to know if letting Bloomberg sell without restrictions would make the firm more profit-

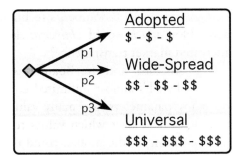

Fig. 3.2 The valuation problem as initially faced by Merrill Lynch, with three unknown probabilities and nine unknown financial variables

able than it was now. And they could not answer the question. As we shall see, that was the wrong question. Reframing allowed Merrill to make their decision in less than an hour.

As Fig. 3.2 shows, Merrill assumed that there were three states of the world that might occur after Bloomberg had been allowed to market freely: *Adoption, Wide-Spread Adoption,* or *Universal Adoption.* Since there were three future states of the world, and Merrill did not know which would occur, there were three unknown probabilities associated with the occurrence of each state after Bloomberg had been allowed to sell to the world's largest banks. These were the probability **P1** of *Adoption,* **P2** of *Wide-Spread Adoption,* or **P3** of *Universal Adoption.* **P1**, **P2**, and **P3** needed to sum to 1, of course, but there is an infinite number of choices that will achieve that. Sensitivity analysis could help, of course, trying a finite number of combinations for the values of these probabilities, like (25%, 50%, 25%) and (33%, 33%, 33%), but there would be a large number of plausible sets of choices to consider.

More problematic was deciding what numbers to use for each of the nine financial variables. If Bloomberg were allowed to sell, and if the system was *Adopted,* how much would Merrill Lynch earn as a result of its investment in Bloomberg (the first $). How much would it lose as a result of general improvements in market transparency (the second $)?[1] And how much would they lose as a result of other competitors gaining a skill advantage comparable to their own (the third $). Needless to say, there were endless arguments. Would Merrill Lynch *really enjoy* a trading advantage over

---

[1]Security firms follow the adage "Buy low, sell high, and pocket the difference!" This requires a counterparty that buys high and sells low, which is invariably the participant in the trade with less information. That's usually the customer. A more transparent the market provides the customer with better information. With better information, customer will get better prices on simple transactions. Wider adoption of Bloomberg would create greater pressure on trading firms.

Salomon if Merrill had sole access to Bloomberg's technology and the market *Adopted* Bloomberg? How *much* would *Universal Adoption* cost Merrill Lynch as a result of increased market transparency?

These arguments were ferocious, and the Board was unable to reach a consensus. Despite Merrill Lynch's almost unlimited computational power, there were simply too many parameters, too many values for those parameters, and too much disagreement over which values to use. Endless computation, and endless fine-tuning of the model, could not produce a single answer that was acceptable to everyone.

Fortunately, although the Board could not determine a unique value for the NPV of allowing Bloomberg unrestricted sales to its competitors, it was not necessary to do so. We developed a simpler way to frame the problem. There was a much easier question that could have been asked, which was also more relevant: "*Will letting Bloomberg sell without restrictions make Merrill Lynch more profitable than it would be if it continued to impose restrictions on Bloomberg's sales?*" That is, rather than compare the value of one strategy *now* to the value of a different strategy in the *future*, compare the value of *both* strategies in the future. Change the base case, the boundary conditions, for the problem.

This is also the correct question to ask! Competitors had seen Bloomberg's system. Competitors like Citi, Deutsche Bank, and Salomon Brothers were not simply going to allow Merrill Lynch to enjoy the competitive advantage they would get by having sole access to Bloomberg's systems. If Merrill did not allow Bloomberg to sell to Merrill's major competitors, eventually the competitors would try to duplicate the systems themselves.

So it doesn't matter if dropping all restrictions on Bloomberg's sales would make Merrill Lynch more profitable or less profitable than it *is now*. It only matters if dropping all restrictions on Bloomberg's sales would make Merrill Lynch more profitable than it *would be if those restrictions were retained*. Fortunately, that's an easy question to answer.

In this reframing, we assume that if Merrill does not allow Mike to sell his Bloomberg system to Merrill's major competitors, some other systems developer would do so. Nothing else changes except who gets the profits from the sales of bond trading systems. The probabilities of adoption, widespread adoption, and universal adoption have not changed. The negative impacts on Merrill Lynch remain the same. The damage from increased market transparency and from loss of trading advantage is the same whether caused by Bloomberg's system or by someone else's. The only difference is that allowing Bloomberg to sell to major competitors produces a revenue stream for Merrill Lynch that is lacking if Bloomberg's sales are restricted.

What we've just done is the commercial equivalent of reframing the watchmaker problem from the previous section. In one, I change the base condition from *9:17 p.m.* to *noon*. In the Bloomberg problem, I change the base condition from *now* to *after someone else sells systems if we don't*.

The problem is now easy! If all other things are equal, it is better to receive a revenue stream than not to receive anything.

Notice that we have not demonstrated that the value of allowing Mike to sell is positive, compared to Merrill Lynch's financial position today. We have not shown that unrestricted sales will be *good* for the firm. We have merely shown that unrestricted sales are *better* for the firm than restricted sales, given that the Bloomberg system already exists.

One more time, we need to ask the right question or ask the question the right way.

In this case, we needed to ask whether letting Bloomberg sell to all banks and without restrictions would be better *than not letting Bloomberg sell to all banks without restrictions*. That's not the same as asking if we will be better off letting Bloomberg sell without restrictions *than we are now*.

The problem of trying to decide if a solution is good, rather than if it is the best available, is common enough to have a name. I call it the *Trap of the Wrong Base Case*. Folk history at American Airlines says that all US carriers in 1984 viewed deregulation of the industry as a potential disaster for their firms. Routes would no longer be protected, allowing competition on routes. Fares would no longer be set by the CAB (Civil Aeronautics Board), allowing competition on fares. As the story was told to me at American, Eastern Airlines' Chairman decided that any strategic response to deregulation would lower his profits, compared to *where he was now*. Thus, no response to deregulation would be *good*, compared to where he was now. He did very little to protect his routes between the Northeast and Florida, and nothing to protect the profitable shuttle between New York and Boston and between New York and DC. Eastern Airlines, of course, has vanished, one of the early airline casualties caused by deregulation. In contrast, the story goes, Bob Crandall, at the time head of Marketing at American Airlines, called a town hall meeting. He said that he did not know the first thing about running an airline under deregulation. The crowd gave a collective sigh of despair. He then promised his audience that American Airlines would know how to deal with deregulation before any other airline had figured it out, and this was met with universal applause. He did not search for a solution that was as *good* and as easy as running the airline *had been*, because the easy, good old days were gone. He searched for the *best* remaining solution he could find, *in the world as it was going to exist going forward*. In contrast to

Eastern, which is gone, American has survived. As of July 2018, American Airlines is the largest airline in the world in terms of revenue, profit, passengers carried, and passenger miles flown.

The failure to plan for deregulation, by comparing the unpleasant results of investments to prepare for deregulation against the rosy results currently enjoyed, is the most common form of *The Trap of the Wrong Base Case*. It involves using a specific form of the wrong base case, comparing the value of a strategy implemented in the future to the best strategy available in a past. The past may have been more profitable, but the past has vanished and cannot be the yardstick by which future strategies are evaluated. This form of the trap has earned its own name, the *Trap of the Vanishing Status Quo*.

3.5   Reframing the Problem so It Looks Like Something You Have Already Analyzed

If you've already solved an identical problem, your work is done!

In the preface, we showed that the Google's control of search was simply an updated and larger version of Sabre's and Apollo's control over the search for flights. Control of the search for everything is clearly larger than the market for control of flights, but the analyses are essentially the same.

We also showed that Uber's attack on the market for taxi services was attacking a newly vulnerable market, much like Capital One's attack on banks with less sophisticated strategies for pricing credit card services. The analysis leaps from "*What's in your wallet?*" to "*Who's in your taxi?*", but the two problems are once again the same.

3.6   Pushing the Problem to Its Limits

Push your analysis to the limit to develop the Theory of Newly Vulnerable eMarkets

This section describes how examining two different industries helped provide early answers to complex questions about the future of eCommerce. Once again, it was impossible to answer the two questions I was initially asked. Fortunately, it was possible to transform the questions in a way that made it possible to answer them, and to answer similar questions for a large number of other industries as well.

The two different industries I was asked to analyze represented extreme cases. The first industry was online travel. This was perhaps the easiest industry for consumers to accept, with simple and unambiguous product descriptions, no need for consumers to inspect the products before purchase, and no need for delivery of physical products. The second industry was online grocery sales. This was among the most difficult for consumers to adopt, with complex products, incomplete product descriptions that required physical inspection of products, and expensive delivery of bulky, low-margin physical goods. Not surprisingly, the travel was one of the first industries to be successfully transformed by online shopping, and not surprisingly, grocery shopping was among the last.

In 1996, I was contacted by the Office of the Chairman of Unilever in London and by the Office of the Chairman of British Airways in London, both on the same day. As a result of something that they had heard at a workshop for UK CEOs, they were interested in the possibility of bypassing their traditional distribution channels, and they both thought that I might be able to help them analyze the risks and the rewards of a bypass strategy. British Airways wanted to know what would happen if they attempted to bypass American Express, Wagons-Lits, and the other large travel agencies that sold their tickets around the world, and instead attempted to sell directly to travelers. Unilever wanted to know what would happen if they attempted to bypass Sainsbury and Tesco in the UK, and Walmart and Carrefour around the world, and again attempted to sell directly to consumers.

My immediate thought was "*How should I know?*" eCommerce had not yet become significant anywhere, and we had very little experience with where it would and would not work. I went to London, and I spoke to executives at both firms, but I still couldn't answer the questions of their Chairmen.

When I couldn't figure out an answer to either question, I thought it might be easier to try to answer both questions together. That is, I laid out the two problems, side by side, and tried to see if I could find a pattern by modeling both. I set up the grid shown in Table 3.1 and compared travel channel encroachment and grocery channel encroachment as if I were using the pattern from the existing work on newly vulnerable markets. Is it easy to enter as a new online travel agency or a new online grocery store? Is it attractive to attack either industry, because of a strong customer profitability gradient? Are incumbents in either industry able to punish a new entrant, or is it difficult for them to defend themselves?

In the mid-1990s, it was newly easy to sell travel online, since a complete description of flights was now easy to provide online, and since there was no bulky physical product that needed to be shipped to passengers. In contrast, the design of an interface for consumer products was more complicated. Every consumer product has different attributes, and while freshness is vital to fish, it has little meaning when describing paper towels, and the attributes used to describe snacks are completely different from the attributes used to describe canned fruits and vegetables. Likewise, shipping is much more of an issue with groceries than it is with airline tickets.

The market for selling travel tickets is attractive to attack, since there is a strong customer profitability gradient. Some customers are easy to serve, like business travelers who know exactly what they want. Other customers are much more difficult to serve, like vacationers who need a lot of help with planning. In supermarkets, most consumers select their own groceries and most pay the same prices, and there are only limited opportunities to distinguish better customers from worse customers based on the profitability of individual purchases.

Finally, I concluded that it would be safe for airlines to attack travel agencies because adoption of online ticket sales would be rapid, and adoption by the most profitable customers would be the most rapid. Because of the speed with which changes would occur, the agencies would have limited opportunities to punish the airlines that attacked them. In contrast, consumer adoption of online grocery sales would be slow, and Walmart and other large retailers would punish any manufacturer that tried to bypass them by selling directly to consumers. Punishment could be simple and direct, such as pulling a manufacturer's products off the shelf. Punishment could be more complex, like making the manufacturer's products more expensive so that they would appeal only to their most loyal customers, or making competitors' products easier to find. Retailers might have reasons to choose one form of punishment or the other, but they did have numerous ways to retaliate.

I had discovered a new pattern. The recommendation to Unilever and other consumer product companies was to be very careful not to offend Walmart and the other major retailers in their distribution system. The recommendation to British Airways and other airlines was to move carefully to develop their own online sales channels.[2]

---

[2]Note that I was not suggesting that online grocery retailing could not succeed. I was suggesting that online grocery retailing would probably not be successfully initiated by a major consumer packaged goods manufacturer.

Table 3.1 Comparing channel encroachment in travel and in consumer grocery sales

Travel channel encroachment		Grocery channel encroachment	
Is the market for selling airline tickets **Newly Easy to Enter?** Are their standard interfaces to describe products for online sales? Is there a physical product for which distribution will be difficult after online sales?	Easy to Attack = YES	Is the market for selling grocery products to consumers **Newly Easy to Enter?** Are their standard interfaces to describe products for online sales? Is there a physical product for which distribution will be difficult after online sales?	Easy to Attack = NO!
Is the market for selling airline tickets **Attractive to Attack?** Is there a customer profitability gradient, so that having a small market share is sufficient for profitability?	Attractive to Attack = YES	Is the market for selling grocery products to consumer **Attractive to Attack?** Is there a customer profitability gradient, so that having a small market share is sufficient for profitability?	Attractive to Attack = NO!
Is this market **Difficult to Defend?** Is it possible for an airline to achieve rapid adoption by customers before punishment by agencies?	Difficult to Defend = YES	Is this market **Difficult to Defend?** Is it possible for a manufacturer of fast moving consumer goods to achieve rapid adoption by customers before punishment by large powerful grocery retailers?	Difficult to Defend = NO!

This pattern has subsequently been useful enough to earn its status as our second pattern. It is our *Theory of Channel Conflict and Newly Vulnerable Electronic Markets*, or more simply the *Theory of Newly Vulnerable eMarkets*. This theory suggests that the following three attributes determine if a supplier can become its own online retailer and compete directly with its existing retailers. We need to assess the following:

- **Is the retailer's market newly easy to enter?** Online travel Web sites are easy to construct. There is very limited information that a shopper requires. For flights, the information includes city of origin and city of destination, time of departure and time of arrival, connections, class of service, seat number, and of course price. Very little additional information is needed to describe a flight. A traveler can pay for his reservation and get an electronic confirmation; there is no delivery of bulky physical products required, since the customer needs to get himself to the plane. Online grocery shopping is much more complex. The shopper needs an array of information on each product, as described above. Freshness may be essential, as when buying shellfish. Delivery speed is essential, and rapid delivery is not free. The design of a Web site to sell everything from canned goods to bakery goods, meats, fish and produce will be complex. Additionally, a manufacturer who could sell only his own goods would probably not have a large enough market basket to justify the customers' paying for delivery.[3]

- **Is the retailer's market attractive to attack?** That is, is there a strong customer profitability gradient in the industry? In the case of air travel, some customers know exactly what they want. I remember how self-important I felt the first time I booked the Concorde. I needed BA 2 from New York to London. I waited for my travel agent to ask me questions. There were none. There was only one class of service. There was only one price. I obviously wanted an aisle seat, since there is slightly more legroom and there is nothing to see out the window at 40,000 feet. The agent earned 10% of a $6,000 ticket for about a minute of work, or $10 per second. No wonder airlines wanted to recapture some of the travel business. In contrast, I remember getting the same travel agent to help me book my first trip to Disney World with my daughter. We spent hours picking the right hotel. Did I want the Polynesian, where I could stay right by the park, where I could get into the park using a launch that left from my hotel, and where the launch dock would allow me to bypass the line waiting to get into the park? Or did I want to stay at the Caribbean, then take a bus to the monorail, and then take the monorail to the park, where I could join a line for admission? We spent hours reviewing our itinerary. I decided that I wanted the Polynesian, which required some negotiations because the rooms I wanted had all been booked for a Microsoft event. Our agent may have earned $45 for three hours of work. That comes out to about $0.75 a minute, or less than $0.01 a second. Compare that to what she earned booking me on the Concorde. *That's* a customer profitability gradient! In contrast, very few consumers represent either a high

---

[3]As I predicted, the initial adoption of online grocery shopping was indeed limited in the USA, where physical shopping was relatively easy. Online grocery shopping was much more quickly adopted elsewhere, where physical stores were less convenient.

end or a low end of the CPG to grocery stores. We come, we buy, we pay, and we leave. No grocery shopper creates the extraordinarily high margins I created for my travel agent when I booked the Concorde; this simple interaction can easily be supported online, directly by the airline. This strong customer profitability gradient ensures that the airlines don't *need* to capture all of the market to succeed; they only want the profitable end that is easy to serve. Airlines and hotels will cheerfully leave any and all complex customer experiences to traditional agencies, like the one that managed my Disney World bookings. It also ensures that they *don't* want to capture the entire market; airlines would prefer that the most complex customer service requests continue to be served by agencies.

- **Is the retailer's market difficult to defend?** The surest form of market defense is threatening a vulnerable attacker with certain destruction. Airlines were certain that they could encourage rapid adoption of online booking by their best customers. They knew who their frequent travelers were, because almost all of them had frequent flyer numbers. They could offer their best customers online booking for simple reservations. That's an effective screening mechanism: "*If you know exactly what you want, book it directly through us online; if you need coaching use an aggregator or an agency.*" They could even offer their frequent travelers a strong incentive: initially, airlines deposited miles to the frequent flier accounts of customers who booked online. Airlines were even able to encourage trial of their Web sites by allowing passengers to use them for information access only, without yet selling tickets in competition with travel agencies. Rather than fight the emergence of these marketing Web sites, travel agents actually encouraged their use. And, when the airlines were finally ready to move into full online sales, they converted their marketing Web sites into sales Web sites, and captured the high end of the profitability gradient so quickly that travel agencies barely had time to respond. Online booking of travel is nearly universal in the USA, except for the most complex passengers who represent the least profitable end of the CPG for booking agents. In contrast, adoption of online grocery sales was slow, and big retailers threatened their suppliers with counter promotions, promoting the competitors of any consumer packaged goods company that attempted to sell directly to their stores' customers. Two decades have passed. Online grocery sales are still a tiny per-centage of the US market. And online sales from manufacturers to consumers, from J&J, P&G, or Kraft, are still virtually nonexistent.

The Newly Vulnerable eMarkets pattern has been used to describe what would happen in a wide range of other situations involving channel conflict. What would happen if a major US insurance company sought to bypass insurance agents who were free to choose which company's products to sell if the insurance company were to become the agents' largest competitor? What would happen to a traditional automobile company that decided to sell directly to US consumers and bypass their dealers? In both cases, this was, predictably, a disaster.

Consumers do not change their insurance companies often. Indeed, they do not even think about changing their insurance companies often. This might happen once a year, at the time the policies were up for renewal, and then most often only if they had a bad experience in the previous year. In contrast, insurance agents think about insurance all the time. When Prudential decided to sell online, like new entrant e-Insurance companies, this initially made very little impression on its customers. However, it produced an immediate, and disastrous effect, among the company's agents. Not surprisingly, agents rebelled. This rebellion helped force a change of the firm's top management. Similarly, when Ford tried selling directly to consumers, dealerships were able to punish them. Large dealerships, which represented Japanese competitors as well as Ford, began moving customers away from Ford and increased their sales of competing brands.

3.7   Using a New Sequence of Questions

Address a complex question you can't answer by looking at two simpler questions you can answer!

Sometimes we need to change the question we are asked to solve. This is especially useful when we can decompose the question we can't answer into two or more equivalent questions that we can answer.

Years ago, I was advising the Board of a charitable foundation that raised money to fund research addressing problems caused by birth defects and childhood diseases. They wanted to know how they should adjust their strategy, given the possible impacts of online giving. None of us knew where to begin. Together, we divided the problem as given—*what should our strategy be?*—into two simpler questions. The first question was *what is the future funding available for charitable giving?* That's basically a question about the supply of services that the foundation would be able to provide. The second question was *what do we do if we actually find a solution to the problems we are trying to solve?* That's not an unimportant problem for a charity. The March of Dimes had to redefine itself decades ago, after research that they had funded resulted in polio vaccines and solved the problem that the March of Dimes had been created to address. The foundation might have to be prepared to do the same. The second question was equivalent to trying to estimate *future demand for their services.*

The foundation then developed four separate strategies, one for each of the four combinations produced by the answers to the two questions. For example, with high giving and an elusive solution to birth defects they might continue their research, and with high giving and a successful research program against birth defects they might search for a new social or medical problem to address.

We will return to this approach to forming strategy in a later chapter on scenario analysis.

3.8   Summary

Reframing a problem can make its solution more obvious. Reframing a problem can also make solving a problem computationally much less demanding. The Newly Vulnerable eMarkets pattern was developed by reframing two problems in channel conflict and has proved to be useful in numerous other settings. Reframing allows us to solve problems we would otherwise be unable to solve, and thus allows us to create superior competitive strategies. If reframing allows us to use existing patterns to adopt a superior strategy, we can gain initial advantage and sustain it over time.

Summary

4

Resonance Marketing in the Age of the Truly Informed Consumer: Creating Profits Through Differentiation and Delight

This chapter introduces our next pattern, *Resonance Marketing*. When *information changes everything*, it changes consumer behavior, which in turn changes corporate strategy. Resonance marketing includes both changes. It is most visible to all of us as a change in the marketplace. When corporations change their marketing strategy today, the first thing we see is a dramatic increase in the range and variety of products that firms offer. We may not actually notice the change in how they promote their large portfolio of new product offerings or the change in our own behavior. This change in corporate strategy is driven by the change in our behavior as consumers. Consumers continue to satisfy basic needs, of course. But we can now find products that satisfy desires, longings, even cravings that were unmet before.

> **Resonance Marketing:** Consumers can find, assess, and fully evaluate new products and can be as comfortable and knowledgeable about them as they are about their old favorites. Firms can introduce novel niche products, including those that are more expensive to produce, without needing expensive advertising campaigns. That means that firms can introduce niche products, with markets small enough that they could not previously promote their new offerings. Firms sell what consumers want, earning higher margins and higher profits. Consumers find what they want, experiencing greater delight.

© The Author(s) 2019
E. K. Clemons, *New Patterns of Power and Profit*,
https://doi.org/10.1007/978-3-030-00443-9_4

You've no doubt noticed the massive increases in the number of available choices in almost all product categories. Where once we chose from a couple of sweet or salty snacks, or from a small number of similar industrial lagers and industrial light beers, we are now inundated with alternatives. Where once we chose from a small selection of jeans, usually from Levi's or Wrangler, we now have thousands of choices, from specialty jeans manufacturers, high style houses, and of course new offerings from Levi's and Wranglers themselves. Why do we have so many choices?

Since the advent of the industrial revolution almost all of us, from the working poor to the upper middle classes, have had a limited range of choices. We choose from small sets of very mainstream products, which were generated through mass production and were marketed through mass advertising. In contrast, we now have an overwhelming range of alternatives in almost all product categories. Why are we supplied with so many new choices? What's changed?

We all understand that computerized control over manufacturing has freed firms from the need to produce limited ranges of alternatives. Firms can make anything. The *complexity penalty* that punished firms that tried to make a large selection is gone. Firms can engage in *hyperdifferentiation* and make products with almost any conceivable combination of attributes. Firms can produce whatever they want. Salesforce management systems, inventory management systems, and supply chain management systems likewise reduce or eliminate the complexity penalty. Firms can distribute anything.

But can they sell anything? Of course not!

But they can sell anything that consumers truly want as long as consumers know that they truly want it. That's the least visible part of the change in product offerings, and the most important. Previously, the introduction of new products had to be preceded with marketing blitzes, advertising campaigns, coupons, and the distribution of free samples. For many new products today, if you can appeal to a passionate group of consumers, you no longer need to advertise. If your product is perfectly tailored for a passionate group of consumers, they sell the product for you.

How? If a beer, or a pair of jeans, or a high-protein, low-calorie power bar, is perfect for me, I *resonate* with it. Figuratively, I *buzz* in response to a product that is perfect for me, and my buzz substitutes for messages the product's creator would previously have had to advertise. Consumers like me find the product online. They buy it. They buzz and create additional new consumers. The buzz creates true *informedness*. We all now know our choices, at least in categories that matter to us. We know what we want. We know how to find it. And this all happens without advertising.

There are two important things to remember about resonance:

1. ***It's additive.*** One soldier walking across a bridge, or a single gust of wind, will have no effect on the bridge. A troop of soldiers walking across the bridge, each maintaining exactly the same cadence over time, can cause the bridge to vibrate as the impact of each footstep is perfectly timed to add to the shock of the steps of the soldiers who crossed before. This can cause the vibrations to get bigger and bigger until the bridge collapses. A gust of wind that lasts long enough at just the right intensity can cause the bridge to vibrate, and the longer the wind blows, the bigger the bridge's vibrations become until ultimately the bridge collapses.
2. ***The match has to be perfect to produce resonance.*** The match between the soldiers' cadence and the bridge's structure, or between the wind's speed and the bridge's structure, has to be perfect. Changing the speed of the soldiers' march, or better yet, letting them walk without staying in step, will save the bridge. Since we don't have control over the wind, we need to design the bridge so that it won't resonate with the wind it will encounter.

It is the online content and the consumer-focused technologies that provide the missing piece for resonance marketing and that allows resonance to occur and to increase rapidly. Industrial technologies like flexible manufacturing and inventory management systems allow companies to produce anything they want. But that's been true for decades. Online content, including chat sites, reviewing sites, Facebook Likes, and a range of other alternatives, all are new. They create the organic buzz that replaces advertising, and the buzz generates more consumers, more products, and more buzz. We won't all resonate in response to all products, but if enough of us resonate to a specific product, there will be a market for it. Resonance marketing guides firms' production decisions and guides consumers' purchasing decisions. It is the least visible, but perhaps the most profound change in business produced by the Internet and the digital transformation of our lives.

But how do we choose what to buy, to maximize our own delight? How do firms choose what to produce, to maximize their own profits? And how can we increase both consumer delight and firms' profits simultaneously? Once we understand resonance marketing, we can answer these and a host of other questions.

As part of our study of resonance marketing, we explore a new form of brand positioning. Historically, firms sought to achieve the largest possible market for their products, like Oreo cookies, Levi's jeans, M&Ms and Snickers, Coke and Pepsi, and popular blockbuster movies. More recently, both producers and retailers are finding that there are higher margins, and sometimes even higher total profits, focusing on niche products. This is especially true in fast-moving consumer products that do not require enormous economies of scale in production or enormous initial investments in research and development. In that case, the firm can make dozens of different varieties, to serve dozens of highly profitable niches, and maximize its total profits. But this is only profitable for product categories where making lots of varieties does not result in crushing increases in operating costs.

This is the third of our *Newly* patterns. The first, *Newly Vulnerable Markets*, was built around pricing efficiency. The second, *Newly Vulnerable Markets* or Newly Vulnerable Distribution Channels, improved the operating efficiency of channels by removing expensive middlemen where they were no longer necessary. Resonance Marketing can also be viewed as *Newly Attractive Markets*, since they are newly attractive to attack. If the seller can make whatever the buyer wants, and the buyer can find whatever the seller made, we have yet another form of efficiency and yet another form of value creation.

And everyone wins. Consumers are satisfying themselves, even delighting themselves, by choosing products that they really want. Producers and retailers are delighting themselves by satisfying consumers and by offering a huge range of products that occupy new highly specialized, highly profitable *sweet spots*, rather than continuing to serve only their traditional mass-market *fat spots*.

We now have hundreds, even thousands of power bars and healthful snacks to choose from, not merely a few dozen candy bars. We now have thousands of brewers and tens of thousands of beers, not just the big three producers of American industrial lager. Levi's makes dozens of jeans, but there are hundreds of more styles to choose from offered by other manufacturers. Product proliferation is occurring everywhere, because consumers are demanding it.

Firms are responding to these changes because it is extremely profitable for them to do so. Competition has reduced the margins on many traditional mass-market fat spots. In contrast, customers are now finding new and highly specialized *sweet spots*. Since the products in these sweet spots offer customers greater delight, consumers are increasingly switching to sweet spot offerings. Since sweet spot offerings are higher margin for manufacturers and retailers, the market is changing and learning to provide them.

It is critical that both manufacturers and retailers understand the drivers of this change. Once they understand the drivers, they can understand the strategic implications of these drivers for their product portfolio and can understand the changes needed in their manufacturing and distribution activities. It is important for consumers to understand their myriad options so that they can ensure they get the most delight from their consumption spending.

4.1 Resonance Marketing: The Changing Marketplace for Craft Beer

Who says academic research has to be dull? Who says it has to be dry?

Did you ever wonder why there are so many different beers and so many different soft drinks and snacks available in the market today?

The flip side of the question is, did you ever wonder, 20 years ago, why there were so few good American beers available in the marketplace? I did. Beer and power bars are interesting product categories. Being really big does not provide a real advantage in either industry.

R&D expenses can keep small competitors out of many product markets. However, there is no real investment in research and development required to be a brewer. When Boeing or Lockheed or McDonnell Douglas developed a new commercial aircraft, the R&D costs for each new product could exceed a billion dollars. If you got it right, like the Boeing 747, you stayed in business. If you made a mistake or were simply unlucky, like the Lockheed L1011 Tristar or the McDonnell Douglas DC-10, you could not survive as a manufacturer of commercial aircraft. There was no room for error.

In contrast, when Dogfish Head brewed a batch of a few gallons of raisin maple beet sugar ale (raison d'etre), either customers bought it or they didn't. At worst, you throw out a few dollars' worth of beer and try again. As it turns out, it was a big hit and is still in production decades later.

There is no real economy of scale in beer production. If you want to make more beer, you buy more tanks. You don't just make bigger tanks. Bigger tanks would generate too much heat, and the yeast would die. It's simply cheaper to use lots of smaller tanks.

So what did the economics of beer production, sales, and distribution look like for America's big brewers?

- Traditional beer companies differentiated themselves through advertising. Promotion was the single largest cost of Budweiser. The beers weren't very different or very special. The advertising was.
- Traditional beer companies manufactured in a few large plants and shipped around the country or even around the world. Packaging and distribution were the second largest cost.
- Equipment is expensive and was probably the third largest expense.
- And ingredients were only the fourth largest expense. Products were differentiated by advertising, not by intrinsic quality. Traditional wheat and barley, used in European beers, are expensive. Corn and rice are cheap and became the basis of most American industrial beers.

Remember that advertising was so expensive that it formed a stable defense against new entrants. Only the largest advertisers were able to play this game, and they gradually forced out smaller producers and divided market share among themselves. Only the most dead-center undifferentiated beers had a large enough market share to afford advertising, so the situation was indeed stable and self-sustaining. We had big brewers of bland beer who defended their market through advertising. Only bland beers had a big enough share to afford advertising, so as long as advertising was key, we were going to have *only* bland beers, and we were going to have brewers who defended themselves and their products through advertising. A circular argument producing a sea of bland beer.

So what would a modern craft beer look like?

- Initially, it would be sold locally, draft, at the brewpub or nearby. Word of mouth, and now social media, would replace advertising and promotion. There would be no advertising needed. So the single largest expense of traditional brewers would vanish for craft brewers.
- Again, initially, it would be sold locally, draft, at the brewpub or nearby. Shipping and packaging costs would be minimal.
- So craft brewers could focus on ingredients, differentiation, and product quality. They could make beers that were perfect for each set of potential customers. Since there was no advertising, they would not need to worry about the cost of dozens of ad campaigns for dozens of products with

small markets. They could make perfect beers, perfect at least for each of their customers.

I picked a brewer I liked, bought shares, and worked with them to design a resonance marketing strategy and watched the company grow. It was the best single investment I ever made.

But it was not a lucky guess. Let's see how I knew what to expect. Let's explore the theory behind resonance marketing.

And, yes, this was *fun!* Who says academic research must be dry and boring?

4.2 Resonance Marketing: Information Changes Consumer Behavior and Corporate Strategy

If you know exactly *what it is, why would you buy it unless you wanted it?*

Somehow, we can now all get the kind of beer we want. Somehow, we can now all get the kind of snack food or soft drink we want. Somehow, we can now all find single-estate Jamaican coffee or single-estate Hawaiian coffee or single-estate Costa Rican coffee. We can find specialty toothpaste and specialty dental floss. We don't have to care, and we don't have to buy products in these exotic categories if we don't care. But, somehow, companies are now producing the widest possible range of choices, and somehow retailers are now providing them to us. How did this happen?

This is resonance marketing at its finest.

Resonance marketing is the study of changes in *consumer behavior* that are caused by consumers' improved *information endowment*. Most importantly, it is about selling *more expensive* bread and cheese, or *more expensive* cars, or *more expensive* beer, or *more expensive* iPods, or *more expensive* hotel rooms. Indeed, it is about selling versions of the same things that consumers already buy, but selling versions that consumers value more. When the products really resonate with consumers, the higher prices still result in greater consumer delight. Of greatest interest to firms, since consumers are willing to pay more for the goods and services they buy, resonance marketing produces higher margins despite higher manufacturing costs. Thus, this leads to higher company profits.

Today's consumers can select from a wider range of products and service than at any time in history. This is driven by increased information available to consumers, manufacturers, retailers, and service providers, from all sources.

Indeed, this change in information endowment is so overwhelming that it needs a new word. This is *informedness*. Informedness in an online world is different from awareness, different from understanding, different from having access to information. Informedness is somehow just knowing. Increasingly, consumers *will know* what is available, at what price, from which suppliers, and with precise and detailed understanding of all of the products new attributes. They will know what it is, what it is worth to them, and why they want it.[1]

Informedness affects producers as well as consumers. Increasingly, producers *must* know enough to deal with informedness among their customers. Producers will need to know everything their customers know. They will need to know what is available in the marketplace, including what is available from their competitors. They will need to know the price of everything. They will need to know exactly what each product is. As importantly, they will need to know every gap in the marketplace. They will need to know the unmet wants, needs, cravings, and longings of potential customers, even when these customers do not yet know what it is that they want.

Informedness is different from traditional branding. In part, it's different because firms can't control it. It's created by information from a wide range of sources, and as a result, advertising plays a diminished role in informedness. Informedness is different from traditional brand strength, and even a new and unknown product that is perfectly positioned for its market segment can be instantly successful. It can be found, evaluated, and purchased despite the product's having no promotions or advertising, no prior history, and no prior reputation.

This is the third of our *Newly* patterns. Resonance Marketing creates *Newly Vulnerable Markets* by making them *Newly Attractive to Attack*. Firms can create and offer anything. Consumers can find whatever they want and will value it fully and accurately even without prior experience with the product or the company. Everyone benefits. This, like the other *Newly* patterns, is truly value-creating.

---

[1]We're all familiar with the hordes of people who line up overnight before a new iPhone or iPad is released. We are less familiar with the fact that people line up to buy a newly released beer from a craft brewer, or a newly released shoe from Nike, or any of a number of new goods that make no sense to most of us, unless *we* actually are the ones who need a new beer from Captain Lawrence or a new shoe from Nike.

4.3   Hyperdifferentiation: With Modern Technology Firms Can Make Anything

Of course, they can make anything. They can make it whether you want it or not!

With modern manufacturing and the range of computer-controlled production technologies, firms can *make* anything. Likewise, with modern production scheduling, modern supply chain management, modern inventory management, and modern salesforce management, firms can control the production, sales, and distribution, a wider range of products than ever before. This does not fully explain why you can *find* anything amid the clutter of new products, or why anyone would want to *buy* some of these things. But, indeed, it is now possible to supply anything. Firms don't just differentiate. They *hyperdifferentiate*.

Where once it looked like America would be reduced to three beer companies, Anheuser Busch, Miller, and Coors, we now have thousands. Where we once had dozens of candy bars, we now have hundreds, or even thousands, of power bars and other healthy snacks. A web site like All Star Health now stocks over 800 bars, divided into categories like breakfast, sports, protein, and weight loss. The most popular, Clif, as I am drafting this offers 84 choices, likewise divided into categories. There is the basic Clif, Luna and Luna Protein (both for women), Builders and Builders Maxx (for bodybuilders, not hungry home builders, I assume), Mojo and Mojo Dipped (simply to taste better than and be different from everyone else's bars), and a granola bar, an organic bar, and a bar for kids. Being different, and being able to make *anything* you want, is basic to hyperdifferentiation.

Perhaps the most extreme examples of hyperdifferentiation occur in beverages and hot sauces. Until recently, the hottest pepper was the habanero, at about 350,000 on the Scoville scale. Pure capsicum, the chemical that gives hot peppers their heat, is 15 million Scoville, and weapons-grade pepper spray is 5 million Scoville. Some of the newer hot sauces weigh in at over 1 million and come with warnings that they are not to be consumed out of the bottle or used as jokes. The Source produces one at 7.1 million Scoville, which is above weapons grade. Obviously, consumers have very different preferences, and manufacturers are trying to delight all of them, even if it has to be done one consumer at a time. Amazon now has hundreds of hot sauce offerings. Some are as fiery as the offerings from the Source. Others, improbably, combine the bite of Sriracha hot sauce with holiday candy canes.

Yes, firms can produce anything, including sauces too hot to use, and beers too hoppy to drink. And yes, we suspect that not all of these products are good ideas. What should firms produce? And why?

4.4   Hyperdifferentiation Plus Information Yields Retailer Profits and Customer Delight

When they make what you want, and when you can actually find it, everyone wins!

More information allows consumers to find what they really want and to assess it accurately. Not surprisingly, consuming what we really want leads to greater delight. More information allows consumers to find what they really want and will really pay for, which leads to more profit for retailers and manufacturers.

My friend Matt Guyer operates The Beer Yard in Wayne, Pennsylvania. He has found a way to use information to expand his market and to transform his business. He sells more beer, more expensive beer, and higher margin beer. Let's see how he uses the net to create *informedness*, and how informedness has changed customer behavior.

Pennsylvania has some of the strictest alcohol controls in the North East, and until recently, you could only find unusual bottles of beer in distributors, who were required by state law to sell by the complete case. That's ok when the customer wants to buy a mass-market beer like a Budweiser, which he knows very well, and which he can drink pretty quickly with his friends. Suppose, instead, he's going to be the best man at his friend's wedding, and he wants to bring a really special beer, perhaps a Karmeliet Tripel, a Scaldis Prestige de Nuits, or something spectacular from the American brewer, Lost Abbey. These are truly extraordinary products, both in terms of flavor and appearance. Each would make a wonderful impression on a wedding party. Of course, the customer wants to try the beer first, before popping for the cost of an entire case, which makes sense since the case may cost him close to $600 if he chooses the Prestige de Nuits! And, until recently in Pennsylvania, he could not buy only a single bottle to try. Beers this good, and this rare, were impossible to find, except from a limited number of large beer distributors, and these distributors could not legally break up a case. Our helpful best man could not buy one bottle to see if he actually liked the beer.

Matt's solution was to link the Beer Yard's Web site (http://www.beeryard.com/) to one of the best online community reviewing sites, Ratebeer (http://www.ratebeer.com/). This has profoundly improved the information available to beer buyers and profoundly altered the profile of Matt's shoppers.

Let's see exactly how this Web site works, how it helps customers, and thus how it helps Matt. I could go to the Beer Yard Web site and click in the upper right corner to find a list of new arrivals. I did that earlier today while researching this section and found Ballantine India Pale Ale was back for the first time in decades. But did I really want to buy a case, just because I'm nostalgic for a beer from a brand that stopped production before I started drinking beer? So I clicked on the Beer Yard's web site and saw a terse description of the beer and some more links. I was still interested, so I clicked on one of the web sites there and was taken to Ratebeer's web site, where I saw a very strong rating of 92nd percentile, and a reasonably solid review from an experienced rater whose ratings conform pretty closely to the norms, and whose favorite style is one of my favorites. I checked his reviews for two east coast IPAs that I know very well and his verbal descriptions are consistent with mine. I trust him. I bought the beer.

Obviously, I appreciate Matt's linking the list of his new arrivals to Ratebeer's Web site, and I'm certain that Matt's other loyal beer-geek customers appreciate this as well. But Matt does not do this as a public service. Matt's Web site has grown his business. Where once 90% of his customers came from within five miles of his store, now more than half are out of county, and about a third are out of state. As Matt explained, out of county and out of state customers are different from local customers. No one would drive twenty or two hundred miles to buy a case of Coors, Bud Light, or Corona, since these are available everywhere. But some of Matt's more exotic offerings are difficult to find anywhere else. Customers have few alternative places to buy these beers, which is why they are willing to drive great distances to buy them from the Beer Yard.

These beers are not only rare; some are also quite expensive. The price for each of them is over $100 a case, and in some instances well over that. Matt *loves* selling these. The margins are higher than with beers that every distributor carries, because the competition is higher on the mass-market beers. The total profit from selling a high-margin $200 case of beer is much higher than the profit on a low-margin $16 case. Expensive beers don't need more floor space than a case of Corona; they don't squeeze out the low-value inventory. They don't weigh a lot more than low-margin cases; they're not much harder to bring to the customer's car. *Of course*, he loves selling these.

Brewers love the fact that they can ship beer to Matt knowing that the Beer Yard will sell it before it goes stale, to customers who know what they are buying. Customers love shopping at the Beer Yard, knowing that they can find things there that they cannot find anywhere else. Everyone is happy.

4.5   Characteristics of a Successful Reviewing Site

Not all reviewing sites are created equally. They have to be informative. And they have to be monitored to keep them honest.

The reviews on Ratebeer can create true informedness because they possess all of the following characteristics:

- **Informative**: Useful reviews need to be truly informative. It does not help me to learn that a reviewer liked a particular beer or disliked a particular hotel. I need to know *why*. If the beer was defective due to poor quality control, that's interesting. If the reviewer hated an IPA because it was too bitter and hoppy, or hated a Belgian Quad because it was strong, dark, and tasted of spices and sweet dried fruit, that's not useful because that is *exactly* how those beers are supposed to taste. If a reviewer hated a hotel because it was dirty and unsafe, that's really useful to me. If he hated the Lodge at Pebble Beach because there was little to do but play some of the world's best golf courses, eat great food, and admire the scenery, that's not useful to me, because that's *exactly* what I would want to do if I were at the Lodge at Pebble Beach. A numerical rating alone is not very useful, maybe not useful at all. An informative review that enables me to understand what the reviewer is saying and how to apply it to my own selections is far more useful.
- **Subject to calibration**: The most prolific reviewers on Ratebeer have posted tens of thousands of reviews. Over time, I have learned to calibrate individual reviewers. Some have preferences very similar to mine, while some disagree with me on virtually every style of beer. The reviewers whose preferences match mine are not *better* or *worse* than the ones who disagree with me, but they are *more useful to me*. I can read a review, identify the reviewer, think about whether his preferences for this style do or do not match mine, and assess the review and the beer with some accuracy. Readers should know how to interpret a review for their own use.

- *Subject to some verification and quality control*: Bud Light is rated among the very worst beers on Ratebeer, both in an absolute sense and relative to other industrial lagers. And yet at the time, I wrote this 27 reviewers gave the beer a perfect 5.0. Most were from newbies, who had rated fewer than 10 beers. They are clearly marked, and their reviews are not included in the calculation of aggregate statistics. Some came from a reviewer who had at least taken the time to review several other beers, and as a result, their reviews were not disqualified. But reviewers who praise a beer with no basis for comparison are now not included in the statistical evaluations of the beer. The rating and reviewing site should consider the quality of the reviewer, and when possible, the reviews of a naïve or malicious reviewer should be flagged and discounted.

I believe that ultimately all reliable Web sites presenting community-generated content will need to possess these same characteristics.

4.6 Hyperdifferentiation Plus Information Guides Manufacturers to Resonance Marketing and Customer Delight

Of course, to make what you want, they have to know what you want! To buy it, you need to know that they made it.

If manufacturers make what the marketplace wants, they can now sell it. If they make the right mix of products, they can earn superior margins. Their products should be different enough from competitors' offerings to survive comparison shopping and to avoid brutal head-to-head price competition. Their products should be differentiated. But they should not be so extreme that consumers find them weird, or worse, nasty.

Notice that we have a new pattern here, which occurs in a wide range of consumer products:

1. The products are extremely differentiated, almost unique. They exhibit their manufacturers' ability to implement *hyperdifferentiation*.
2. This hyperdifferentiation provides the products with *virtual monopolies*. If I want a Graeter's Black Raspberry Chocolate Chip ice-cream sandwich, that's really what I want, and I don't care much what it costs or what other less expensive ice creams cost. Health concerns limit my ice-cream

consumption, not expense. There are no direct substitutes for my resonance products.

3. Online content enabled *informedness*. I knew exactly what these products were, even before I bought them. They were like familiar old favorites, even when I bought them for the first time.

4. Since their producers knew I could find them and knew I could assess them, their producers actually provided them. *Informedness* also guided producers.

This combination of factors leads to *Resonance Marketing*. Resonance marketing and resonance marketing strategies represent our next recurring pattern.

4.7 Unrewarded Excellence and the Need to Be Better Than Good Enough

When everyone knows how to make something good enough, it's necessary to be better than merely good enough!

Consumers are abandoning products that are *good enough for everyone*, in favor of products that *fit them perfectly as individuals*. This is not *trading up*, in the sense that consumers are not always choosing products that are more expensive or that are better in any absolute sense. Customers are abandoning traditional candy for power bars and moving away from Coke and Pepsi in favor of flavored water, ice tea, and other non-carbonated beverages. Bud, Miller, and Coors still dominate the market for beer in the USA, but thousands of new craft beers have captured an unprecedented share of the market. Canned coffee still dominates supermarket sales, but specialty bagged coffee and premium and near-premium offerings from Starbucks and Peet's, Green Mountain, and single-estate coffee growers in Hawaii and Jamaica are likewise capturing an unprecedented share of the market.

Resonance marketing is not about having a product that is *better for all customers*. It's about having an array of products, one of which is *better for each customer*. There are now hundreds of power bars. Some are designed for men, like Clif, and some are designed for women, like Clif's Luna. Power bars for weight lifters, like Detour, have whey protein for muscle gain, and chocolate and caramel for quick energy bursts; weight lifters do not worry about fine motor control. Power bars for golfers can't have chocolate coatings; how could you play a course in Hawaii or Florida and deal with hot, soft, drippy chocolate? How could you eat a bar and then touch the grips of your clubs? Fine motor control matters, so jitters are a serious issue; power bars for golfer need to provide slow, controlled energy release. Of course, if you're exhausted by the front nine, you're going to need a boost that's slightly faster for the back; that's why power bars for golfers use a different formula for the front and back sides of the course.

If a product sells for a premium price, it's because someone *loves* it!

There is no single best energy bar. There is no single best beer. There is no single best physical product of any kind. There is no single best hotel. There is no single best airline, or best bank or best securities broker. There is no single best service provider of any kind.

There is only what is best for each consumer. The highest margins and the highest profits do not go to *good* firms, making *good* products. The highest margins and the highest profits go to firms with products that *resonate!*

4.8 Not Just *Better* Enough to Be *Liked*, But Also *Different* Enough to Be *Loved*!

It doesn't matter how many guys like you, all that matters is how many guys love you. Or, "Oh, great! They're spitting it into the sink!"

The extreme differentiation of resonance marketing really does require an entirely new mind-set. With traditional products, you want the largest number of customers to *like* you and your product. If you run a focus group for a traditional product, or run comparisons among your products, you look for things that everybody likes. Anyone grimacing after sampling your product, or worse yet, spitting, would be taken as a very bad sign! You want the largest possible number of people *satisfied.*

With Resonance Marketing, you don't focus on getting *most* guys to *like* your product. Instead, you focus on getting *some* guys to *love* your product. That's not as crazy as it sounds. With resonance offerings, having customers merely like you and your product and having customers absolutely hate you are both equivalent for your sales. Of course, customers who hate you won't buy your product no matter what it costs. But customers who merely like your product also won't pay the higher prices that resonance offerings command. Only the guys who love you represent potential customers.

The experience of Victory Brewing is instructive. Victory Dark Lager is an easy beer to like. However, it uses expensive ingredients, which makes it more expensive than most mass-market beers, and it's just not different enough from a traditional mass-market beer to justify the higher price for most people. Everyone likes it, but no one really loves it. Victory's founders are still proud of it, but they have relegated it to a seasonal draft, no longer bottled or available year-round.

In contrast, Victory Hop Devil sells well. It most definitely is not a beer for beginners. When it was introduced it far hoppier than anything, Americans were used to drinking. When I started pouring Hop Devil at beer festivals, it was the beer most likely to be spat out by tasters. It was also the beer that other tasters were most likely to come back to for a second taste. It was our *most hated* beer. It was also our *most popular* beer, initially counting for more than half of our total sales.

How can a beer be most loved and most hated? How can we explain this apparent paradox? It's explained by resonance marketing.

- *If you merely* like *a resonance product, you probably* won't *buy it*. If you *like* Victory All Malt Dark Lager, you'll probably like something dark from Michelob, such as their Dark Wheat (Dunkel Weisse) almost as much. It's not the same as the Victory Dark Lager, it's not even made with the same grains, and you won't like it *quite as much*. But it's a lot cheaper, and you'll like it *enough*. Although you might prefer the Victory Dark Lager, you won't buy it, because you don't like it quite enough to justify the higher price.
- *If you* love *a resonance product, you probably* will *buy it*. At the time Victory introduced Hop Devil, it was the most bitter, most flavorful, and most authentic Indian Pale Ale available in the northeast of the USA. If you loved it, and you wanted an authentic fresh local American IPA, you almost certainly were going to buy Hop Devil. I learned to say something at Victory's tastings that I would never have said at a tasting for Budweiser, Kraft, Nabisco, or General Mills: *"Oh great, some of them spat it in the sink!"*

Resonance strategies need to be monitored and updated. As time passed, and as more beer drinkers came to appreciate IPAs, competition in this category has increased. Tastes changed, and even more complex flavors and more nuanced bitterness were demanded. Customers demand hoppier and stronger Double IPAs now, and Victory responded with Dirt Wolf. It's even more bitter. It's even more hated, as well as even more loved. It's even more expensive than Hop Devil. And sales have been fantastic.

4.9   Information Changes Everything for Producers and Retailers

Sellers need to be better than everyone else for at least some of their customers. And they have to learn how.

Why has consumers' purchasing behavior shifted so dramatically? Why are previously successful firms finding their reliable old strategies now ineffective, why are their profits declining, and why are they suffering from unrewarded excellence? The answer is that customers finally know—accurately and with certainty—what is available to them. The customer can now *trade out, trade up,* or *trade down* because the customer knows what he wants, knows what is available, knows where to find it, and knows what it costs.[2]

These changes in consumer behavior are driven by information. They directly change the incentives and behavior of firms, through three factors:

- *Competition*—For categories that do not matter to the customer, he is able to find the lowest possible price for an offering he considers adequate. With perfect information now available online, the *competition discount* is as large as it has ever been. Thirty years ago a discounted airfare between Philadelphia and San Diego on United was close to $500; with excess capacity and easy online price comparisons, the fare as I wrote this chapter was under $400 on the same carrier, despite an 80% increase in fuel costs.
- *Compromise*—The customer can find and can get exactly what he wants; he will no longer accept a product that does not fit his preferences unless it is substantially less expensive. Perfect information and the increase in choice combine to make the *compromise discount* as high as it's ever been. We now see why merely being good enough is no longer good enough.

---

[2] *Trading up* means that consumers buy better products, which are better in some sense that is absolute and agreed upon. *Trading down* means buying cheaper products, maybe generics, in categories that really don't matter to you. And trading out means buying something that you really want because it is better for you, even though other people may not agree with your rankings or with your choices.

- *Certainty*—Finally, and most importantly to the success of resonance marketing, the customer can find what he truly wants and can determine what it truly is and what it truly offers. With perfect information, he knows what he is getting and he knows that he is getting exactly what he wants, even for first-time purchases and even if he is not familiar with the product or its producer. The customer is no longer paying less because he worries about whether he is getting a perfect fit with his preferences; the customer knows he is getting a perfect fit and the *uncertainty discount* has been eliminated.[3]

These changes are so profound they go beyond mere awareness and become true *customer informedness*.

While most of the best examples of resonance strategies can be found in small companies, resonance marketing is becoming a strategic necessity for many companies that were already dominant in their industries. The Dutch conglomerate Unilever owns the super-premium craft ice-cream Ben & Jerry's, but it also owns Breyers, Fudgsicle, Klondike, and Popsicle, among others. The super-premium craft ice-cream Häagen-Dazs is now owned by Nestlé, which also owns Edy's, Dreyers, and Mövenpick. Nestlé owns a range of bottled water companies including Perrier, Poland Spring, and S. Pellegrino. Anheuser Busch owns Goose Island Brewery, Kona Brewing Company, Blue Point, 10 Barrel, Old Dominion Brewing Company, and Boxing Cat in Shanghai, among others. It's clear that major food and beverage manufacturers have figured out that the profits from resonance marketing are simply too great to ignore. As importantly, they have learned how much they need to relearn about marketing in the age of the informed consumer. They have decided that acquisition of firms that have successfully implemented resonance marketing strategies is the fastest way for them to learn about resonance marketing strategies and the fastest way to duplicate them.

---

[3]The uncertainty discount is a little more complicated to explain. Suppose, I believe that my perfect Pilsner, a Czech Pilsner Urquell, is worth $5.00 because of the amount of beer happiness it produces when I drink it with a sausage pizza. Suppose, I believe that an industrial Pilsner, like a Miller, is worth $2.50 to me. And suppose that a great American Pilsner, like Victory Prima, is worth $4.50. And now my pizza restaurant offers me a Pilsner with my sausage pizza, but I don't know which of the three I am going to be getting. What would I be willing to pay? If that's all the information available to me, the average of the three turns out to be $4.00 in beer happiness. That's the most they can charge me, even if they are selling Urquell. There is a $1.00 difference between the $5.00 I would pay for a perfect Urquell and $4.00 I am willing to pay when I am not sure what I am getting. That $1.00 is the uncertainty difference. It's not because I'm *irrationally afraid* of what I might get. It's because I am *hyper-rationally* aware that I might have to compromise. With better information, the uncertainty discount is reduced, and with perfect information, the uncertainty discount is eliminated.

4.10 This Is Global: Resonance Marketing Is Everywhere

Information Changes Everything for producers and retailers outside the US as well.

Resonance marketing is not only a US phenomenon, and it is not only about the pursuit of luxury goods by the wealthiest consumers in the most developed nations. Shopping in upmarket grocery stores in Beijing and Shanghai is like shopping in their counterparts anywhere else in the world. The selections of imported pasta, imported olive oils and cooking oils, coffees, preserves, and chocolates are indistinguishable from selections anywhere else on earth. The signage is in Chinese, and the prices are in Yuan; otherwise, they could be anywhere on earth.

Likewise, the craft beer movement is slowly emerging in China. New brewpubs are emerging. They brew excellent beer, comparable to many of the best American craft brewers. Great beer bars are emerging as well. Originally, they catered mostly to expats, but increasingly their patrons are local Chinese as well.

On a recent trip to Copenhagen, I found War Pigs, an American style craft beer bar and barbecue restaurant. I had a couple of pints of purple IPA, brewed the week before by the brewmaster of Great Leap in Beijing. American craft beer, in Copenhagen, brewed by an artisan from Beijing. It doesn't get more global than that.

4.11 The Rise of Astroturfing and the Threat of Fake Grassroots Support

It's not easy to fake resonance marketing, but it's cheaper to pretend to be good than to really be good.

It has been an article of faith among craft brewers, organic bakeries, and other producers of resonance products that their consumers cannot be influenced by paid content. Craft brewers don't advertise. Organic bakeries don't advertise. They rely upon word of mouth and community content sites like Ratebeer.com and TripAdvisor.com. But what if they are wrong? What if consumers really cannot judge products confidently, still rely upon reviews, and can be deceived by well-written and well-placed false reviews? What if customers not only make a bad initial purchasing decision, but then continue to return to their bad choice because they just can't tell the difference? Could this actually happen?

The newest form of false or misleading advertising involves faking grassroots support. Reviewers paid by competitors might write false and terrible things about your restaurant, your hotel, or your beer. Reviewers paid by competitors might write false but wonderful things about a competitor's restaurant, hotel, or beer. One or two fake reviews are not likely to have much impact for a product or service that has hundreds or even thousands of reviews. But what if the paid reviewers submit a large number of reviews? What if they submit enough of their false reviews to alter the readers' sense of the quality of the product or service being reviewed? What if they can actually create the credible appearance that a doctor or dentist is competent and caring, when he is not? What if they can create the credible appearance that a daycare center is competent, caring, and safe, when it is not?

The industry of creating the false appearance of grassroots support for a product or service is called *astroturfing* or *astroturf marketing*. It may be more harmful than traditional false advertising. Most traditional advertising is in the form of paid promotional messages, such as newspaper ads, paid commercials on radio or television, billboards, and ads on online web sites. We can apply appropriate filters and use appropriate caution when interpreting messages that are obviously ads. Astroturfing may be different. Astroturfing may be more difficult to detect and more dangerous to consumers.

Interestingly, many retailers are surprisingly slow to pull obvious astroturfing. The text below shows a reviewer's response to discovering astroturfing on Amazon. The reviewer notes that a product purporting to be Harissa is actually more of a tomato sauce than a fiery Moroccan mixture of chili peppers and spices. As significantly, the reviewer has detected that the producer of the fake Harissa has engaged in an effective campaign of astroturf marketing to inflate the product's ratings. The following paragraphs are taken from the full text of the review.

> I started to read the 5-star reviews and noticed that almost every single one had all sorts of hyperboles -"This is the best harissa ever!", "It goes with everything!", "Amazing!", "I love Mina Harissa!!!!!" (yes, five exclamation points). You get the idea.

> So then I looked at how many other reviews these enthusiastic customers had written. The far majority had written only one review on Amazon - coincidentally for this product. Most of the others had only written 2 total reviews. And there's the person who has written a total of 5 reviews on Amazon — all for Mina Harissa.

This review was originally posted in 2012. Although 165 people have seen the negative review and have noted that it was helpful, at the time I wrote this Amazon has left the high rating in place and has not pulled the astroturf reviews. Unless web site curators enforce standards of honesty and integrity, astroturfing may actually work.

4.12 Summary

We've covered a large number of phenomena and combined them into a single pattern, Resonance Marketing. *Hyperdifferentiation* means that firms can make anything, or any combination of things. The *complexity penalty* no longer limits how many products firms can market. We call this hyperdifferentiation because it so much more extreme than differentiation in the past.

Informedness allows consumers to find anything they want, assess and evaluate it, and decide whether or not to buy it. Informedness reduces the importance of prior experience and advertising. Firms can sell whatever consumers really value.

Perfect information amplifies the *Competition Discount*: With perfect information, if products, goods, or services are directly comparable and fully equivalent, consumers will locate and find the cheapest one. Firms with undifferentiated products will be forced into brutal, head-to-head price-based competition.

Perfect information makes the *Compromise Discount* more important. When consumers know they are not getting exactly what they want, and know that alternatives that are better for them are available, consumers are less willing to settle for compromise offerings.

Finally, perfect information reduces or eliminates the *Uncertainty Discount*. As consumer informedness increases, consumers are more willing to purchase products that are unfamiliar or even totally unknown to them, if they know with certainty that these new offerings are perfect for them.

These changes lead to a new marketing strategy in the *age of the informed customer*.

- *Advertising*: Advertising is less important for many consumer products, since word of mouth and online content are sufficient to eliminate the uncertainty discount.
- *Scale*: Scale is now less important for these products as well. For products like aircraft or computer chips or operating systems, research and development still creates barriers to entry and economies of scale. But for

products like soft drinks, beer, snacks, or blue jeans, advertising was the greatest expense, not ingredients, technology, or research. And traditional advertising is less important and less likely to create barriers to entry.

- *Loved or liked?* Firms no longer need to be loved at mass-market fat spots simply to survive. It is now possible to thrive by being loved by a smaller number of consumers.

Firms' strategies now must change, because consumer behavior has changed:

- Because firms *have to*—the competition discount is so high that head-to-head competition is brutal.
- Because firms *want to*—the compromise discount is so high that firms certainly want to avoid the desperation strategy of dumping products into the market and hoping that someone, anyone, will value them enough to pay for them.
- Because firms *can*—uncertainty discount is now so low, and the cost of advertising is now irrelevant. If firms can identify what consumers want and can produce it, consumers will find it and will buy it.

Understanding resonance marketing can allow us to capture an extremely profitable market, can allow us to expand into additional profitable segments, and to protect those profitable segments over time. Capturing and protecting profitable market segments is a source of sustainable competitive advantage. Unfortunately, most firms do not yet know how to implement a resonance strategy. This will be reviewed in the next chapter.

5

Online Brand Ambassadors and Online Brand Assassins: Master the New Role of the Chief Perception Officer

This chapter does not introduce a new pattern. It shows the implications of a previous pattern, that of Resonance Marketing and Newly Attractive Markets, and it shows how firms can work effectively with their customers to implement Resonance Marketing strategies. This discussion of *Online Brand Ambassadors* and *Online Brand Assassins* concludes our discussion of Resonance Marketing as an aspect of the digital transformation of everything.

> **Online Brand Ambassadors and Online Brand Assassins:** Resonance marketing strategies are critically dependent upon user-generated content to eliminate the uncertainty discount and create demand for new offerings. Delighted customers can serve as *Online Brand Ambassadors*, by posting reviews that create demand. In contrast, strongly dissatisfied customers often serve as Online Brand Assassins, writing reviews that deter future customers from trying the product and can destroy the perception of a product's quality. The newly emerging role of the *Chief Perception Officer (CPO)* is to coordinate all aspects of a product's quality, and thus manage customers' perception of the brand.

This chapter focuses on the tactical problems associated with implementing and sustaining a Resonance Marketing strategy. Most important is integrating all aspects of product design, production, distribution, and service,

Much of the research on brand ambassadors and brand assassins reported here was done jointly with Chris Dellarocas, but never published in English; we did publish it in *China Long March to Quality*, as "重视消费者评价 提升整体管理质量" in November 2012.

to ensure that all customers are delighted and to reduce or eliminate catastrophic quality problems that destroy a firm's reputation. This is the role of the CPO.

The CPO ensures that the firm consistently delivers what it promises so that its customers know what to expect and get what they want.

5.1   Tactical Implications for Companies: The New Role of the Chief Perception Officer

The Chief Perception Officer never sleeps!

In an online age, reputation matters more than ever before, and advertising budgets are not the best way to create and manage reputations for resonance brands. This has created a new corporate role, the *Chief Perception Officer*, whose job is to coordinate all of the organization's activities so that they create and manage reputations in place of explicit communications drafted by the company and its advertising agencies. Actions now speak much, much louder than words in the marketplace. Of course, with the advent of reputation officers, reputation management consulting services were not far behind, and there is a range of support available for the CPO once he has defined his job.

Reputation matters because it translates into higher sales and higher margins. With a great reputation, products can command very high prices. Westvleteren 12 is often regarded as the best beer in the world. But at US$28.50 for a small bottle when you can find it in the USA, it is not cheap! The brand is too small to permit advertising. To a large extent, community content Web sites like RateBeer.com have allowed Westvleteren to convert the quality of its products into a highly visible reputation.

We have already discussed in Sect. 4.4 how RateBeer.com helped launch the craft beer industry. In this chapter, we will explore how TripAdvisor helped launch the online travel industry as well. When I was just starting to travel as an assistant professor, I knew almost nothing about hotels or airlines. My travel agent, Anna Maria, had actually flown on most of the airlines I needed to use, had actually visited most of the cities I needed to visit, and had actually stayed in most of the hotels I needed to consider. She was an endless source of vital information. I needed a hotel close to the InterContinental on Rue de Rivoli in Paris but could not afford it; she booked me into the Hotel Regina in Paris, a short walk from the InterContinental, directly across the street from the Louvre. The hotel was convenient for my meetings, comfortable, and in a great location. Another time I needed to meet someone for breakfast at the Savoy in London, at the time one of the best and one of the most expensive hotels in London. There was no way I could afford that on an assistant professor's budget. She booked me into the Strand Palace, a favorite of World War II prostitutes and now not exactly a palace, but serviceable and directly across the Strand from the Savoy. Anna Maria knew everything and was indispensable.

Online travel made it possible to book quickly and easily, without the use of a human intermediary. This was initially a great saving for hotels, since they no longer had to pay the 10% commission charged by travel agents. But the use of online booking systems created problems for users. How did I know if I could trust an online recommendation from one of the major travel sites? I quickly adopted TripAdvisor, an unbiased and apparently independent Web site that rated hotels, restaurants, and travel destination sites like museums and other attractions. I never wondered who created TripAdvisor or why, or where their revenues came from. Initially, TripAdvisor did not seem to take ads. Initially, TripAdvisor did not redirect users to booking sites. It appeared to operate almost as a charitable foundation to help travelers make informed online booking decisions without consulting a travel agent.

Who would have an interest in helping travelers make informed online booking decisions without consulting a travel agent? That would be online booking systems, of course. A little research indicated that TripAdvisor was owned and operated by InterActive Corp (IAC); IAC also owned Hotels.com, Expedia.com, and Hotwire.com. TripAdvisor was created as an independent source of reviews, enabling users to assess the recommendations that they received from IAC's booking systems. IAC has since spun off all four of these Web sites. But TripAdvisor had already done its work, contributing to the creation of the online travel industry.

Online content is now important to an unprecedented degree. The new role of the *Chief Perception Officer* is to manage online content in a way that strengthens the firm's reputation. The first job of the CPO is to *eliminate the negative* and to keep bad reviews off Web sites. The second job is to take actions that lead to the widest range of positive reviews and to *accentuate the positive.*

You can't ethically manipulate online reviewing sites or perform your own astroturfing to generate false grassroots support. Likewise, you can't ethically control what the *customer writes* online, and you can't ethically *write your own online reviews*. But to a large extent, you can control what the customer *wants to write.*

A couple of years ago, I noticed a man at Roy's Restaurant in Waikoloa, Hawaii, who seemed to be studying every guest at every table. From time to time, he would stride decisively over to one table or another and then return and resume watching. I started watching him more carefully. If a guest cut into a steak or a piece of fish and then put his knife and fork down, this mystery man would walk over and determine if the customer believed that the dish was cooked too rare, or too over-cooked. If someone were leaning forward to try to hear the conversation at his table, the mystery man would walk over to see if the guests needed a quieter location. The mystery man was the restaurant's manager, and he was my first exposure to a real CPO. He described himself as the restaurant's Yelp and TripAdvisor control officer. He described his job very simply. *"I can't control what you write online, but I can control what you want to write online. I can make sure that every guest leaves delighted, and no one leaves wanting to write damaging reviews."* This self-appointed CPO managed online content by avoiding mistakes before they happened, or before the customers had a chance to be disappointed by them.

The role of the CPO is to control the public image and perception of the company, by aligning all aspects of the company's operations with its intended image. Sometimes this requires changes to the company's product portfolio. Sometimes it requires hands-on management of service operations. Sometimes it requires reverse-engineering hostile online content, to see what breakdowns in quality were responsible and how they can be avoided in the future. This is entirely different from using traditional advertising for image management.

5.2   The First Role of the CPO

"Eliminate the Negative" and Eliminate Brand Assassins

The successful implementation of resonance marketing sounds like a popular song from the 1940s, which talks about accentuating the positive, eliminating the negative, and avoiding "Mr. In-Between." We've already seen that resonance marketing strategies avoid Mr. In-between, since consumers who merely like a product produce no more sales than those who hate it. A good CPO eliminates the avoidable negatives caused by operational breakdowns.

There are many parts of the CPO's job and they need to interact in a consistent way and amplify each other so that the activities of the firm likewise interact in a consistent way and amplify each other. The role of the CPO is to do whatever is possible to eliminate mistakes that would result in negative reviews, since these reviews would damage the firm's image. Individual activities include:

- Working with the operations team to design practices and empower employees to avoid mistakes or respond to mistakes immediately, at the time they occur.
- Monitoring activities as they occur, allowing the firm to respond to any mistakes that have occurred, in order to avoid the bad reviews that would result.
- Monitoring all activities over time, detecting patterns, identifying procedures that need to be corrected, and fixing the underlying causes of quality breakdowns before problems occur again.
- Working with HR to ensure that hiring practices, training, and orientation result in "service heroes," employees who understand the role of hospitality in their interactions with customers, and who understand the role of caring and personal initiative in performing their jobs.
- Monitoring online reviews, detecting and removing fraudulent content, and where appropriate taking legal action against fraudulent content.
- Developing a strategy to manage suppliers, to ensure that their actions contribute to and support the mission of the firm and do not interfere with or damage the firm's reputation.

Online *brand assassins* are lurking, ready to turn any mistake into a public relations disaster. Bad reviews really matter. Experimental economics suggest that a disappointing surprise makes us *unhappier* than the amount of happiness we get from a pleasant surprise. That's called *status quo bias*. Anything that makes us better off than we are now is good, but anything that makes us worse off than we are now is *really* bad. We *really* want to avoid being made less happy.

When working with a major international hotel group in 2007, I became acquainted with one of their properties in Chicago that was proving to be a serious problem. The hotel's *average* reviews were actually acceptable for its chain, but its *worst* reviews were among the worst of any reviews of any comparable property on the net. The worst reviews were among the worst not only *numerically*, consistently 1 star out of 5, but *linguistically*. Their negative reviews were the *longest* and the *most detailed*. Their unhappy guests were not just disappointed. Their unhappy guests *hated them* and were actually *vengeful*. Its occasional bad reviews were truly dreadful reviews, and this was destroying its ability to attract online bookings.

It appears that no one within hotel management made any attempt to identify the cause of reviews like this or to rectify the problems that were the source of these reviews. The problems would not have been difficult to address. Ten years later, the hotel had changed brands and was affiliated with a different hotel group. And yet the reviews continued to show similar problems. The hotel was capable of satisfying guests and continued to attract its share of positive reviews. But the hotel was also prone to the same set of problems that horrified guests in 2007. The two most recent reviews at the time I drafted this chapter were a 5-star, followed by a 1-star. In the hospitality industry, reviews are driven by service quality, and clearly this hotel was suffering from serious service breakdowns. The breakdowns were not constant, but they were frequent enough to demand attention from management.

Reviews matter, and bad reviews *really* matter. Bad reviews affect the number of customers as well as their willingness to pay. With bad reviews, both elements of a firm's revenues, head count and average ticket size, are reduced. It's hard to say this more clearly.

Sometimes bad service can be averted by *simple rules to avoid mistakes*— nobody wants a dirty, moldy room, and you especially don't want bloggers to have them. Sometimes the problems of bad service can be averted simply by *observing and adapting*—we don't all agree on how cooked fish or steak should be, or how much noise makes a table too noisy. But to avoid service mistakes, someone needs to be empowered to notice an unhappy customer and respond immediately.

Moreover, someone needs to care, and someone needs to *empower employees to care*. Inside many service employees is a *service hero* waiting to be unleashed. I once showed up at Philadelphia's International Terminal at 10.58 p.m., absurdly late for an 11.30 flight to London. The terminal was dark, and there was only one USAir employee behind the counters. Anyone senior enough to be left to shut down the operations was apparently senior enough to do a manual override and get me added to the passenger list, which had already been closed. I ran to Terminal C. I boarded the plane seconds before the doors closed, and the plane pulled back as soon as I sat down. A service hero averted a personal disaster that would otherwise have been entirely my fault.

The second element of managing bad service is to understand what caused it and to eliminate it. There's no need to scramble desperately to undo the impact of truly inferior service if service breakdowns don't occur. This allows the firm to eliminate the bad experiences before they occur, which eliminates the bad reviews before anyone even wants to write them.

If everything is now perception, then everything is part of marketing. Operating practices that produced a few dissatisfied guests might have been acceptable once, if the negative experiences were justified by achieving full occupancy and maximizing short-term revenues. Our own research has shown that for mid-price hotels, negative online reviews have the greatest impact on future occupancy, more impact than average or even excellent reviews. The CPO must eliminate negative experiences, in order to manage what the customer wants to write. To succeed, the CPO needs to understand trade-offs and interactions among different measures of performance, so that he or she can balance the immediate profit from full occupancy against the cost of allowing the hotel's reputation to slip. Renting small rooms, dirty rooms, and rooms still under repair will initially yield a small amount of additional revenue. But this will reduce revenues over the long term by destroying the property's reputation. In firm after firm, in industry after industry, the CPO must understand what leads to inferior service and inferior reviews and must improve operations to eliminate the problems.

The CPO can't anticipate everything. The CPO must work with the organization's human resources department to hire employees who *want* to be service heroes and to empower them sufficiently to *allow* them to be service heroes. We've all seen service heroes in the expected locations. Disney World provides some of the best examples. I've seen a young child take the Nautilus submarine ride twice, to make sure that she saw what was out the portholes on both sides of the "sub." She burst into tears when she realized that she was going to be on the starboard side a second time, but one of the "sailors" noticed her distress, asked about the problem, and immediately whisked her off to the port side. We expect this from Disney employees. Increasingly, we are coming to expect flawless service from all organizations, and increasingly firms are going to need to demand this from all employees, in order to eliminate costly public relations disasters.

The next element of the CPOs' responsibilities is to monitor the online posts reviewing their firms' products and services and to recover from the negative reviews if possible. Restaurants and hotels monitor their reviews in Yelp and TripAdvisor and often respond to bad reviews by providing apologies and explanations. Merchants in the Amazon Marketplace respond to bad reviews in similar ways. Many of the best will respond to bad reviews by contacting the seller and offering to fix the problem; I have had a rusted part of a pasta maker replaced within hours of posting a review in which I mentioned how disappointed my daughter was when it arrived rusted. Amazon did not allow me to alter the negative review, but they did allow me to remove it.

The CPO also needs to prevent fraudulent attacks on the firm's reputation. Since online reviews have become so important, firms now often have to deal with fraudulent reviews. Sometimes fraudulent negative reviews are posted by organizations trying to damage the reputation of direct competitors. Occasionally, fraudulent reviews are posted by criminals who offer to remove them in exchange for payment. Of course, the CPO must work with the firm's legal department to have fraudulent reviews removed. When possible, the firm should file charges against fraudulent reviewers and seek prosecution against fraudulent reviewers.

Why don't firms all do a better job of managing their reputations? The implications of online reviewing have been visible for at least a decade to anyone interested enough to look. Why has it been so difficult for firms to adapt? Why has the process of managing perceptions been so complicated? Why have so few firms learned how to manage online content by *managing what the customer wants to write*? Part of the problem arises because senior management is often focused on managing the averages of their reviews, rather than being focused on avoiding their worst reviews and encouraging their best reviews. Part of the problem is caused by senior management continuing to believe that average reviews and mass-market fat spots are the strengths of their business. Part of the problem occurs because senior management believes that it can control perception through its own publications and its own advertising content, rather than through deeds and managing what the customer wants to write. That is, much of senior management understands the world before the Internet, before resonance marketing, and before the need to focus on the impact of extremes. Their world has changed, and service management needs to change with it.

5.3   Tactical Implications for Companies

"Accentuate the Positive" and encourage Brand Ambassadors

Section 5.2 concentrated on the negative aspects of the CPO's role. The CPO needs to eliminate the negative. This section focuses on the more positive aspects of the CPO's role.

The first positive role of the CPO is to observe customers and understand their unmet wants and needs. When craft brewers Victory Brewing, Dogfish Head, and Stone were still very small, their brewpub operations were essential to their success and enabled their future growth. Brewmasters drank with their customers. They saw what their customers liked and didn't like, and altered their products accordingly. Even when the breweries had grown enormously, had multiple locations, and produced one hundred times more beer than when they had started, watching customers at the bar remained essential. Tastes change, making some products less novel than before, and creating openings for new offerings that will now be popular. Competitors change, making some products less distinctive. And, frankly, customers get bored and from time to time need variety. Brewmasters of the largest craft brewers can no longer know all of their customers personally. But the best still function as CPOs and hang out in their bars watching customers' reactions to old favorites and experimental new offerings.

The second positive role of the CPO is to observe the customers' own innovations and incorporate the best ones into the firm's products. Eric von Hippel has published extensively on the role of customer-driven innovation. One of my favorites of his examples is the history of the skateboard. Early skateboards were cobbled together by users, from a slab of wood and a single traditional roller skate separated into two halves. In contrast, corporate manufacturers make today's modern high-performance boards. And yet, manufacturers of these high-performance boards work closely with the best professional boarders, to ensure that their products attract sweet spot customers with their highly focused needs and preferences.

The third role of the CPO is seeding demand and seeding online content. Part of getting online customers is to provide samples to very demanding, very experienced, very committed customers. This is not cheating. When you get your product exactly right, you give some of it to people who will recognize its quality, appreciate it, and review it. Paradoxically, when you have only a limited quantity of your new product initially, your most profitable strategy might be giving a lot of it away, if you can direct it to the right people.

Once again, the craft beer industry provides an excellent example. Craft beer festivals like the Great American Beer Festival in Denver in the Fall and Philadelphia Beer Week in the Spring provide gatherings for dozens, even hundreds of brewers and for thousands of experienced beer drinkers. This is the best time to try out a new beer, get it into the hands of highly motivated potential customers, and wait for the reviews to start appearing. If you have done everything right and produced exactly the right beer for the market, you will see wonderful reviews start appearing. Again, this is not cheating. You are not controlling what your customers write. You are managing what your customers want to write.

Any industry that focuses on its key users, and on its most influential customers, is following the same model. Think of computer electronics shows, air shows, or Star Trek conventions, to name just a few.

Just as there are many activities that the CPO performs to reduce or eliminate bad reviews, there are many activities that the CPO performs to maximize positive reviews.

5.4   Summary

Online content provides an essential element of Resonance Marketing strategies, by eliminating the uncertainty discount and enabling the introduction of new goods and services. Online content rapidly helps consumers achieve informedness and to become fully familiar with offerings they have never tried before. This is an essential part of the digital transformation of consumer behavior.

Online content matters. Dissatisfied customers can become Online Brand Assassins and destroy a product by damaging other customers' perception of the product or even the entire company. Likewise, delighted customers can become Online Brand Ambassadors, influencing other customers' perceptions and allowing them to feel comfortable purchasing new resonance offerings.

The Chief Perception Officer coordinates all of the firm's activities to manage customers' perceptions. There are several concrete steps that the CPO can coordinate to accentuate the positive and eliminate the negative. This is the most important element in the implementation of a firm's Resonance Marketing strategy. The CPO maximizes the gains from your Online Brand Ambassadors and minimizes the harm from your Online Brand Assassins. This is an essential part of implementing a Resonance Marketing strategy, and thus an essential part of gaining and defending the competitive advantage that Resonance Marketing can provide.

Part II

Patterns for Power, Control, and Harvesting of Profits

6

Resources, Platforms, and Sustainable Competitive Advantage: How to Win and Keep on Winning

This chapter introduces one new pattern, but first it reminds us of an old pattern that has been known to strategists for centuries. Whether you are in a competitive business, in complex political negotiations, or engaged in outright military warfare, it's helpful to have valuable stuff that the other guy doesn't have. If you want to sue someone, it helps to have more money and better attorneys. If you want to fight a war, it helps to have better fighter aircraft and better tanks. For obvious reasons, this pattern is called *resource-based sustainable competitive advantage.*

Resource-based sustainable competitive advantage is surprisingly difficult to achieve in an information-based business. Software that innovative firms develop can usually be duplicated by competitors, who may even improve upon the original. However, sometimes the resources the firm owns, the skill base of the firm, and the environment in which it operates cannot be fully duplicated by any competitor. These resources and skills, and occasionally the operating environment itself, can be sources of sustainable competitive advantage when leveraged through software, even if the software itself can be copied.

This chapter's new pattern is *platform envelopment as a source of sustainable competitive advantage.*

> **Platform Envelopment:** Platform envelopment is a form of resource-based sustainable competitive advantage. In platform envelopment, the firm creates the resources that it later combines and uses to protect and defend

© The Author(s) 2019
E. K. Clemons, *New Patterns of Power and Profit,*
https://doi.org/10.1007/978-3-030-00443-9_6

> its sustainable competitive advantage. Microsoft gained advantage from the interactions among Windows, Office (Word, Excel, PowerPoint, and Outlook), Media Player, and Internet Explorer, all of which Microsoft created.

Google has a platform envelopment strategy. Facebook and Uber both pursue platform envelopment strategies. Platform envelopment strategies create lasting value for their creators, in part by creating so much value for customers that it is almost impossible for any other firm to steal the customers away. This, in turn, may give the platform creator enough power to reduce competition, limit consumer choice, and as a result increase consumers' prices. I view platform envelopment strategies as a transition between the value-creating patterns of the first part of the book and the value-harvesting patterns of the second half.

6.1   Introduction to Sustainable Competitive Advantage

First get ahead, then stay ahead!

Competitive advantage is easy to recognize. When a firm has competitive advantage, the firm does something better than its competitors, from which it earns more money. This generally translates into higher profit margins, greater market share, or some combination of the two. *Sustainable competitive advantage* is more difficult to recognize, because it involves competitive advantage that is maintained for a long time, even in the presence of competitors who seek to copy a firm's offerings and erode its advantage.

It's difficult to sustain advantage with skill alone. Whether you're making great India Pale Ale, writing great operating systems, or building great automobiles, if you're making enough money doing it, competitors will eventually duplicate what you are doing. If you want to keep earning extra money from your competitive advantage, you will need to learn to do whatever you're doing even better. There's a limit to what you can do with an IPA; after you've exhausted the possibilities you need to come up with a new style, or open a better brewpub, or do something to protect your advantage. There's a limit to how good a car can be; with great gas mileage, great fit and finish, and great styling you need to find some other way to compete. BMW, Mercedes, Nissan, and Toyota are about as well engineered as they need to be. As a result, BMW, Mercedes, and the Japanese Infiniti and Lexus brands are now competing through the superior service experience they can offer for their customers. But constantly improving the quality of a traditional automobile on any one dimension *hits the wall* eventually. Cars can't have fewer than zero defects. Cars can't be more efficient than the laws of physics permit. At some point, constantly improving the quality of the service department will eventually hit the wall as well. Any skill-based competitive advantage will erode over time. Skill-based competition based on electric vehicle power will also erode over time. Some skills are difficult to obtain and require years of practice, but every expert and every champion athlete should understand that their skill advantage will erode.

A promising alternative for extending competitive advantage is to base it upon some unique collection of resources that competitors cannot match. This is extremely difficult in athletics, where competitions are supposed to be fair. Every sport has rules that govern the equipment that can be used. The maximum "springiness" of golf club surfaces, the maximum length of a tennis racket and the maximum size of the racket's hitting surface, and the composition and length of a baseball bat are all regulated in formal competition. In contrast, every business tries to compete, at least in part, by obtaining an advantage in resources that cannot readily be duplicated. For years, the De Beers Company enjoyed a near monopoly on the supply of diamonds. All of their expertise, including their wonderfully efficient inspection and quality rating rules, was available in the public domain. The only advantage they had was their ownership of the principal source of diamonds. As other sources of supply have emerged, even this source of competitive advantage has been eroded.

6.2 Sustainable Competitive Advantage Based on Acquiring a Unique Set of Resources

One way to stay ahead is to acquire and learn to use resources that no one else can get!

Controlling critical assets can be a source of sustainable competitive advantage. And this idea itself is a reoccurring pattern, as old as competition itself. It's certainly been true in the innovative use of information systems, almost since the advent of information systems. Merrill Lynch earned superior profits for years when it introduced the cash management account and paid higher interest than any traditional banking product was allowed to offer. But only uniqueness provides advantage. All banks and credit card companies prepare monthly statements. All savings institutions have ATM networks. No one gets advantage by doing what everyone else is able to duplicate.

Online grocery shopping provides a recent example of advantage from the innovative use of systems in ways that other firms cannot duplicate. The home page for the online grocery site for Amazon and the equivalent site for Walmart are almost indistinguishable. I may prefer Amazon, and you may prefer Walmart, but it's hard to argue that one site is fundamentally better than the other, or that one firm gained sustainable competitive advantage over the other through its use of software alone. And yet, the two are coming to dominate online grocery in a way that few other firms can match.

Both Amazon and Walmart achieved competitive advantage *somehow*, since both are ranked among the top US online grocery sites. Both obtained competitive advantage through resources that they enjoyed that most competitors did not have and that most competitors could not easily acquire. Both firms enjoyed an enormous distribution network that spanned all of America. And both offered the widest array of choices, which they could afford because they had the largest possible customer base.

Why couldn't *any* firm just duplicate the distribution systems of Amazon and Walmart? Both firms developed their distribution for other products, not originally for groceries. Both originally sold a wide range of shelf-stable items, from books to bikes, and towels to tableware. That's actually quite important. The adoption of online grocery sales in the USA has been quite slow compared to other countries. It would have been prohibitively expensive to develop a distribution network only for online grocery sales. In contrast, it's relatively cheap and easy just to piggyback online grocery sales on an existing distribution network.[1]

And why couldn't *any* firm just duplicate the wide array of products offered by both Amazon and Walmart's online grocery stores? With a large number of customers, customers' average behavior becomes predictable. Imagine you are a small health insurer, insuring only five people, all of them in Philadelphia. It is not impossible that all five might come down with the flu in the same week. Now imagine that you are a huge insurance company,

---

[1]And why stop there? It was easy to sell books online because consumers didn't need to inspect a book before deciding if it was fresh or ripe; those words apply to produce, not to books. But many consumers trust Whole Foods enough not to require inspecting produce before buying from them; I expect to see increasing integration into Amazon's online sales and distribution.

insuring 500,000 people all across America. It is now virtually impossible that all 500,000 might come down with the flu at the same time and you can estimate in any given week just how many of your clients you could expect to be sick with the flu or any other common condition. Likewise, for Amazon and Walmart weekly sales become far more stable and far more predictable. That means that Amazon and Walmart can order just enough from their suppliers with less concern for running out or excess supplies spoiling. That means that their customers can count on getting the products they want, getting products when promised, and getting products that are fresh.

Amazon and Walmart can have sustainable competitive advantage in online grocery sales, even with software that could easily be duplicated. Both firms already enjoy resource advantages over potential competitors because of their existing distribution networks and their existing scale.

Interestingly, they gain advantage because of the interaction of their new businesses with businesses that they had already created. This is the start of a platform envelopment strategy.

6.3   Introduction to Platforms and Platform Envelopment

Another way to stay ahead is to spin a web of software applications that competitors can't match and customers won't ever abandon!

Platform envelopment requires a platform, of course. And it requires a strategy for leveraging that platform for sustainable competitive advantage. A *platform* is what it sounds like—software, or an integrated software, and hardware installation, that can readily be extended. A *platform envelopment strategy* starts with a simple platform and additions are then built on it. These additions create incremental value for users through their interactions with the initial platform. As the platform grows, the new additions add value through their interactions with each other, as well as with the original simple platform. These interactions are critical to the value creation; they make the platform more valuable, and they also make the additions more valuable. Strategy geeks call this *super-additive value creation*.

An example is helpful. Microsoft's Windows is a platform. Once Windows is installed, the laptop or desktop computer finally can deliver value to its owner. And once a machine has Windows it becomes extensible. Microsoft Office interacts well with Windows, and each element in the Office Suite interacts well with the others. Indeed, the ease of interaction between Windows and Office, and the difficulty other software vendors had integrating their own office software, ultimately led to the death of Lotus 1-2-3 and WordPerfect, the first widely adopted spreadsheet and word processing programs. Likewise, when Microsoft's Internet Explorer came pre-bundled with Windows, and when IE became the most popular browser at the time, Microsoft was able to make tight integration with Windows into a platform envelopment strategy that contributed to the death of Netscape. Microsoft continues to add applications and continues to ensure that they interact to create super-additive value. This ensures that each application is part of a platform envelopment strategy and not merely an addition to a software application portfolio.

Microsoft's platform envelopment strategy is a form of resource-based sustainable competitive advantage, as are most platform envelopment strategies. In platform envelopment, the key resources are not possessed by other firms and are not easily duplicated. The Intel-based world simply did not have room for another dominant operating system, and Microsoft got there first. A superior resource endowment can be a result of superior planning, historical accident, or even luck. But once a firm enjoys a resource advantage, and can leverage it in a platform envelopment strategy, its position is secure. Microsoft's dominant position was secure from competitors until the world shifted; as we move more toward mobile access, and more toward Internet, cloud-based access, and search, power shifted to Apple and to Google. There was nothing that another word processor vendor, another spreadsheet vendor, or another operating system vendor, could have done to shake Microsoft's dominant position until users' view of computing had shifted.

A platform is not the same as critical infrastructure. AT&T enjoyed a monopoly over America's telephone infrastructure. But strict regulation prevented AT&T from leveraging its communications infrastructure into control of radio or television. The Internet may be a platform, in the sense that almost any application developed today is written for the Internet and distributed through the Internet. But no single company owns the Internet, and no single company is able to determine who can, or cannot, access the net.

Successful platform envelopment strategies almost always involve software in some way. It's just more difficult to integrate numerous physical products into a platform, instead of just combining them into a portfolio. When Berkshire Hathaway acquired See's Candies, this was a portfolio investment; See's was acquired for its latent value as a stand-alone company, and not because of its potential synergies with Berkshire Hathaway's energy company holdings, its financial services holdings, or its holdings in other consumer packaged goods companies.

6.4   An Early Example of Platform Envelopment at Rosenbluth Travel

Platform envelopment is not new, and smart software companies have been using it for decades!

One of the earliest modern examples of a robust platform envelopment strategy was developed at Rosenbluth Travel in the years immediately following the deregulation of the travel industry. This is also one of the earliest examples of the *digital transformation* of a firm and of an entire industry.

Rosenbluth Travel had been one of the regional players, perhaps the largest travel agent in Pennsylvania, and one of the 50 largest agencies in the USA. Like most travel agencies in the 1980s, Rosenbluth focused on leisure travel, because there simply was not much that could be done to add value for corporate travelers. The Civil Aeronautics Board (CAB) controlled the routes that airlines could fly, the schedules that they followed, and the fares that they charged. There were very few fare possibilities, generally coach, first class, night fares, and advance purchase excursion fares. With so little complexity and so little change in routes and prices, there was little need for corporations to work with travel agencies. Most corporate travelers were served directly by the airlines.

In contrast, when air travel was a novelty, leisure travelers needed coaching. Where should a vacationer go for the best beaches in Hawaii? What was an inexpensive hotel close to the Louvre in Paris? In fact, the industry standard 10% commission that airlines paid to travel agents was invented by the airlines, to provide an incentive for travel agents to advise vacationers and to help create the leisure travel industry.

All of this changed after deregulation of air travel and the abolition of the CAB. Airlines were free to alter their routes and their schedules. Airlines were free to alter their fares at will, often issuing hundreds of thousand or even millions of fare changes in a single day during industry-wide fare wars. Airlines introduced complex pricing mechanisms, trying to identify which reservations were from leisure travelers and which were from corporate travelers so that they could charge higher prices to business travelers. Corporate travelers and corporate travel managers were outraged, paradoxically considering travel one of the largest controllable corporate expenses that they had not yet learned to control.

At this point, Rosenbluth transformed itself and began to focus on corporate travelers almost immediately after deregulation. Rosenbluth's first innovation was a system called *Readout*, which allowed them to price tickets based on fare, rather than on airline or time of departure. Rather than announce that they had a United Airlines flights at 10:45 a.m., 2:15 p.m., and 6:30 p.m., with *Readout* Rosenbluth agents could announce that they had flights at $345, $590, and $1700. Agents could then coach travelers so that they could pick the least expensive fare that was compatible with their scheduling requirements.

Hal Rosenbluth announced *Readout* to his corporate customers and immediately doubled the size of the company. Their daily sales volume doubled the day of the announcement, increasing from an annualized level of $10 million in air sales to $20 million.

Rosenbluth was attacking a newly vulnerable market for corporate travel. It was newly easy to enter after deregulation, because there was finally something for agencies to do that was not being done by the airlines themselves. It was attractive to attack because of the strong customer profitability gradient for business travelers compared to leisure travelers. Corporate travelers still on average bought more expensive tickets than leisure travelers, so they generated higher commissions. Corporate travelers knew where they wanted to fly, and why, and generally required very little coaching on restaurants and sightseeing. They were easy to serve and produced higher commissions. And the industry was difficult to defend because no one trusted the airlines to perform honest price-based competition, and because other agencies initially had very different strategies.

Rosenbluth introduced other applications in quick succession.

- *Vision*—Vision provided complex expense account verification and analysis, including flight by individual, by department, by airline, and by city pairs. It provided other analyses that companies might request, like who was using more expensive fares, or staying in more expensive hotels, when less expensive alternatives were available.
- *User Vision*—User Vision allowed corporate travel departments to download their data and run their own analyses.
- *Scripting Languages*—Rosenbluth was able to persuade United Airlines Apollo to add a scripting capability that was useful when Rosenbluth agents were taking reservations. This allowed Rosenbluth to avoid certain common errors, like accidentally booking a passenger on a flight into one airport while reserving a rental car at another airport. If you are landing at New York's JFK, a rental car at La Guardia or Newark is of very little value. The scripting language also helped Rosenbluth agents guide travelers to the best fares available for their firms.

- *Negotiated Airfares*—Once Rosenbluth had gotten large enough, it was able to negotiate special airfares for its corporate travelers. In exchange for guaranteeing an airline a certain percentage increase in traffic, or a certain guaranteed level of traffic, the airline would offer Rosenbluth special discounted airfares. This discount had two components, the discount that the traveler saw, and the *override,* or increased commission, that Rosenbluth received. The airline had higher load factors and more passengers. Rosenbluth earned higher commissions on each ticket, even while selling less expensive tickets. And the customer paid less.

This created a *virtuous circle.* Successful deployment of technology made Rosenbluth more attractive to customers, which allowed them to grow. Increased scale made writing additional applications more cost-effective, which led to more technology. The deployment of additional technology made them more attractive, which led to more scale, which further drove their technology development.

As importantly, each new application interacted with Rosenbluth's existing application base. It made the existing applications more valuable. They, in turn, made the new application more valuable.

Rosenbluth's negotiated fares may provide the best examples of this. *Negotiated fares* only work if you already have the scale to demand concessions from a single airline as your preferred carrier—you have to be large enough to make demands and make promises that are credible. Negotiated fares only work if you have systems like *Vision* and *User Vision,* so that you can demonstrate the effectiveness of your negotiated fares program both to your corporate customers and to your selected airline partner. And negotiated fares are most effective if you already have a *scripting language,* which helps you direct corporate passengers to your partner airline. Private, negotiated fares gave Rosenbluth an advantage, one that allowed it to increase its market share still further. Rosenbluth divided the discount from these special fares with its clients, allowing its clients to enjoy lower fares while simultaneously allowing Rosenbluth to enjoy higher profits on each ticket sale.

This portfolio, or platform, is very effective. It enabled Rosenbluth to continue to grow, which enabled it to continue to offer negotiated fares. Importantly, this platform funded continued development of new applications, which served as platform extensions.

Platform envelopment is not just the same as continuous improvement, although the user did experience continuous improvement as Rosenbluth's platform was extended. Each of the applications in the platform is integrated with the others. Each adds value in a way that requires prior successful implementation of the others. Each gains value from the others and each contributes value to the others.

Like Microsoft with its platform envelopment strategy, Rosenbluth's platform provided sustainable competitive advantage, even after other agencies were able to duplicate some of its earliest services, like *Readout* and *Vision*. Rosenbluth enjoyed sustainable competitive advantage, based on the interaction of resources that it had created. Rosenbluth's advantage was secure from attack by other agencies and would last as long as users continued to purchase travel services through agencies.

Rosenbluth's platform envelopment strategy clearly created enormous value for its customers. As a result, it provided enormous value for Rosenbluth as well. Rosenbluth grew until it was one of the three largest agencies in the world. And with the added profits that came from negotiated fares, it enjoyed higher margins. Both contributed to sustainable competitive advantage.

Sustainable competitive advantage is seldom *permanent competitive advantage*! Rosenbluth was a dominant player for years, when it was merely competing with other travel agencies. With the advent of eCommerce and eTravel, airlines began offering their own reservations services online. As we discussed previously, airlines began serving the industry's *love 'em* customers, leaving the *kill yous* to the agencies. Rosenbluth Travel and its successor, Rosenbluth International, are no more.

6.5   Platform Envelopment Strategies in Two-Sided Markets

Platform envelopment is now an important pattern in information-based strategy, with its own structures and its own winners and losers.

Two-sided markets exist when the seller buys from one or more suppliers and sells to one or more buyers. The term can be broadened to include the market's *value-adding activities*: Dell buys processing chips and memory chips and other parts from its suppliers and although it does not resell processing chips or memory, it does sell complete assembled laptop and desktop computers, tablets, and servers to its customers.

Since the goal of many two-sided markets is to develop a platform envelopment strategy, it's easy to confuse two-sided markets with platforms because so many of the most visible platforms started as two-sided markets. Many of us deal with Amazon several times a week now, ordering physical products, or using their music service, or their TV service or unlimited access to Kindle books. Some of us interact with Amazon constantly, every hour we are home, through Alexa. Amazon started as a classic two-sided market, a bookseller. Uber started as a two-sided market, and as it adds services like UberEats it clearly is attempting to become a powerful platform operator. Google and Microsoft have maintained such dominant platforms that both have endured antitrust judgments, but neither is primarily a two-sided market.

For a concept as broad and general as two-sided markets to be useful, it must allow us to subdivide the huge constellation of markets it describes along several dimensions.

- The first dimension is whether or not the market is **symmetric**. Stock exchanges are symmetric because the investors are buyers at some times and sellers at others. Stores, reservations systems, and ride-hailing services are not. In contrast to investors on an exchange, roles in the other markets are more limited. I never go to Walmart to sell, I never use a reservations system to offer flights, and I never use Uber to offer a ride.
- The second dimension might be who has the **power** in the market and thus **which party pays for the market's services**. This is a measure of the extent of competition. As we will see in the next chapter it is possible to have several participants but if the structure of the market limits the competition, as it did in airline reservations systems, then the owner of the market can still exercise considerable power. Large chains like Walmart often have enough power to demand payments from producers for including their goods in Walmart's inventory.
- The third dimension might be **extensibility**, which can allow the market to be developed into a **platform**. Amazon was launched as an online bookseller, but it was rapidly extended. Amazon now sells books, eBooks, and eReaders, and a wide range of other physical products. It is a dominant player in online books. Apple started by selling computers and the operating system for their computers; gradually, Apple added laptops and other devices, like the iPod, the iPhone, and the iPad. Most importantly, they are all bound together by Apple's operating system and iTunes, creating an integrated ecosystem that serves as a valuable platform. "*iTunes to rule them, iTunes to find them, iTunes to bring them all, and in the Ether bind them, in the Land of Cupertino ...*". This is not just a successful platform, this is a successful platform envelopment strategy.

The most interesting two-sided markets we will study in this book provide significant power to their operators and are extensible. They are dominant. And they are profitable.

6.6 Summary

This chapter introduces a new pattern for sustaining competitive advantage. It is difficult or even impossible to gain competitive advantage from software alone. When a firm can create a unique portfolio of interlocking applications, this can enable a platform envelopment strategy, which in turn can provide sustainable competitive advantage.

Platform envelopment can create value for the platform's users and can allow the firm to harvest enormous value for itself.

7

Understanding the Power of Third Party Payer Businesses and Online Gateways

This chapter introduces our final two patterns, both of which represent powerful, even potentially dangerous, business models for the Internet. Individually, each can be very profitable. Together, they can engage in almost unlimited harvesting of profits from the rest of the online ecosystem. The first pattern is *Mandatory Participation Third Party Payer Systems* (MP3PPs).

> **Mandatory Participation Third Party Payer Systems:** A Third Party Payer System is a platform where Party-1 (the customer) uses Party-2 (the platform) to interact with Party-3 (the merchant or service provider who needs to interact with the customer). The platform is free for Party-1 because Party-3 values it enough to subsidize it, or even to pay enough to make it available without charge to Party-1. A Mandatory Participation Third Party Payer System is one where the platform has become so essential to Party-3 that Party-3 *must* participate, almost without concern for the cost of its participation.

The second pattern is *Online Gateway Systems*.

> **Online Gateway Systems:** Online Gateway Systems are platforms that can be used to link buyers and sellers. Sometimes there are effective competitors for a gateway, as when multiple markets can be used to trade securities, or when the eCommerce sites of multiple big box stores sell the same appliances. Sometimes an online gateway develops enormous importance to buyers, and as a result becomes essential for sellers, such as Amazon in books or Google in search.

© The Author(s) 2019
E. K. Clemons, *New Patterns of Power and Profit*,
https://doi.org/10.1007/978-3-030-00443-9_7

MP3PPs are not restricted to online systems, although as we explore in this chapter they achieve their greatest impact in conjunction with online systems. The combination of an online gateway with an MP3PP represents one of the most powerful and most useful innovations enabled by the Internet. They have transformed individual behavior, online marketing, and the balance of power between new entrants and powerful established brands.

There is very little that limits the prices that these MP3PPs can charge Party-3, the sellers, once sellers have become dependent upon them for access to buyers. Interestingly, there is also surprisingly little that limits the power that an MP3PP has over Party-1, their customers, provided they maintain certain minimum standards. These standards can on occasion be surprisingly low.

We usually can rely upon competition—market forces—to limit a firm's prices and profits and to drive a firm to offer the best possible products and services. To a surprising degree market forces and competition do not force MP3PPs to lower their prices or to achieve the best possible quality. Indeed, as we shall see in a range of examples, competition among MP3PPs can actually lead to a *reverse price war*, in which competitors seek to gain market share by actually *increasing* the prices they charge to Party-3, in order to pay subsidies to attract a larger share of Party-1 users, which will make them even more important to Party-3. Likewise, to a surprising degree, competition does not force MP3PPs to offer the best possible service to their Party-1 customers. Historically, when market forces do not and cannot control the behavior of a business or an industry, society has turned to regulation.

The MP3PP pattern and the online gateway pattern differ significantly from the previous four patterns. While the previous patterns principally created value by increasing efficiency, these two patterns have a significant element of value harvesting, which may be more significant than their value creation. Surely their profitability comes from harvesting, rather than from value creation, since the *value is created for Party-1* but the *revenues and profits are harvested from Party-3*.

While MP3PPs are both the most interesting and the most problematic innovations associated with the Internet, they are certainly not the first innovative use of technology to force society to rethink its policy on regulation. Railroads opened up the American continent, but they also developed the ability to abuse farmers whose rural locations were served by only a single rail line. When short-haul transit to Chicago on a monopoly line cost more than the rest of the shipping from Chicago to the east coast, we started to regulate interstate commerce. Telecommunications, both traditional land-based telephony and broadcast radio and television, initially had significant monopoly power and initially required innovative regulation.

Chapter 8 explores more of the power and the potential for abuse of power associated with MP3PP online gateways. Chapter 9 explores the ways in which MP3PP power might affect consumers and the potential roles for regulation as well as the potential forms such regulation might take to create the greatest benefit and cause the least disruption to the online business environment.

This chapter and the two chapters that follow are important for a variety of reasons. First and foremost, every business and every individual, both online and off, interacts with one or more Third Party Payer Systems today. It is important to know how they can help you, how they can hurt you, and, on occasion, how they can destroy you. Second, there are additional opportunities to create third party payer businesses, and some of these opportunities may be quite profitable if they are deployed properly. Finally, we need to be informed consumers and informed citizens. We all interact with third party payer businesses constantly in our private lives. We need to know when we are beneficiaries, and when we are actually harmed by systems that appear to be free, so that we can protect ourselves and exert appropriate influence upon our legislators and our regulators.

7.1 Introduction to Third Party Payer Systems

It does look free, doesn't it!

Third Party Payer Systems (3PPs) include all services that are heavily subsidized or even free for users because a third party pays the system provider to make the systems available. Since these systems are offered to users at such low prices, it's hard for any other business model to compete with them. This is great strategy for capturing and growing market share. Third Party Payer Systems are everywhere. Network radio broadcasting is a Third Party Payer System: I listen to my favorite stations and advertisers pay the cost of programming, broadcasting, and all the other expenses associated with providing radio service. Traditional TV works the same way: I watch my favorite programs and advertisers pay all the costs.

Mostly, Third Party Payer Systems are not dangerous. That is, mostly they provide useful services, and mostly they are not too expensive even for Party-3, since competition among alternative third party payer limits what they can charge Party-3. If ads on a New York TV station become too expensive, advertisers could switch to another station, or they could switch to radio advertising. There are entirely too many TV and radio stations today for collusion and price fixing to be a problem for firms that need to advertise. But if collusion and excessive pricing did become a problem, advertisers could switch how they choose to advertise, and could place their ads in the New York Times and USA Today, or they could use local editions of magazines.

MasterCard and Visa, health insurance, and broadcast radio, and TV are well known, decades-old examples of Third Party Payer Systems. For more modern Internet-based examples, think in terms of online travel reservations systems like Hotels.com or Orbitz. For individual users, these modern online systems are free, because hotels and airlines pay commissions to these systems' operators to subsidize our use. Search engines like Google, file sharing systems like YouTube, and social media networks like Facebook, are free to individual users because they are all Third Party Payer Systems, and they are obviously all very important now.

7.2   Mandatory Participation Third Party Payer Systems: Third Party Payer Systems in the Absence of Effective Competition

You can feel the power!

Over time some Third Party Payer Systems have developed an almost unlimited ability to charge the payer. Hotels and airlines really do need to be found by travelers. Reservations systems developed the ability to charge hotels and airlines for being found. But they also developed the ability to threaten and to misdirect users to other locations if hotels and airlines did not pay them for their services. The business model moved away from charging hotels and airlines *to be found*, which is a *profitable* business model for Party-2. Instead, these systems began to charge hotels and airlines *to not be not found*, which is *even more profitable* for Party-2.

In Third-Party Payer business models, Party-1 uses a facility that he truly values, which is provided by Party-2, and he uses it in order to find or interact with Party-3. Party-3 needs Party-2 to allow Party-1 to find him, so Party-3 pays Party-2 in order to obtain access to Party-1.

Think about search: Users value search, and hotels need users to be able to find them. Users don't always know what their hotel choices are in every city, so search is vitally important.

Hotels invest in their brands so their users will search for them and not search for some other hotel in the same city. Hotels also pay search engines, but paying search engines is different from the hotels' usual investments in brand creation. Brand creation leads users to *want* to find a particular hotel and to search for that hotel, but that doesn't automatically mean that users *will* find a particular hotel, or that they will find it *easily*. Search engines can report search results in whatever order they wish. That means that even though you specifically requested an individual hotel, there is no reason to assume that hotel will be the one that shows up first on the list of hotels you are shown. Hotels therefore pay search engines to ensure a preferred location on the page of search results that you will be shown when you search, and to ensure that they *"won't be not found."* They need to do this even when you search specifically *for them*.

When I was working with a major American hotel chain we found that every dollar we saved by not paying Google for the use of our own name as a keyword cost us between $30 and $40 in lost revenues. That is, if we did not buy our name from Google, someone else would buy our name and our Web site would be less likely to be found, even by travelers explicitly searching for us and for our brand.

Controlling the point at which consumers interact with the net creates the ability to misdirect users to alternative sites, if those sites pay a fee. This in turn creates the ability to charge all other sites a fee, even the ones that users are actually searching for, so that these users will not be redirected elsewhere. Misdirection is a proven business model, as is the threat of misdirection. This was already clear in the 1980s, when misdirection and payment to avoid misdirection were the bases of two powerful airlines reservations systems. Interestingly, these two businesses also made it clear in the 1980s that the power of mandatory participation Third Party Payer businesses may not be reduced by competition.

Let's start with a little history lesson. Let's start with a form of search that is almost half a century old and can be discussed today with little or no ambiguity about the power and the abuse involved. After half a century's experience, we can honestly say that we know what happened in the older form of search. Studying older forms of search provides insight and enables us to understand newer search-based business.

In the late 1970s, American Airlines and United Airlines both decided that they needed additional hub cities, and they decided to use the manipulation of search to enable them to win over their new hub cities. For historical reasons, both had originally chosen to locate their hubs in Chicago. American decided to locate its new hub in Dallas/Fort Worth and United decided to locate its new hub in Denver. The weather in the Southwest was certainly more amenable for air travel. And the Southwest was growing economically, while the "Rust Belt" was stagnating. These were good business decisions. However, American and United found that they were facing stiff competition in their new hub cities. Dallas was already the hub for Braniff, and Denver was already served by Frontier.

Fortunately for American and United, and unfortunately for their two competitors, control over a reservation system allowed American and United to destroy the established competitor airlines in their newly selected hub cities. American Airlines dropped Braniff (Airline **A** in Fig. 7.1) out of its Sabre computer reservations system (CRS **I** in Fig. 7.1). Travel agents whose agency used Sabre could no longer book flights on Braniff. If they tried to book passengers from Dallas to Chicago or other destinations served by Braniff, no Braniff flights were listed on their screens. They naturally assumed that there were no Braniff flights at the requested times, and they booked passengers on other airlines, mostly American Airlines. Passengers were not harmed; they got seats on American, perhaps at promotional prices, and they got to Chicago. Agencies were not harmed; they still got to book flights for their customers and they still received their commissions.

This was, however, disastrous for Braniff. Agencies that used United Airlines' Apollo could still book Braniff, but Braniff's loss of traffic from agencies that used Sabre was sufficient to bankrupt them. Air travel is a

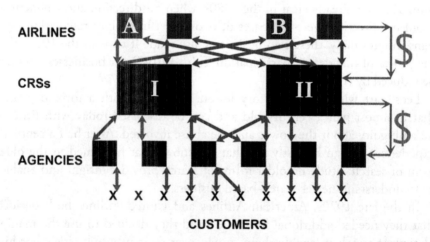

Fig. 7.1 Two computerized travel agent reservations systems, I and II, provide services to numerous airlines and to numerous travel agencies. Most agencies used only one system, so most airlines needed to work with both reservations systems

largely fixed cost business for the airlines; reducing the number of passengers on each plane does not affect fuel costs, equipment costs, crew salary, or fees for the use of airport gates. And being dropped from Sabre reduced Braniff's passenger load and revenues by close to 40%. Note that most agencies "*single homed*"; that is, most agencies used *either* Sabre *or* Apollo but *not both*. That's why American could crush Braniff by dropping them from their reservations systems; if agencies had routinely used both Sabre and Apollo to compare search results on both systems, then being dropped by one or the other would have had very little impact on Braniff.

United Airlines also dropped Frontier (Airline **B** in Fig. 7.1) out of its Apollo reservations system (CRS **II** in Fig. 7.1). Now travel agents whose agency used only Apollo could not book flights on Frontier. If they tried to book passengers from Denver to Chicago or other destinations, they found that no Frontier flights were listed on their screens, and they booked passengers on other airlines, mostly United. Once again, agencies that used Sabre could still book Frontier, but the loss of traffic from agencies that used only Apollo was also sufficient to bankrupt Frontier. Once again, it's important to note that most agencies "*single homed*"; that is, most agencies used Sabre or Apollo but not both.

It's interesting to ask why neither agencies nor their customers complained. Most did not even notice that Braniff and Frontier had been dropped. While dropping multiple airlines simultaneously from a single reservations system would almost certainly be noticed, dropping only one from each CRS made very little impression. Dropping several airlines might significantly reduce the usefulness of the reservation system, reduce its credibility, and even lead to agencies' switching reservations systems providers. However, dropping one airline at a time had little or no impact on agencies or passengers.

7.3 Learning the Lessons of Power

When firms have that much power they always figure out how to use it!

The reservations systems operators learned an interesting lesson about the power of controlling an airline's interaction with potential passengers, and they began charging airlines for inclusion in their reservations systems. And the airlines had already learned the same lesson, and they paid whatever fees the reservation systems demanded.

This was the start of a *reverse price war*, perhaps the first reverse price war in history. American Airlines introduced a fee of $10 per reservation made through Sabre, and the money collected was available to provide subsidies to travel agencies to buy their loyalty and increase Sabre's market share; increased loyalty and increased market share among travel agencies would increase Sabre's bargaining power with airlines when it demanded higher fees from airlines. United saw American's fees, and realized that it would also need to charge a fee for listings, to increase the loyalty of its own agencies and to increase its own bargaining power when demanding fees from airlines. United executives realized that if they also charged $10 this would look like price fixing, and they decided that they needed to charge a different price. Interestingly, they realized that there was no need to charge a lower price! The fees were paid by airlines, which needed to be found and needed to be listed in both systems; they would pay the fees for *both* CRSs if they possibly could. Likewise, United's higher fees would not discourage agencies, which were the users of the reservation systems but were not actually paying for service. United charged a slightly higher fee, call it $10.30. Notice that competition did not limit what Sabre or Apollo could charge airlines to be listed in their reservations systems.

When American realized that United's Apollo was charging the airlines more than its own Sabre, it realized also that United would have more money to use to buy the continued loyalty of the agencies that used Apollo. Executives at American believed that they too would have to charge more, to avoid being at a competitive disadvantage when trying to retain travel agencies' loyalty. American therefore added a fee for writing tickets after the reservations had been made on Sabre; airlines had to pay a fee to Sabre every time an agency made a reservation and every time an agency issued a ticket for one of the airline's flights. United now in turn was concerned that American's Sabre might have more money to use to buy the loyalty of the agencies that used Sabre than United had to buy the loyalty of users Apollo. This might have placed Apollo at a disadvantage. United responded by adding a fee for writing tickets and an additional fee for reservations with multiple segments. Once again, competition did not limit what Sabre or Apollo could charge airlines to be listed in their reservations systems. More interestingly, competition actually led both Sabre and Apollo to increase their prices.

Again, this reverse price war was possible only because airlines had to be listed in both systems, which was because most agencies used only one of the two major CRSs. This is clear from our discussion of Fig. 7.1. Thus, if an airline chose to pay one CRS fee and not the other, and thus was listed in one system and not the other, the airline would lose enough passengers to be forced into bankruptcy. Airlines had to participate in both CRSs, which essentially eliminated competition between the systems

By paying subsidies to agencies both Sabre and Apollo ensured that their reservations systems were "more free than free" for agencies; agencies were actually paid for using them. And yet, these apparently free systems led to real costs and real harm to consumers. First, the fees paid to reservation systems operators became one of the airlines' largest costs of doing business. American Airlines made more money selling Delta's flights than Delta made operating them, and United Airlines made more money selling reservations than operating its own airline. This increased the cost of air travel for consumers. Additionally, by controlling distribution, American and United were able to limit competition on their own routes, reducing consumers' choices and again increasing the cost of air travel for consumers.

Interestingly, prices airlines paid for participation in Sabre and Apollo did not increase *despite* competition; prices increased *because* of competition.

7.4 When Mandatory Participation Third Party Payer Systems Combine with Online Gateway Systems

This combination provides unlimited power!

Controlling consumers' interaction with sellers and service providers is a tremendous source of power. This power over customers is naturally a tremendous source of profits. Gateways can turn power into profits by selling access to consumers, and by directing customers to Web sites that pay a fee.

Many factors contribute to a gateway's ability to redirect and misdirect consumers. First, the buyer may not even be aware that he is being misdirected. When he cannot book Braniff to Chicago he may simply conclude, "*I guess they don't fly there anymore!*" It's true that over the *long term* the intermediary would die if it lost buyers' trust through excessive manipulation of reservations information. However, over the *very short term* any individual seller would die if the intermediary cut off its access to its customers. This allows the operator of the reservation system to discipline airlines by threatening to cut them off from their passengers. The threat is usually sufficient, and usually the reservation system operator does not need to drop a carrier. Consequently, the customer usually is able to find whatever he wants.

Gateway systems are especially powerful under a range of conditions. Gateway systems often have a high degree of flexibility in choosing what to offer customers, because gateway bias is especially difficult to detect. Perhaps this was best said by Sergey Brin and Larry Page in *The Anatomy of a Large-Scale Hypertextual Web Search Engine*, in which they wrote "*Since it is very difficult even for experts to evaluate search engines, search engine bias is particularly insidious.*"[1] Similarly, Hotels.com has enormous power because it can list an uncooperative hotel as sold out; since most potential travelers interpret this to mean fully booked, they are unlikely even to use the hotel chain's own Web site once they see the sold out indication on Hotels.com. This ability to choose what to show customers and what not to show customers provides gateway system's power, which is a great source of profitability for gateway operators.[2]

There are at least three conditions under which search engines have a great degree of flexibility in choosing what to offer customers, and therefore considerable leverage in charging sellers for visibility to customers. Anyone of these would suffice:

- The buyer *does not already know* what he wants; this allows the gateway to omit results that are not profitable for it to recommend.
- The buyer *is easily deceived*, and confuses the item offered to him for the item that he actually wants; once again, this allows the gateway operator to offer something that is more profitable for it, rather than something that would be as good or better for the customer.
- The buyer *does not care* what he gets and shops largely on basis of price, at least from a small set of items that he considers largely equivalent; again, this allows the gateway operator to demand concessions from sellers that wish to be included in the gateway's set of available choices.
- The buyer does not care enough to use multiple search engines. The buyer may comparison shop among sellers or service providers, but only those on a single search engine.

---

[1]See http://infolab.stanford.edu/~backrub/google.html.

[2]Once again, this power depends on the fact that most consumers *single home* when they search. A shopper who used Google and Bing, or who used TripAdvisor, Trivago, Kayak, Orbitz, and Expedia would find what he wanted. If *all* consumers did this then search engine's power to misdirect, and to charge for not being not found, would be eliminated. But most of us don't.

When the buyer does not know what the available alternatives are, he or she is most easily influenced by the suggestion of items that are acceptable. They may not be ideal, but if the buyer doesn't know what the alternatives are, he or she may easily be persuaded to choose one of the first offered to him. This is especially true of buyers who did not know that the top search results were usually paid placements, and thus represent attempts to purchase access and redirect or even misdirect shoppers.

The second case may be the most dangerous to consumers. When customers are easily deceived gateways do indeed have enormous freedom to decide what to show to consumers. Sometimes consumers' lack of awareness merely allows the gateway to redirect the customer from one legitimate merchant or service provider to another. Merchants who want to increase their sales can buy keywords, even the names of competitors' businesses or competitors' products, in order to get more customer traffic. Sometimes, however, this can be extremely dangerous to an uninformed buyer.

The Department of Justice documented hundreds of millions of dollars in sales to American consumers of pharmaceuticals that were sold by Chinese or Indian suppliers through Web sites masquerading as legitimate Canadian drug retailers.[3] Sometimes these products were genuine, but sometimes they were not. Google helped these foreign suppliers bid for keywords, pass themselves off as legitimate sellers, and capture traffic. The Department of Justice imposed a fine of half a billion dollars, recovering the profits that Google earned from the illegal sales.

The final source of gateway power is the most interesting. A search engine never wants to disappoint its users, so users with a strong preference will see what they really want to buy. Customers without strong preferences will see whichever brand is more profitable for the platform operator. In the absence of strong brand loyalty, brands once again have to pay to _not_ be not found.

---

[3]See http://www.huffingtonpost.com/eric-k-clemons/google-doj-prescription-drugs-_b_936063.html. The Department of Justice's press release noted the following:

> The shipment of prescription drugs from pharmacies outside the United States to customers in the United States typically violates the Federal Food, Drug and Cosmetic Act and in the case of controlled prescription drugs, the Controlled Substances Act.

> The importation of prescription drugs to consumers in the United States is almost always unlawful because the FDA cannot ensure the safety and effectiveness of foreign prescription drugs that are not FDA-approved because the drugs may not meet FDA's labeling requirements; may not have been manufactured, stored and distributed under proper conditions; and may not have been dispensed in accordance with a valid prescription.

That is, the Department of Justice believed that there was a serious probability of real harm. The DoJ did not believe that this was a victimless crime.

Google has a brilliant business model. It's one we can best understand by reminding ourselves of a little history. Google has great power, as evidenced by its profitability. But as we have just seen, competition is unlikely to reduce Google's prices. Competition is more likely to result in a reverse price war.

7.5   Power Is Not Unlimited

It's not easy to escape the grip of the MP3PP but it may be possible!

There are limits on the power of a gateway. An online gateway cannot charge any amount it wants. The amount taken by the gateway is limited by the smallest of the following three thresholds.

- *The bankruptcy threshold*—If the amount charged by the gateway is high enough, the sellers may be forced into bankruptcy. This is probably the highest threshold. The gateway operator cannot charge its participants more for access to customers than the participants earn from their sales to those customers. The seller will fail and exit the market. This may be ideal if the gateway wants to force the seller to exit and then enter that market itself. But that is a vertical integration strategy, not a pricing strategy.
- *The exit threshold*—If the amount charged is too high, the seller may decide not to work with the gateway. But the exit threshold is highly variable. Some small restaurants and food trucks may refuse to participate in some payment systems. Some airline operators with very strong brands and high customer loyalty, like Southwest Airlines, may refuse to participate in gateway reservations systems entirely. eBay is one of the Web sites that is so well known it does not have to pay for keywords in search. But these are the exceptions, firms that are able to avoid the high fees of an MP3PP. Most retailers need MasterCard and Visa, most airlines need reservation systems to supply customers, and most web sites do need to buy keywords at least some of the time.
- *The regulatory threshold*—If the operator of a gateway charges too much it will attract regulatory attention. At some point, regulators would notice that competition is not working to limit the prices that Party-2 intermediaries are able to charge. If the cost of search became high enough, regulators would notice that bankruptcies among Party-3 players were limiting offerings available to consumers. And regulators would notice that the fees charged by Party-2 intermediaries, in the absence of effective competition, had started to harm consumers.

7.6   The Origins of the Credit Card Industry, Before It Became an MP3PP

Remember, the game starts off safe. It always does!

It's important to remember that Third Party Payer Systems, even Mandatory Participation Third Party Payer Systems, are not unique to online systems, to search, or to gateway systems. MasterCard and Visa are both Third Party Payer Systems. These systems are mandatory participation because of rules adopted by MasterCard and Visa, and not because of the essential geometry of the card payment systems.

MasterCard and Visa's rules were designed to create powerful payment systems that would be adopted by the greatest number of merchants and the greatest number of consumers, which required adoption by the greatest number of banks. From their inception, the two card associations required that if a merchant accepted the cards issued by one of their banks it would have to accept cards issued by all of their banks. If a store accepted Chase or CitiBank MasterCard it would have to accept the MasterCard customers from all banks. This simplified brand recognition and made MasterCard and Visa more attractive to merchants and to customers.

The initial design of MasterCard and Visa created a first party payer system. The fees that they imposed on merchants were very low and much lower than American Express's fees at the time. This made the cards attractive to merchants, but contributed to the cards being first party payer rather than Third Party Payer Systems.

While both associations were first party payer systems, their fees were initially lower, in order to attract consumers. Annual fees were usually $12 or less. This made the card more attractive to consumers.

MasterCard and Visa association rules required that merchants charge the same price for cash and for credit transactions. At the time, merchants could not impose a surcharge for using the card or offer discount for using cash instead of the card. This made the card more attractive to consumers. As we shall see, this also enabled the transition to a Third Party Payer System once MasterCard and Visa had attained sufficient power.

Fees were not set jointly by MasterCard and Visa. Some fees were determined by competition between MasterCard and Visa. Many of the fees were actually determined by competition among individual banks.

The original structure of the credit card payment network is shown in Fig. 7.2. The two credit card systems, MasterCard and Visa, are shown

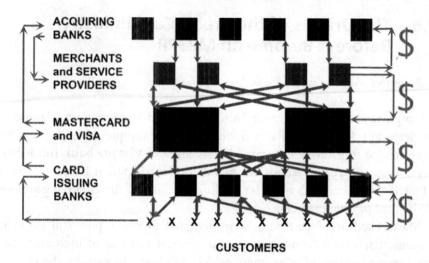

Fig. 7.2 This figure shows the flow of funds and profits in the MasterCard and Visa payment systems early in their history. The left side of this figure shows the flow of funds among MasterCard and Visa, their member banks, their participating merchants, and the merchants' acquiring banks. The right side of the figure shows the flow of profits

in the center of the diagram. Merchants and service providers that accept MasterCard or Visa are shown just above the systems operators MasterCard and Visa; the figure shows only a few of the hundreds of thousands of merchants and service providers that accept the card. Acquiring banks are shown on the top of the figure; these banks acquire the merchants' debt and pay the merchants almost immediately. In the earliest days of MasterCard and Visa, processing was quite slow, and it might take several days for payments to work their way through the system. The acquirer ensured that the merchant was paid immediately for purchases. The acquirer received a small fee from the merchant for providing immediate access to cash. Card issuing banks are shown below MasterCard and Visa, and customers are shown below their banks. Some merchants accepted MasterCard, and some accepted Visa; many, but not all, accepted both. Some banks issued MasterCard and some issued Visa; initially banks did not issue both, but that has changed over time. Some banks acted as both issuer and acquirer; very large banks like Citibank and Bank of America were both retail banks that issued cards, and commercial banks with strong relations with local merchants.

Cash flows among the participants in the entire card payments ecosystem are represented by the green arrows on the left of Fig. 7.2. Issuing banks sent statements to their cardholders. Cardholders paid their banks, their banks paid MasterCard and Visa, MasterCard and Visa paid the acquiring banks, and the acquiring banks paid their merchants. The timing might vary. Acquiring banks paid merchants quickly. MasterCard and Visa paid merchant banks almost as quickly. Issuing banks paid MasterCard and Visa quickly. But each of these payments was independent and did not wait for one of the others for completion. Cardholders paid their issuing banks much more slowly. Sometimes cardholders paid by the end of the month after they received a bill. Sometimes customers did not pay their balances in full by the end of the month and finance charges were added to their bills.

Issuing banks, MasterCard and Visa, and the acquiring banks, each took a small percentage of the total payments made to merchants, called the discount rate. The acquiring banks' fees were low as a result of competition. The other fees were low in order to encourage both merchants and consumers to adopt the card. The principal sources of profit for issuing banks were finance charges and annual fees.

The flow of profits is shown on the right-hand side of Fig. 7.2. Acquiring banks, MasterCard and Visa, and the issuing banks, all earned small profits from the discount rate, that is, from the fee charged the merchants. Issuing banks also earned a fee from finance charges.

7.7 Mandatory Participation Third Party Payer Systems Outside of Search: Credit Cards' Transition to a Powerful MP3PP

The game starts off safe. It always does!

Credit card associations started off as first party payer systems. They eventually made the transition from first party payer systems to Third Party Payer Systems. And, like Sabre and Apollo in airline reservations, and Google in search, once they realized their power they began to use it in ways that neither they nor their users had fully anticipated.

Sabre and Apollo were not abusive to airlines at first. They became abusive when they were able to do so. Sabre and Apollo first needed to get all major airlines to participate in their systems before they were able to get travel agents to use them. Once most travel agents used Sabre and Apollo, they became essential gateways that airlines needed to fill their flights. After Sabre and Apollo became essential gateways, they were able to impose massive new fees on the airlines that had become dependent upon them for access to travelers.

Similarly, MasterCard and Visa were not initially expensive for merchants. However, once card adoption was sufficiently large that participation in credit card systems was essential to a merchant's competitive survival, MasterCard and Visa were both able to increase their fees. The transition from first party payer to third party payer occurred, as in air travel.

Additionally, the simple cards of the 1970s and 1980s have evolved into a large collection of rewards cards. American Airlines pioneered the rewards card, where cardholders got credit toward the frequent flyer *AAdvantage* accounts based on their purchases using the card. Discover pioneered the cash back rewards card, where customers received a rebate on their card purchases. The number, variety, and complexity of rewards cards increased enormously, so that consumers can choose between single airline loyalty cards, generic mileage loyalty cards, single merchant cash back cards like the LL Bean Visa card, or generic cash back cards. Some issuers like Capital One allow consumers to design their own rewards program.

As cards' rewards programs became more complex, they became more powerful competitive weapons. Issuing banks used their reward programs to differentiate their cards, to appeal to consumers, and to compete, and to gain market share. As these programs became more complex and more attractive to consumers, they also became more expensive for merchants.

Remember, banks do not fund their rewards programs by reducing their own profits. They voted to have MasterCard and Visa increase the charges that could be imposed upon merchants who accepted MasterCard and Visa. Thus, it is not Capital One that funds your rebate on your Capital One MasterCard, or Barclays that funds the miles you receive on your American Airlines Aviator MasterCard. The merchants who accept these cards actually fund the banks' rewards programs. That means that the small retailer who sold you your last camera, or the giant retailer who sold you your last laptop, actually gave you a refund through your credit card reward program while your bank took credit for it and earned your loyalty.

MasterCard and Visa have changed their competitive strategies. They no longer need to worry about getting their cards accepted. They now need to keep their largest issuers happy. The system as it exists now is shown in Fig. 7.3. (There are of course more large banks than are shown in the figure.)

The most significant changes in the figure when comparing it to Fig. 7.2 are:

- *Number of issuers.* The number of issuing banks is down significantly, making each of them more important to MasterCard and Visa.
- *New rewards programs and large new cash flows.* The largest issuers have new rewards programs. These programs are powerful competitive tools that banks use to attract customers away from competitors within MasterCard and Visa and away from American Express. These programs have increased the market share of the largest card issuers.
- *Power of the largest issuers.* As the banks with these rewards programs grew even larger, they became even larger and even more important to MasterCard and Visa.
- *Increased payments by sellers for their participation in the system.* MasterCard and Visa charge much higher fees to participating merchants. These highest rates are not imposed on all cards, but are associated with the most popular rewards cards, like frequent flyer miles and cash back rewards cards.

The structure of the lower three levels of Fig. 7.3 is strikingly similar to Fig.7.1, which showed the flow of profits through the CRS platforms. Merchants have become dependent upon MasterCard and Visa as parallel

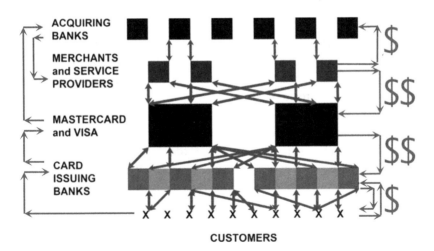

Fig. 7.3 This figure shows the flow of funds and profits in the MasterCard and Visa payment systems as the systems matured, and after significant consolidation among issuing banks. Once again, the left side of this figure shows the flow of funds among MasterCard and Visa, their member banks, their participating merchants, and the merchants' acquiring banks. The right side of the figure shows the flow of profits, with merchants' funding MasterCard and Visa and their own acquiring banks, and with customers funding the profits of their issuing banks

monopoly credit card systems, just as airlines became dependent upon Sabre and Apollo as parallel monopoly reservations systems. We would expect to see the same sort of reverse price war in credit cards that we saw in airline reservations systems.

Once again, we *do* see a *Reverse Price War*. MasterCard and Visa independently increased the maximum amount that their members could charge to merchants. As they increased the amount that banks charged merchants, they increased the amount that they transferred from merchants to their member banks. This in turn allowed banks to increase the attractiveness of the rewards programs they offered to their cardholders. Increasing rewards led to pressure to compete by offering still-more-attractive rewards, which led to a greater need for funds from merchants and a further increase in the discount rate. As issuing banks competed for customer business, the amount charged to merchants increased. This is another example of competition increasing prices. Competition among banks increased rather than decreased the price that merchants pay for access to the credit card payment system.

Moreover, in some instances, merchants pass higher selling costs through to consumers, just as they would pass through higher costs for rent or for utilities, or higher prices charged by their own suppliers. In essence, all consumers are now paying slightly higher prices, and consumers with reward program credit cards are getting small subsidies from merchants and all other customers.

This does not actually imply that there are *no* limits on the charges that banks can impose on merchants and service providers that accept their credit cards. There are three separate sources of limitation, the same three sources of limitation we saw previously in Sect. 7.5.

- *Bankruptcy threshold*—The *bankruptcy threshold* suggests that if the cost to merchants for accepting the cards gets too high, merchants and service providers will go bankrupt as a result. If too many merchants and service providers fail, this will limit the market available to credit card issuers, and to all Party-2 players in all Third Party Payer Systems.
- *Escape threshold*—The *escape threshold* suggests that if fees get too high at least some merchants and service providers may simply find ways to exit the market. Many food trucks and small merchants have found credit card fees too high, and rely upon alternatives like PayPal, Square, Apple Pay, or Google Wallet, or only accept cash.
- *Regulatory threshold*—The *regulatory threshold* suggests that if the costs of accepting the cards get too high, regulators will notice that competition is not working to limit the prices that Party-2 intermediaries are able to

charge. Regulators will notice that bankruptcies among Party-3 players are limiting offerings available to consumers. And regulators will notice that the fees charged by Party-2 intermediaries, in the absence of effective competition, are harming consumers. At the time I am writing this, class action lawsuits in Canada are challenging credit card agreements with merchants, suggesting that merchants should be allowed to accept or refuse some of the cards that have higher fees, and that merchants should be allowed to offer different prices for cash customers and for credit card customers. There has not yet been a resolution of these disputes, but they may be indicators of regulatory changes to come.

The fact that at least some participants *have* been able to escape MP3PP Systems demands that we ask the question: Can MP3PPs still be dangerous in the Internet Age? If Southwest can escape the grip of reservations systems, why can't all other carriers? We examine the continuing power of MP3PPs in the next chapter.

We'll return to the issues of MP3PP power, profitability, and regulation in Chapter 12.

7.8 Summary

Mandatory Participation Third Party Payer Systems can have enormous power. Online Gateway Systems have enormous power. When the two are combined they result in extraordinarily profitable businesses. If users engage in single homing, then the systems that appear to compete are actually parallel monopolies, with pricing power that is not subject to market discipline. Third Party Payer Systems are often not constrained by normal market forces, and competition can actually force prices up in a unique form of reverse price war. These systems often provide real value to consumers. However, they can also distort what consumers see, can limit consumers' choices in goods and services, and can increase the prices that consumers pay for goods and services.

Operating a successful MP3PP gateway is obviously a source of sustainable competitive advantage, since even competition does not reduce the prices you can charge. On the other hand, becoming dependent upon someone else's MP3PP gateway can negate whatever competitive advantage you previously enjoyed.

8

The Continuing Power of Third Party Payer Businesses

In the previous chapter, we saw the enormous power and profit that can be gathered when online gateways operate as Mandatory Participation Third Party Payer Systems. We've seen how difficult it is for companies that become dependent upon these MP3PP gateways to escape their grasp or to limit what they pay to the gateway operators.

In this chapter, we see that even the perfect efficiency and perfect transparency promised by the Internet do not limit the power of these MP3PPs; MP3PPs are even more powerful than they were forty years ago before the net, because they are even larger than they were forty years ago. They are potentially even more dangerous. We see that even MP3PPs that initially appear safe, moderate, and temperate in their demands have the ability to become exploitive. And we explore one of the greatest sources of danger, which occurs when MP3PP gateway operators expand into additional lines of business, and use their control of a critical gateway to destroy competitors and limit consumers' ability to choose. This chapter explores the power of two patterns introduced in the previous chapter, but does not introduce additional patterns.

Online gateways that operate as Third Party Payer Mandatory Participation systems are complicated. They add value for users, Party-1, which is why they attract users in the first place. As they become more valuable to users, they develop enormous ability to charge Party-3, sellers, and they switch from value creation to value harvesting. As they become more profitable they spend more on buying customer loyalty, which makes them more popular immediately. By increasing their value to Party-1, increased loyalty from Party-1 increases the system's importance to Party-3, making them even more profitable over time.

© The Author(s) 2019
E. K. Clemons, *New Patterns of Power and Profit*,
https://doi.org/10.1007/978-3-030-00443-9_8

8.1   MP3PP Systems in the Internet Age: How Can They Still Be Dangerous?

We all understand our choices, and everything is just a click away, *right?*

When the Internet was emerging as the backbone of all online interactions, *digital optimists* expected that all commercial interactions would now be transparent, fair, and unbiased. We expected that platforms that made commercial interactions possible would likewise be efficient, and thus inexpensive for both buyers and sellers. Our reasoning was simple. Choice would be just one click away. A platform that biased its results in any way would be abandoned by users, ensuring that all systems were fair and unbiased. The net was transparent; if a platform or gateway biased its results, *someone* would know immediately, and then *everyone* would know immediately after that. Since all platforms were fair and unbiased, they would have to compete for business by being as efficient and inexpensive as possible. A gateway system that overcharged consumers would be abandoned immediately. But a gateway system that overcharged sellers would be abandoned by sellers just as quickly, destroying value for buyers trying to use the system and ultimately destroying value for the gateway operator as well. There was simply no way a harvesting MP3PP like Sabre and Apollo could emerge again. We were so *certain* of this.

And we were wrong.

Indeed, we supported the deregulation of the air travel reservations systems, now called Global Distribution Systems or GDSs.[1] Yes, we knew that the MP3PP business model had been dangerous in the 1980s, even if we didn't call them MP3PPs yet and even if we didn't understand exactly why it was dangerous. But it seemed impossible that unfair behavior or abuse of power could continue when all customers were one click away from an airline's own reservations system. It seemed unlikely that misrepresentation could survive in the presence of complete online transparency. Who would need agencies or GDSs? Who would use any gateway that distorted its results or that prevented consumers from accessing what they really wanted to find? Consequently, GDSs were deregulated in 2004.

We expected that in our brave new digital marketplace, the market for airline seats would look nothing like the market structure in the early days of Sabre and Apollo. Passengers might still use travel agencies, while others

---

[1]When discussing the current market for air travel, we will use the more recent term.

might use GDSs, but most would go directly to the airlines' own Web sites. Agencies might still use GDSs, but most agencies would connect directly to the airlines' own Web sites.

There were going to be so many ways to bypass the GDSs that they would be powerless and almost irrelevant. Connections between agencies and GDSs would still exist, as would connections between GDSs and airlines. However, we expected that they would receive very little use, since both passengers and agencies would primarily interact directly with airlines' own Web sites. GDSs would have little relevance and little power. Payments from airlines to GDSs might still exist, but they would be payments for services rendered, not payments to ensure the airlines' survival. Payments would be much, much smaller.

Again, we were certain. And again, we were wrong. The arrival of the net did not eliminate the power of online gateways and MP3PPs. Consumers and agencies did not behave the way we expected. Let's see why.

The actual evolution of air travel distribution[2] did not match our expectations. The current structure of the marketplace, the resulting distribution of power, and the flow of funds have surprised us. They all look much more like the market in the 1980s. There is far less direct access to the airlines' own web sites than we expected. Customers still like agencies, especially online agencies, because it is not necessary for consumers to query multiple individual airlines' reservations systems. As long as customers con-tinue to book through agencies, and as long as agencies are paid by the GDSs to use the GDSs and not the airlines own reservations systems, GDSs will continue to have power over airlines and will continue to demand fees from the airlines. Current airlines' lawsuits against the GDSs look remarkably like the litigation from the 1980s. The *Digital Optimists* were wrong.

Let's see why Party-3 has to participate in all MP3PPs even in an online world; that is, let's see why participation is still mandatory.

Many consumers still believe that they can get a better price from an online agency than they can get from the hotel or the airline directly. It doesn't matter if the airlines advertise that they sometimes have Internet-only fares that are lower than any fares available elsewhere. It doesn't matter how many times hotels advertise that their best prices are available from their web sites. Online agencies spend much, much more on advertising than any hotel chain or airline can afford to spend. As a result, many customers simply believe that they get a better price from Priceline, or that they

---

[2]See http://www.huffingtonpost.com/eric-k-clemons/why-is-there-still-litiga_b_887252.html.

get a better price from Expedia than from any airline or hotel. Likewise, consumers believe that if they use an online agency it will find a better price than if they went directly to the Web sites of their favorite hotels or airlines. It doesn't even matter if this is true or not. What matters is that customers believe it. If enough customers insist on booking through Priceline or through Expedia then hotels and airlines will have to deal with them, even if they would prefer customers use the hotels' or the airlines' own systems. Indeed, hotels and airlines have to deal with every system that has enough loyal consumers to direct or redirect a significant number of travelers. This is true even though airlines and hotels do have their own systems, and even though customers can always access them directly, without the use of any agency or online agency.

Likewise, almost all merchants and service providers have to bid for Google key words. Bing's market share does not substitute for Google's market share. When doing online research before a significant purchase many of us will go to several web sites to check out different offerings and to compare prices, but very few of us use several search engines to find those Web sites. I may look at product selections and product reviews at Amazon, Home Depot, and Consumer Reports. However, I never look for these Web sites using Google, Bing, and DuckDuckGo. For sellers who need to ensure a steady flow of traffic to their Web sites, there is no substitute for Google, and Google remains an MP3PP even in an online world.

With Mandatory Participation Third Party Payer gateway systems, any one system is not a substitute for the other; you have to be in all the major ones as long as users single home. And this is still true in an online world.

8.2 The Recurring Pattern in Third Party Payer Models: When the System Can Really Use Its Power

They never start off abusive! How do they become so expensive and why is Party-3 always so surprised?

There is a recurring pattern in Mandatory Participation Third Party Payer Systems. They start off as inexpensive for everyone, and as long as the platform operators create systems that function well, both Party-1 and Party-3 come to love them. Party-3 sellers enter because the platforms are initially better, cheaper, more efficient, or more widely used than any alternatives. Airlines initially found that Sabre and Apollo were the best possible ways to reach agencies, and the agencies received so much value from Sabre and Apollo that they actually paid most of the costs of operating a GDS. Member airlines were initially called "co-hosts," which sounds so much better than being called "my future lunch." Key word prices were initially low on Google, and commissions on Hotels.com were likewise quite reasonable at the time of Hotels.com's launch.

Over time, Party-3 becomes *vulnerable* because it has become dependent upon Party-2. As we have seen in Chapter 5, much of the power of an MP3PP system results from Party-3's need to work with all of the Party-2 system operators. This in turn reduces or eliminates the role of competition, which would otherwise limit the prices Party-3 could be charged.

Once the vulnerability of Party-3 is clear to all, Party-2 is able to exploit Party-3's vulnerability. That is, the system operator increases the cost to Party-3. This has been the model in Sabre and Apollo, and MasterCard and Visa, which we have already discussed.

It's important to remember that Sabre and Apollo were not advertising systems. They were access systems. Advertising might influence a traveler so that he *wanted* to book Frontier, or Braniff, or Eastern Airlines. Advertising did not ensure that a traveler actually *could* book Frontier, or Braniff, or Eastern Airlines, since Sabre and Apollo controlled so much of the flow of customers to airlines. In the late 1980s, virtually all corporate travel was booked through travel agencies. Sabre and Apollo were the mechanisms that agencies used to locate seats for their customers. If an airline had been dropped from Sabre or Apollo, advertising was of very little assistance to the airline that had been dropped. Advertising might create traveler awareness. Advertising would not create passenger bookings. American and United operated Sabre and Apollo, the dominant reservations systems of the 1970s and 1980s. Continental, Eastern, Northwest Airlines, Pan Am, TWA, and USAir no longer operate as independent carriers. All airlines advertised. Only Delta survived without a dominant reservations system.

The similarity between Google and the buyers of key words today is remarkably similar to the profit flows between CRSs and airlines in the reservations business in the 1980s. Very few agencies go directly to airlines. Some consumers do go directly to sellers' Web sites without search. Still, most of us use search for all but a few giant Web sites that are our most frequent destinations. We use search either to find an airline like American or an online comparison site like Kayak or Orbitz.

However, although the structure of the search market and the travel markets appear very similar when illustrated graphically, the <<*online search for everything market*>> is much, much larger than the <<*GDS airline search market>>* ever was. The role of loyalty is important in search, since consumers are not contractually obligated to use a single search engine. The power of single homing is important, since single homing limits competition and increases the prices that gateways can charge. And the potential for the reverse price war we saw with Sabre and Apollo and with MasterCard and Visa still applies in modern search. Competition between Google and Bing provides little pressure to reduce the prices that either is able to charge for key words.

8.3   And Now—Coming Soon to a Search Engine Near You—Platform Envelopment and Vertical Integration

Why just charge for access? Why not take the customers, serve them yourself, and keep all the profits?

As we saw in Chapter 6, platform envelopment is the process whereby a Party-2 platform operator integrates more and more interrelated functionality into its core offering. When pieces fit together well, like the pieces of Microsoft's Office Suite, this process provides additional value to users and may provide marketplace power and competitive advantage to the platform operator. Microsoft has long followed a platform envelopment strategy. Google, likewise, is following a platform envelopment strategy, integrating its numerous offerings into a coherent whole.

Vertical Integration is the process whereby a business, online or off, begins to bring in-house activities that used to be performed by outside companies. Apple has always been extremely vertically integrated, selling desktops, laptops, iPads, iPhones, and their operating systems, and using iTunes to knit them together into a coherent ecosystem. Microsoft's Surface tablet, and Google's Android operating system and Chrome devices represent more recent examples of vertical integration.

Why would we assume that a sufficiently powerful search engine provider would use its power only *indirectly* over Party-3? Why wouldn't the search engine provider be tempted to compete *directly* against Party-3? The search engine provider can become a ticket agency and compete with Orbitz. It can operate a local marketplace and compete with the Amazon Market. It can earn commissions on *everything* while becoming even more attractive and even more convenient for its users. It can increase the effectiveness of its platform envelopment strategy and destroy competitors at the same time.

As I drafted this chapter, a search for flights between Philadelphia and Boston took me to Google's travel site. Interestingly, it took me there even before I complete the query, and thus even before I got to specify that I want flights on American Airlines. I could still book American, but American would not have the advantage of commission-free bookings through their own site. A search for Yoder barbecue grills gave me the chance to "shop on Google." Strikingly, the Yoder Grill I wanted was absent from the list. Yoder did show up below these offerings from Google, but it was below the sites that Google would prefer I use, and those sites all had images of the products they were offering. A search for Manchester's *The Last Lion*, a biography of Winston Churchill, took me to Google's own book-selling site. Once again, Google could complete entering the search string for me and took me to its own choice of retailing sites, without my ever completely typing my request and without my seeing competitors' sites.

Yes, I can find American Airlines' site and Amazon's site easily if I want them, but I can easily end up buying directly from Google. Yes, it's very convenient, since I don't even have to finish typing! It's also scary, since it gives Google even more power as a gateway.

Not surprisingly, a search engine operator is tempted to give its own businesses preferential positioning in search results, which makes its own businesses easier to find and makes them appear more relevant and higher quality than competing businesses. Microsoft provided an extra boost for Internet Explorer. Google did this when it immediately displaced Yahoo Finance with its own financial information systems at the top of the search list as soon as Google's system was available. It did the same thing when nearly crushed Foundem when Google's own comparison shopping system was available in the UK.

In the most extreme cases, intermediaries who compete with Google might not even get a chance to see customers. Intermediaries who used to pay for showing up on a search for Marriott or Holiday Inn or Lakers tickets or Nikon cameras may almost disappear from search. More importantly, hotels and other sellers likewise may see traffic to their own web sites reduced. This will be more profitable for Google, and very expensive for hotels themselves since they will pay booking fees on more of their traffic. Competitors may be destroyed, consumers' range of choices may be reduced, and prices may be increased. These were the very arguments used to regulate CRSs in the 1980s. We have seen that the net has not eliminated the power of MP3PPs. Vertical integration by search engines is potentially very important. At least part of the promise of the Internet—free and efficient commerce, and free and efficient interaction between buyers and sellers—may be destroyed.

Often a platform operator can take some of its extraordinary profits and invest in expanding its platform envelopment strategy. At the peak of its power, Microsoft was able to take the extraordinary profits from Windows and invest them in a range of services, from Word and Excel to Internet Explorer. Each of these rapidly displaced and ultimately destroyed existing competitors. We have seen that it is possible for a platform operator with a successful envelopment strategy to become extremely powerful, and it is tempting for the operator with such power to become abusive. The US Department of Justice brought Federal Antitrust Litigation against Microsoft for, among other things, alleged abuse of competitors through a platform envelopment strategy.[3] It is possible that the very features of the platform envelopment strategy that make Google so attractive to consumers can be used to exclude competitors from Google's platforms or even to destroy them entirely. Not surprisingly, this was the basis of the EU's Competition Commission's complaint against Google for abusing Foundem. Foundem had been reported first in Google's search results for a comparison shopping site in the UK, but when Google decided to offer a competing service Foundem virtually disappeared. One might wonder how Google's own offering immediately showed up first, without user experience or links to its web site, if rankings had been determined by algorithms as Google usually claims. But then presumably Foundem would have dropped to second place; instead, Google moved it down dozens of positions. Google essentially hid Foundem several pages below the top of the search results when it chose to compete directly with Foundem.[4] Abuse of platform power is also the basis of the Competition Commission's most recent complaint against Google, claiming that Google's Mobile Application Distribution Agreement (MADA) gives Google almost total control over Android devices. Indeed, the MADA allows Google to determine which Apps *must* be preinstalled on Android devices, which *may* be preinstalled, and which *must not* be preinstalled. This severely limits competition.

The case was still ongoing as I wrote this chapter[5] but the Competition Commission announced its decision as I finished the draft.[6] Google has been fined a record $5 billion for abuse of its control over the apps on Android devices. Google used the MADA to limit what other applica-

---

[3]See http://en.wikipedia.org/wiki/United_States_v._Microsoft.

[4]https://www.nytimes.com/2018/02/20/magazine/the-case-against-google.html.

[5]See https://www.politico.eu/article/google-android-antitrust-competition-fine-margrethe-vestager/.

[6]See https://www.wsj.com/articles/google-to-be-fined-5-billion-by-eu-in-android-case-1531903470.

tion developers could expect to see installed on Android devices and limited smartphone manufacturers' ability to develop their own variants of Android. The MADA has been judged anticompetitive. Google immediately announced its intention to appeal.

So we see that even in an online world, MP3PPs continue to wield enormous power. An MP3PP can charge high fees for access, even when Party-3 creates its own web sites. Moreover, in cases where Party-3 is itself a gateway or intermediary, like a comparison shopping engine or a travel booking web site, the MP3PP can vertically integrate into the intermediary's own business. An MP3PP with a vertical integration strategy can easily promote its own offerings ahead of existing high-quality products from competitors. Ultimately, with Party-3 dependent upon the search engine either for direct access to consumers through search or vulnerable to bypass in favor of the MP3PP's own businesses, Party-3 is indeed desperately vulnerable.

In the next chapter, we explore implications of this power for businesses, for consumers, and for regulators.

8.4   Summary

Online gateways as MP3PPs have not lost their power as a result of the Internet. When gateways are combined with platform envelopment strategies they become even more powerful, even more profitable, and potentially even more dangerous. And, as we have seen, there is half a century of experience suggesting that MP3PPs almost always become more dangerous and more exploitive over time.

Once again, since competition does not reduce the power of an MP3PP gateway, creating a successful MP3PP gateway can be a source of sustainable competitive advantage. And, again, becoming dependent upon someone else's MP3PP gateway can negative whatever competitive advantage you previously enjoyed.

9

Power and the Potential for the Abuse of Power in Online Gateway Systems: An Analysis of Google

In Chapter 6, we introduced the pattern associated with platforms and platform envelopment. Chapter 7 introduced two additional patterns, Mandatory Participation Third Party Payer Systems (MP3PPs) and online gateways, and showed how they combined for a unique form of power that was one of the most important and most profitable innovations enabled by the Internet. Chapter 8 showed how these three patterns become even more intertwined online. We argued that the net has not reduced the power of online gateways that function as MP3PPs. Indeed, the net has increased their power. In this chapter, we will explore how dominant MP3PPs can protect and extend their power, and how they can make the transition from value creation to value harvesting. We explore the harm that this may cause, and the inability of traditional forms of competition to limit or to correct this harm. Finally, I suggest why regulation of online MP3PP gateways may indeed be necessary, and what forms this regulation might take.

My friend Jaron Lanier has just written a book on why you should delete your social media accounts right now.[1] He's also drafted manifestos on how to deal with technology and how to reclaim your role in the future machine-dominated economy. Perhaps even more so than Jaron, I am a professional worrier and have been paid by executives to worry for their firms about a range of topics including the impact of eCommerce on retail stores and on traditional brands, the impact of social media on the stability of regimes in the Middle East, and the impact of social media on the future

---

[1]https://www.amazon.com/Arguments-Deleting-Social-Media-Accounts/dp/125019668X.

© The Author(s) 2019
E. K. Clemons, *New Patterns of Power and Profit*,
https://doi.org/10.1007/978-3-030-00443-9_9

of elections. I first worried about online search in 1991, when I was clearly not worrying about Google; I first worried about Google's potential anti-trust problems in 2009, within 6 months of their launch of Android and the start of their march toward domination of mobile computing. Consider this chapter as my mini-manifesto about our future in a world transformed by technology. I want you to understand the impacts of technology on your privacy, on the prices that you pay for goods and services, and even on the quality of your elections. We will come back to this in Chapter 12, when we explore what *might happen*. This chapter explores what has *already happened*.

Search is critically important to the future of every online ecosystem. Let's suppose that I do convince you that some form of regulation of Google is needed. What would you want to know before you regulated a high-tech company? I suggest that we should start by demonstrating the following:

1. That the firm had *considerable market power*. That is, that competition and the usual market forces did not limit the prices the company could charge or did not force the company to improve the quality of the services it offered its customers. The company therefore was in general free of the market discipline that normally limited the behavior of most companies.
2. That the company's *power was not going to be limited by future changes in the market*, such as the imminent entry of new competitors or a shift away from the current hardware platform.
3. That the company had *acted to defend and extend its monopoly power*, which violates antitrust law in the USA and antimonopoly law abroad.
4. That the company had already *abused its power*.
5. That *consumers had been harmed, or inevitably would be harmed by the higher prices* charged by the company's customers. If the high-tech company can force higher prices on its customers, this in turn would usually result in higher prices for consumers. This is true except in rare instances when retailers, manufacturers, or service providers are not able to increase prices at all, even when their costs are increased.
6. That *consumers had been harmed, or inevitably would be harmed, by reduced competition*. Again, this could be the result of consumers having to pay higher prices, having reduced choices, or being sold inferior and defective products.
7. That *current regulations were not adequate* to deal with this market structure or this business model. If current regulation could be shown to be adequate, there would be no need for additional regulations or additional legislation.

8. That there were *precedents for introducing new regulation to deal with new market structures and new business models* enabled by new technologies and new uses of technologies. We have a tradition in the USA of not retroactively enforcing criminal laws on actions that were not illegal at the time they occurred. But we also have a tradition of adapting laws and regulations to respond to problems that did not exist before the introduction of a new technology. And it is indeed possible that some technology businesses, like Google, Microsoft, Apple, Amazon, and others, might require additional regulatory analysis.

Point (2) above was addressed in Chapters 7 and 8. The entry of additional MP3PP competitors does not force down the prices charged to Party-3, indeed, competition leads to *reverse price wars* and higher prices for Party-3. Moreover, Google's successful transition from dominating the desktop browser, to dominating mobile computing with Android, to their introduction of a wide array of additional services, suggests that they are not about to be displaced by changes in our computing platforms. We will address each of the other points in turn below.

Like any good manifesto, I'm going to start by explaining things that reasonable people might not have worried about, might not even have thought about yet, and don't think of as problems. But these things make me crazy, and let's see if I can get them to make you crazy too. Let's start with the secret component to Google's ranking algorithm, quality scores.

9.1   Quality Scores and the Power to Make and Defend Arbitrary Decisions

Don't blame me. My quality score algorithm made me do it!

If Google always provided the best search results that its algorithms could possibly generate, the company would make consumers very happy, but it would earn nothing from search.[2] But as Larry Page and Sergei Brin realized

---

[2]Search results have two parts, the *Organic Search* results generated by one algorithm and the paid ads/*sponsored search* results generated by the second algorithm. Sponsored search is a major revenue source, while organic search doesn't directly produce any revenue. Of course, if organic search results were always perfect, consumers would never click on sponsored search results, and companies would no longer pay for placement in sponsored search.

That doesn't mean Google would earn nothing. It has numerous other revenue sources, most based on highly informed targeted advertising. Highly informed means based on your search history, your texting, the contents of your e-mails sent and received, and the GPS data from your Android phone.

even before they started Google, organic search does not have to be perfect. It simply has to be good enough to keep consumers from abandoning their company. So they provide good enough organic search, and then you see paid search on top. These paid search results were originally called "*sponsored links*," which sounds innocuous. They are now called "*paid ads*." More honestly, they could originally have been called "*deceptive and camouflaged attempts at misdirecting consumers to alternative sellers, for a price.*"

But consumers learn and consumers notice when search results are really bad, and certainly, they learn when the top (paid) search results are worse than the organic (free) search results underneath them. This means Google couldn't provide inferior paid search results forever. If consumers learned that the paid links were inferior, that would have destroyed consumers' confidence in Google's paid search results. If that had happened, then consumers would have stopped clicking on them, which in turn would have destroyed Google's revenues.

That's where quality scores come in. Quality scores are nearly perfect for making sure that search results serve both Google's desire to earn as much as possible from search and consumers' needs for the best possible search results. To be clear, the design of quality scores is a brilliant balancing act, aligning relevance with consumers' needs with Google's desire to maximize revenues. A single hypothetical example should help explain how it possible to do both. We consider the market for a nonexistent electronic part for the engine of a nonexistent luxury car manufacturer.

Assume we have two resellers of replacement Flodgets, an exotic electronic control subsystem for Barbarian Motor Werkz 128 sedans.

- *Munich Auto* (Munich.com) sells authentic, genuine, high-quality parts. They're expensive for Munich to import, and they are expensive for consumers to buy. But they're great.
- *Billy Bob's Bait Shop and Best Auto Parts* (BBBB.com) sells inexpensive, low-quality counterfeit parts. Billy Bob's pays very little for the counterfeits, and although he sells them for less than the genuine Flodgets from Munich, they are still very profitable for him. They are also very low quality, and consumers are often very quickly disappointed. Consumers often need another replacement very soon after buying from Billy Bob.

Because the profit margins on counterfeits are very high, BBBB can afford to pay more for key words related to the sale of Flodgets. And because BBBB doesn't enjoy a strong reputation, it needs the Internet sales more than Munich. Obviously, BBBB will bid more for key words than Munich, and in the early days of paid search, BBBB would automatically have shown up higher in the list of paid search results than Munich.

When BBBB was allowed to buy the top spot in paid search results, this was bad for consumers; they were clicking on, and purchasing from, an inferior vendor. It was also bad for Google, in two ways. It weakened Google's reputation. And as consumers learned not to click on BBBB or other top companies in paid search results, Google's revenues from the sale of key words declined.

This is where quality scores come in. For concreteness, assume that Munich is in some sense 10 times *better* than BBBB as a retailer of Flodgets. That is, consumers are 10 times more likely to be *satisfied* with a purchase from Munich and 10 times more likely to *click* on Munich. This limits the value to Google of placing BBBB in the top spot. Why waste the top spot, the most valuable piece of *real estate* on a page of search results, on a URL that won't produce clicks or click revenue? So, as long as Munich bids *enough*, Google should put Munich on top of paid search.

But how much is enough? Enough in this case is defined as 10% the amount that BBBB bids. If BBBB offers $10.00 per click on "Flodget" as a key word, then Munich will get top spot as long as it bids $1.00 or more.

Clearly, this use of quality scores is good for consumers. Inferior sellers like BBBB no longer show up in temptingly high places in search results. And it is good for Google. Inferior sellers no longer can easily bid to occupy a high spot, which resulted in few clicks and only limited revenues for Google. Additionally, inferior sellers can no longer dominate the top spots and damage Google's reputation.

Google can even argue that this is fair. Good companies pay less than bad companies for key words. New companies that need to grow their business are willing to pay more than established companies in order to break into the market. If companies didn't want to bid for key words, they wouldn't bid. If companies didn't lose sales when they failed to buy key words, or if they didn't gain sales when the succeeded in buying key words, they wouldn't do so. Clearly, it is better to be present in paid search than to be absent from paid search, so companies bid for key words. But, Google argues, companies don't have to bid unless they believe that buying key words will increase their revenues.

How could anyone complain? Google doesn't set the prices for companies to pay. The algorithm made them use the prices they use!

Of course, competition does not place restraints on the price of key words, as we saw in Chapters 7 and 8. And indeed, as we shall see in the next section, Google can manipulate quality scores in ways that allow it to extract almost as much money as it wants both from Billy Bob and from Munich.

9.2   Vickrey Auctions, Pseudo-Vickrey Auctions, and the Power to Charge Whatever You Want

Don't blame me. That's what the seat cost. Sorry you went down with the Titanic.

This section sounds pretty technical. It's about quality scores, Vickrey Auctions, and Pseudo-Vickrey Auctions. It's really not that hard to follow, and it explains a lot of Google's power over search.

Vickrey received the Nobel Prize in Economics for designing an auction with two desirable properties:

- *Honest Revelation*—Everyone has an incentive to bid honestly and bid his or her actual valuation of the item being auctioned, rather than shave his or her bid to try to save a little by bidding less than they think the item is worth.
- *Revenue Maximizing*—No other auction design consistently produces more revenue for the seller.

It's what's called a *sealed bid second price auction*. The design is brilliant in its simplicity:

- Everyone bids, and no one sees anyone else's bids.
- Everyone bids what he or she believes the item is worth, and what they are willing to pay.
- After the auction, everyone actually pays the same price, so there is no winners' curse, or buyers' remorse, and no reason for anyone to shave a bid to avoid paying more than anyone else.
- The price that all winners pay is set as the price of the highest losing bid.

Imagine you are on the Titanic and it is sinking. What should you bid for a seat on one of the lifeboats? Obviously, you should bid as much as you can since you don't want to try to save a few dollars and risk going down with the ship. But you don't want to be foolish and to pay too much. How should you set your bid? You could count the number of seats, estimate your wealth compared to that of other passengers, and decide what you need to bid to be sure of getting a seat.

Let's keep this concrete. Imagine that there are 400 seats available in the lifeboats. If you want a seat, you don't have to bid everything you have.

You only have to bid more than the 401st wealthiest person on board the Titanic. You might want to rush out and try to find a list of all the passengers, to help with your calculations.

Now the skipper announces that the seats are being sold with a Vickrey Auction. Now you don't have to look at the passenger list, estimate anyone else's wealth, or perform any calculations. You bid everything you have and you *automatically* get the seat if you have more money than the 401st wealthiest person on board. *And* you only pay what the 401st wealthiest person would have paid if he had been rich enough to get a seat.

Vickrey Auctions keep things very simple.

Now let's see what the skipper could do if he wanted to raise more money. First, he could control the number of seats he offers to sell. He may have only 400 seats, and he may have far more passengers than seats, but that doesn't mean he has to fill the seats. With a Vickrey Auction, he may make more money by changing the number of seats he offers after seeing the bids. Suppose there are 400 seats, but there are only 350 really wealthy first-class passengers on board. Suppose that the 350th bid was for $1,000,000, but the 351st bid through the 401st bid were all for $100,000. The most that the skipper could earn selling 400 seats at $100,000 each would be $40 million. But if he sold 349 seats, all 349 winners would be charged the highest losing bid, or $1,000,000. That would generate $349 million. So the skipper, after looking at all of the bids, could determine his profit-maximizing price by adjusting the number of seats he sells. He's still following a Vickrey Auction, but with a slight tweak. He, and only he, looks at the sealed bids and based on the distribution of the values adjusts the number of items he actually sells.

But can he do better than that? Sure, if he is willing to deviate even further from the spirit of a Vickrey Auction. Suppose all passengers are *not* created equal, at least in the eyes of skipper. Suppose the skipper had a bad experience with a divorce attorney, but he had a great time as an undergraduate at Oxford studying Elizabethan drama. So, based on his experience, he gives a high *quality score* to professors, but a low quality score to lawyers. A lawyer who bid $1,000,000 might not be given a seat, while a professor who specialized in Shakespeare might get a seat for $500,000. You don't know what your quality score is. You don't know what the other passengers' quality scores are. You don't even know how the scores are computed. You just know that even if you were the high bidder, you still might not get a seat on a lifeboat.

So how does this change anything? It doesn't change your behavior. You still bid everything you can, of course. The only thing that changes is that now the skipper looks at all the bids and can control both quality scores and the number of seats in order to maximize the revenue from sale of seats.

Why should you care? You still bid everything you can. It doesn't change your strategy. Well, maybe it's not efficient to leave seats empty while people drown? Maybe it's not fair to value a professor over a lawyer? But, again, it doesn't change your strategy.

Why do I care? I care because I may have to pay more for a seat. I care because we *all* may have to pay more for our seats. Quality scores are not usually used simply to punish someone. Google uses quality scores in ways that allow them to charge bidders whatever they want to charge them. Often a seller following a profit-maximizing strategy moves far, far away from the original Vickrey Auction. We don't all pay the highest losing bid. We all pay the highest losing bid multiplied by an arbitrary measure that cannot be appealed, questioned, or even viewed.

I also care because it's deceptive to call it a Vickrey Auction. It provides the illusion of fairness where no fairness exists.

Mostly, I care because search may be the most important application on the net and no other form of critical infrastructure is allowed to charge multiple individualized profit-maximizing prices in the absence of competition. Google has enough information about every seller, and enough power over the process, to charge whatever it decides to charge for search listings. And make no mistake—as we have seen, there is no effective competitive pressure to limit prices.

9.3   The Illusion of Choice

No one is forced to use our Search Engine. Choice is just a click away!

OK, so we've seen that Google search is expensive for the companies that use it. What about the argument that no one is forced to use Google? Isn't choice just a click away? Doesn't choice provide competition? Companies don't really have to buy Google key words, right? They can always choose to participate only on Bing, right?

Well, no. Not if most of the companies' potential customers are using Google. If the shoppers are on Google, companies have to participate on Google.

What does it feel like to have no choice? Suppose you decided not to buy a seat on a Titanic lifeboat. Even a fair Vickrey Auction might seem too expensive, and you decided to buy a seat on a lifeboat from a different ship. The closest available ships, the SS Carpathia and the RMS Californian, arrived too late to offer assistance before the Titanic sank. Choice was not just a click away on the Titanic. And as long as Bing delivers only 10% or less of a company's customers for products and services, choice is not just a click away for companies trying to be found in search either.

But, really, what is the point of this allegory? Does Google really sell anything as critical as seats on the Titanic's lifeboats? *Paying to be found* is a complement to advertising; if you advertise, people know your name and search for you. But *paying to not be not found* is far more powerful, since even when consumers shop for a specific seller, they can end up at a different web site if the seller didn't pay enough to not be not found. Google is usually pretty good about making sure consumers don't often end up someplace terrible, but Google has enormous power over deciding what consumers find. Google sells key words and adjusts prices with quality scores, allowing it to influence what gets found. And beyond that, Google has decided that registered trademarks are like any other key word. Thus, Google will sell the use of a company's trademark to one of the company's competitors if the rightful owner does not bid enough, further influencing what gets found.. Disappearing from search, even after you advertise, or being dropped way down in the search lists even after you advertise, can cause a company to drown just as surely as being dropped from the list of passengers assigned to lifeboats.

So why do consumers use Google? Because it's very good, and a lot better than brute-force search. It's not as good as it *could be*, but neither was Sabre or Apollo. There is no law that says a product has to be perfect, or even as good as it could be.

And why do sellers pay Google? Because as long as consumers are happy enough with Google, companies really have no choice. There is no alternative supplier of customers for most sellers, just as there was no alternative supplier of lifeboats for passengers on the Titanic.

Why does this matter? Because providing free search that is subsidized by key word auctions may be the most expensive possible way to provide free search.

We have shown through our analysis of MP3PPs that Google and companies with similar business models enjoy monopoly power, even without actually functioning as a monopoly. However, the Appendix shows that by traditional measures Google actually does have monopoly power. Choice is an illusion. Google's power is real.

9.4   Can We Show That Monopoly Power Has Been Abused in Search and Extended Beyond Search? Is There Evidence?

There are numerous complaints, and several admissions of responsibility. At least you might want some forms of protection.

It is not my intention to prove Google abuses its power. That's an exercise best left to the courts. I don't want to try to provide an extensive list of alleged problems or of problems for which Google has signed consent decrees. But I do want to go beyond purely theoretical arguments about what might be possible, and at least surface the idea that Google may have already committed real abuses of the monopoly power we have discussed above.

Numerous examples are alleged of Google's abuse of its power. Some examples come directly from search, involving the cost of key words. Others involve abuse of companies that compete with Google in other areas, where Google's control of search may provide it enormous advantages over these competitors. Still, others focus on using monopoly in search to fund additional monopoly lines of business.

Let's focus on examples from outside of the cost of key words. My concerns about Google's market power fall into four major categories. Additional concerns about privacy will be discussed in the final chapters of this book. My four areas of concern are listed below.

1. *We can hide you if we want to!* When Google began to compete with UK comparison shopping engine Foundem, Foundem was dropped from its top spot on the first page of search results and buried below more than 100 other Web sites. Foundem is perhaps the most significant example currently used by the European Commission in their arguments against Google and its anticompetitive behavior.[3] Perhaps the tersest summary is offered by Foundem itself:

   While the [European] Commission is clearly heading towards a robust Prohibition Decision, we are concerned that if it does not act conclusively in the near future there may be little competition left to protect.

---

[3]https://www.theguardian.com/technology/2013/nov/19/google-european-commission-row-vertical-search, current as of 25 October 2016.

2. *We can replace you if we want to!* Google can place itself ahead of any seller it wants, giving its own emerging retail and travel operations status available to no other competitors. We saw in the final section of the previous chapter that search engines can engage in vertical integration as part of a platform envelopment strategy. They can hide competitors' offerings in a variety of ways, including dropping them down in the search list, or moving their own offerings way up in the search list. They can even complete a user's search query, acting as if you are looking for Google's own offerings, and then place their offerings on top of the search results, automatically. Users see Google's own offerings, even before the users complete typing their searches. It's very convenient for the user, which makes it a successful platform envelopment strategy. And it can be fatal to any seller that Google targets as competition.

3. *We can use your content if we want to!* Google scraped content from Yelp in order to bootstrap its own review services. It was hard for Google to launch a service to compete with Yelp. Why would anyone post on a review Web site that had no readers? Why would anyone try to read from a review Web site before it had any reviews? Google understood the problem: reviewers need readers before they'll post, readers need reviews before they'll read, which circles back to reviewers need readers before they'll post. Google solved the problem by taking content from Yelp and moving it to its own Web site, to create the first content on Google's site and create initial interest in the site. Now that Google has a self-sustaining community, it signed a consent decree and no longer scraped content. Why did Yelp tolerate this? Google offered Yelp the same choice it offers newspapers that object to having their content scraped and provided in Google's news service:

   - You can let us take your content now, for as long as we need to. We'll try to build the best competitor to your web site that we can. You're free to try to compete over the long term, if you can. You can wait and see what happens to you over the long term.
   - Or you choose not to let us see your content. But then we won't even look at your content, and we'll drop you out of search entirely. So the second alternative is we won't read your content, we won't scrape your content, and we won't use your content to provide the initial content for our own web site. However, we also won't include you in any search results and you will vanish from the net. See what happens to you immediately!

4. *We can help you sell anything for a high enough fee!* The Department of Justice imposed one of the highest fines in its history on Google for facilitating the smuggling of prescription medications, including counterfeits, into the USA from China and India through online pharmacies in Canada.[4] This complaint is impossible to refute. Articles 2 (a) through 2 (q) list 17 offenses that Google and the government agree are the "Relevant Facts" and article 14 precludes Google or any attorneys, agents, officers, directors, or employees from contradicting anything contained in 2 (a) through 2 (q).

5. *And we can build more monopolies if we want, and fund them with the profits from search.* Google's Android mobile operating system has catapulted ahead of Microsoft's Mobile Windows and Apple's iOS operating systems. And by bundling and tying its mobile applications to Android, it is developing monopoly power in additional areas. Google's initial claim was that the Android operating system was *open,* which meant that all other software vendors had an equal chance to develop software, in direct contrast with Apple's more closed system. In fact, the Mobile Application Distribution Agreement (MADA) provides over a dozen pages of confidential rules that govern exactly which applications *must* be preloaded onto an Android device, and that even specify *where* many of these applications must be preloaded. Additionally, the rules specify which applications *cannot* be preloaded onto an Android device. Google can enforce these rules by declaring that a manufacturer whose devices are not fully in compliance with MADA rules can be blocked from accessing Google Play. A device that cannot access Google Play cannot download content and apps; that is, it cannot be tailored and customized to meet its user's needs. Denying a manufacturer access to Google Play basically removed the manufacturer's devices from the Google ecosystem, converting a smartphone into a limited capability brick with phone service and e-mail. Combining revenues from search with the power of Android and the control provided by MADA has given Google monopoly power over software in a variety of areas that have nothing to do with search, such as Google Maps and Google Earth. The abuse of Android is the basis of the third of the EU Competition Commission's complaints against Google, which was resolved just before this book's publication. The Commission imposed a record $5 billion fine on Google for abuse of Android's monopoly power.

Again, I am not attempting to prove that Google abuses its power. Nor is it my intent to review all allegations made against Google over the past ten years and review the disposition of each case. However, Chapters 7 and 8 argue

---

[4]https://www.justice.gov/opa/pr/google-forfeits-500-million-generated-online-ads-prescription-drug-sales-canadian-online. Yes, this really did happen.

that abuse is certainly *possible* in an MP3PP system. Sections 9.1 through 9.4 of this chapter argue that Google's power is real and that there is reason to believe that this power has been deployed to protect, defend, and extend monopoly power. And, while I have singled out Google as the primary example of abuse of platform envelopment in the west, it was not the first. And, when I argue for regulation, it is because Google will not be the last abuser of platform envelopment unless platform-based competition is regulated.

In this chapter, I simply want to argue that Google's power is extreme, and that "trust us, we won't be evil" may be a leap too far.

So, while "don't be evil" and "do the right thing" both sound like part of a great corporate philosophy, I might want to add the following as a more realistic assessment of Google's corporate philosophy, based on the complaints that have emerged about Google around the world[5]:

- If we have monopoly power, we'll use it.
- If we have access to content that belongs to others, we'll share it with our users; users will love us for it.
- If the price is high enough, you can get us to do almost anything.
- Why should we stop with only one or two monopolies?

But maybe the company really doesn't intend to "be evil." Maybe it intends to "do the right thing." Even if you trust Sergei, Larry, and Eric completely, this much power in the wrong hands may be truly dangerous. And Google and Alphabet may already be the wrong hands.

9.5   Should You Care About Reverse Price Wars? Do Higher Prices Charged to Sellers Really Affect Consumers? Some of the Money Goes to You, Right?

Bread and Circuses, YouTube and Gmail — I've got Android, who could ask anything more?

You are the beneficiary of much of Google's investments in purchasing online users' loyalty. Unlike Sabre's and Apollo's payments to travel agencies, the money search engines invest in buying loyalty goes to you, the user.

---

[5]"Don't be evil" was part of Google's code of conduct for years. When they restructured as part of the holding company Alphabet the phrase was replaced with "do the right thing."

As Google argued in front of the Federal Trade Commission, how can there be consumer harm from services that are so popular, and so much cheaper than just free. Think of how much you get from Google, in addition to free search.[6]

So why should you care how much Google charges companies for key words? That doesn't cost you anything, ever, does it? What's the last time you as a consumer paid for key words? What was the last time you as an individual actually paid Google for anything? How does the lack of competition in search make search expensive for you? Actually, how could the lack of competition in search *possibly* affect you in any way?

Advanced economies around the world protect competition, because the absence of competition almost invariably leads to higher prices, lower quality, and reduced choice for consumers. This was the reason given for declaring that Sabre and Apollo had engaged in anticompetitive behavior. How do higher prices for key words lead to higher prices for consumers? That's pretty straightforward.

Sometimes higher prices for sellers get passed through directly as higher prices for consumers. Often higher gas prices are passed through as fuel surcharges for passengers in taxis. Higher fuel prices lead to higher prices for air travel. Increases in sellers' costs are not usually directly visible to consumers as separate charges. Still, it would be hard to deny that higher costs for retailers and service providers usually increase the prices consumers pay for goods and services. Why would an increase in costs for search be different from an increase in any other costs?

Moreover, I expect to see additional abuses in the future, especially as Google continues to offer additional services, which allows it to compete against additional companies in additional markets. I expect to see additional abuses as long as Google's platform envelopment strategy provides opportunities to destroy these competitors. Regardless of how much you may choose to trust Google now, the possibility for future abuse cannot be safely ignored. Indeed, while Sabre and Apollo had the ability to limit consumer choice in air travel, Google has the ability to limit consumer choice in almost any market they wish to dominate.

Again, we're seeing unregulated marketplace domination, in ways that regulators never tolerated from AT&T in the USA, or from any other tele-

---

[6]See https://www.google.com/intl/en/about/products/ for a list of more than forty applications, from Web search, mobile computing, entertainment, social networking, online storage, and office systems support that Google provides consumers without charge. Android devices are among the most popular in the world, just as Google Maps and Google Earth are among the most widely used personal navigation tools.

communications giant or from any other key provider of critical infrastructure. Recent European experience indicates that it is almost impossible for a European company to compete against an American firm like Google or Facebook, which can subsidize their operations out of monopoly profits not available to anyone else. How would a French *Livre des Visages* or a German *Buch der Gesichter* compete with Facebook, which already has billions of users to connect to, and is already free?

The experience of Microsoft's Bing teaches us a similar lesson. Microsoft has been unable to break into the market for search, despite developing superior algorithms and investing in broadcast attack ads targeting Google search as dangerous. Even Microsoft's ability to absorb massive, billion dollar losses year after year, has not enabled them to break into the market for search.

9.6 Why Should Anyone Do Anything About Monopoly Power in Search? Won't Technological Progress Fix Any Problems Better and Faster Than Regulation?

Fixing a hole where the rain gets in …

Even if you agree that Google has monopoly power over search, and even if you agree that at present this power is harmful, it may not be necessary to do anything. Some monopoly markets really do fix themselves. General Motors and other competitors quickly followed Henry Ford's lead in manufacturing affordable cars on an assembly line. Sometimes the market corrects monopoly power by moving toward newer products that make the previous monopolies almost irrelevant. IBM no longer dominates computer sales because there are so many alternatives to its traditional *big iron*. Kodak's ubiquitous yellow boxes no longer dominate film sales because, as most photographers today would say, "*What's film?*"

So, if you believe that the market for search will correct itself quickly, regulation is unlikely to be justified. Regulation would be unnecessary. And, perhaps, it would also be counterproductive. Given unforeseen technological progress, unnecessary regulation today could lock the market into a structure that blocked future innovations and locked the market out of better competitive structures that would have emerged if the market had been free to adapt.

However, sometimes a hole in the roof, or a hole in regulation, really does need to be fixed. Unfortunately, for reasons discussed in the previous two chapters, market forces are unlikely to improve search quality or reduce the total cost of search. Google offers only limited transparency into their algorithms and their quality scores, so that most users do not immediately notice quality issues or *misdirection*. And almost no consumer is aware of the costs that the current MP3PP structure creates for Party-3 and ultimately for consumers as well in terms of reduced choice and higher prices.

Additionally, Google appears not only free to users but *free-er than free*. Google provides us so much great stuff, which successfully buys most of our loyalty. We've already seen that this comes with a price. Why don't we leave Google for a new search engine that would be better for merchants and therefore might lead to lower retail prices for us?

- *Why would we leave?* Google appears to be free for us.
- *How would leaving help any one of us?* If a couple of us leave Google for Bing, or DuckDuckGo, or a new search engine of my dreams, how much would that save the merchants? Would the first users see any differences at all in the retail prices they paid when shopping?
- *How could we replace any single part of our Google world?* The Google/Android/YouTube ecosystem links together so well, and we've already seen how Google's Mobile Application Distribution Agreement makes it difficult to replace single pieces of that ecosystem.
- *And isn't Google better?* As we saw from Bing's experience, part of what makes a search engine good is its ability to learn from users' experience. A search engine with large market share has vast amounts of data from its users' recent search history. Without enough data to drive its algorithms, a new search engine is almost certainly going to start off inferior, even if it is entirely unbiased and attempting to provide the best possible search results.

And, finally, the brilliant use of quality scores in their modified Vickrey Auction helps reduce or eliminate the most obvious errors in the ranking search results without reducing Google's earnings. This allows a search engine to extract as much money as possible from Party-3 sellers, while most of the time still reporting search results in the order that Party-1 users would want.

As we have seen in the earlier sections of this chapter, and in Chapters 7 and 8, our current system of providing free search may actually be the most expensive way to provide search.

9.7   Is It Fair to Complain? After All Google Has Done for Us?

That's not the right question! Ask if this the best way for us to run the Internet!

My students often ask if it is fair even to consider regulating Google now. They agree that some of what Google did may have been creepy. Some of what they did in the past might even have been illegal. But surely they don't need to be creepy or do anything illegal any more. Why not live and let live? Is it fair to change the rules? Isn't that just punishing them for success?

Regulation is not a punishment. But it may be a necessary response to power in some circumstances, either to mitigate past harm or to limit future harm.

Fairness is an odd word for an economist to use. As we shall see in the final chapter, it is almost impossible to agree on what fairness would be in many situations. Is it fair to protect consumers, competitors, or anyone else, from a company attempting to realize the profits associated with having made innovative and risky investments? Surely Google did make extraordinary investments. Aren't they now entitled to whatever they can earn?

The answer to that is complicated: In Europe and in much of the rest of the world, benefitting from monopoly power is suspect, no matter how that monopoly power was obtained. In the USA, most of the time we allow a monopolist to profit from a monopoly legitimately attained, but not to take active steps to protect, defend, or extend its existing monopoly. However, in rare instances courts or regulators in the USA have determined that even a monopoly legitimately attained may still require regulation and limitations on profit-seeking behavior.

I believe that integrated MP3PP Gateways represent one of those instances when regulation may be required even without proof that monopoly was attained deliberately and thus was obtained illegally. My reasons for suggesting regulation are drawn from a range of historical precedents.

1. *Historical Precedent 1: Sabre, Apollo, and control of an* essential facility— If agencies couldn't connect to airlines through Sabre and Apollo, they almost always booked flights on a different carrier. Travel agent reservations systems were truly critical to the industry in the 1980s and accounted for the bulk of air reservations. Moreover, more than half of all flights were booked from the top line in Sabre or Apollo Search, and more than 90% were booked from the first page. Not surprisingly American's Sabre tended to place American's flights on the first page and

tended to hide flights from direct competitors, while United's Apollo did the same for United's flights. Consequently, by using their control of the two largest reservations systems American and United gained the power to grow their own business and to destroy competitors. We have already seen the power that Sabre and Apollo were able to exercise over all competing airlines in the 1980s. There is no indication that Sabre or Apollo initially set out to attain monopoly power. But there is clear evidence that they used this power to bankrupt competitors, resulting in higher prices to consumers and to reduced choice for these consumers. Moreover, it would not have been feasible for smaller airlines to break into the reservations systems market, for a variety of reasons.

Additionally, as we have already noted, the *market for everything* is larger than the market for air travel, and as an essential facility Google may pose even greater problems than Sabre and Apollo did.

2. *Historical precedent 2: Railroads*—When I was in junior high school we studied what was poetically called "*the long haul short haul evil.*" Short routes connecting small towns to bigger cities were likely to be served by a single railroad. Farmers that needed to get their crops and livestock to processors in Chicago depended upon that single rail company, and as a result, farmers were forced to pay higher prices for short distances served by a monopoly carrier than the prices charged processing companies for shipping much longer distances. The route for a few dozen miles into Chicago might cost more than the rest of the route connecting Chicago to New York or Atlanta. No one argued that rail carriers were not entitled to fair profits. But nothing in the structure of these markets led to the creation of competing carriers over these short distances, and consequently, nothing in the structure of these markets created the competitive pressures that would have limited prices. The abuse of small farmers continued. Since the market would not have limited the power of these carriers, the Interstate Commerce Commission was created to regulate rail tariffs.

Again, the market for everything is greater than the market for agricultural products.

3. *Historical precedent 3: AT&T and the creation of the Bell System*—The limited capability of telephone technology in the early 1900s ensured that you could only make phone calls within a single carrier's network.

We now take cross-system interoperability for granted and would be surprised if an AT&T phone could not call a Verizon phone, or Rogers phone in Canada, or a T-Mobile phone in Germany. This was not the case in the early stages of telephone service. Originally, you could only call an AT&T phone from another AT&T phone. As the AT&T network grew it became more attractive. As the network gained more subscribers, this increased the likelihood that the people anyone wanted to call were already on the network, which meant that new subscribers were more likely to join AT&T than any competing network. This is called a positive network effect, meaning the bigger the network got, the more valuable it became.

As a nation, we faced the following paradox: We wanted to have only a single carrier, in order to maximize network effects and ensure that all telephone subscribers could talk to each other. But we feared monopoly power in an industry as important as telecommunications already had become.

The solution was *The Kingsbury Commitment*, an agreement to let AT&T remain a monopoly and make all important decisions itself, subject to two overriding concerns. First, AT&T sought to ensure that every home could have a phone—AT&T agreed to advance the objective of universal service. And second, AT&T agreed to limit its profits so that an investment in AT&T seemed more like an investment in bonds than in shares in a risky corporation.

Since market forces would have led to a single phone company without restrictions on its power, regulation was imposed on AT&T. Unlike most of the rest of the world, the US Federal Government stayed out of the telecommunications industry, neither owning nor setting policy for the phone system. And for decades, the USA had the best phone service in the world.

And yet again, as important as telephone service was to business and to society a century ago, the net is more important today.

4. *Historical precedent 4: AT&T Long Lines and AT&T's early move into broadcast radio networks*—The first successful commercial radio station with scheduled programming funded by advertising was operated by AT&T. As broadcast radio networks became more important, regulators realized that competing radio network operators were going to be dependent upon AT&T long lines to "ship" their programming to their affiliates. AT&T's monopoly over long-distance communications had positioned it to extend its monopoly into broadcast services, had it cho-

sen to do so. Since market forces would not have eliminated AT&T's competitive chokehold over network broadcasting, the company was forced to divest its share of ownership of WEAF and to exit broadcast radio.

And yet again, the power that AT&T would gain through dominating broadcast radio networks a century ago is not as great as the control that Google is gaining through control of search, mobile computing, and smartphone operating systems.

So, yes, there are precedents for imposing regulation on companies with monopoly power, even after they have made significant investments, and even if there had been no clear evidence that they acted deliberately to obtain their first monopoly. But even given those precedents, would it be *fair* to regulate Google now?

Economists do not often use the word *fair*, although politicians, political scientists, philosophers, and sociologists often do. Something that's fair to Google and its shareholders might not seem fair to Foundem and its shareholders, or to Yelp, or to merchants who participate in key word auctions, or to consumers who end up paying higher prices for virtually everything they buy online. Fair is subjective and personal.

Economists talk about efficiency, and that entails prices that do not distort the market. Ok, what on earth does that mean? Suppose the Federal Communication Commission declared that long-distance rates should be regulated and set very high, with excess profits from long distance used to lower the cost of rural phone service. That might seem socially desirable, since everyone needs a phone. But any time someone took a subsidized Amtrak train to DC for a two-hour meeting instead of making a two-hour phone call, that's a market distortion caused by regulation. While the price of the train ticket might have been lower than the price for 120 minutes of long-distance conversation, the actual cost to provide a seat on the train was much higher than the cost of providing the two-hour phone call. Historically, that happened, and avoiding these strange behaviors was one of the objectives of the deregulation of AT&T and the telecommunications industry in the early 1980s.

So, really, what would I want to see? Something that served a purpose similar to the Kingsbury Commitment, or the Interstate Commerce Commission, or the regulation of Sabre and Apollo. Something that prevented economic harvesting that was enabled by exploiting an essential piece of infrastructure. Something that served a purpose similar to AT&T's divesting ownership of WEAF, so that its control of long-distance telecommunications couldn't be extended into dominance of radio.

Remember that at least some of the higher costs of sponsored search are paid by you, every time you shop.

9.8 But What Should Regulation Look Like?

What form of regulation do we need?

I would start with several forms of regulation. We probably need to start with new regulations, rather than relying upon distorting existing regulatory regimes designed for different technologies, for different business models, and for different forms of market competition.

The first thing I would do would be to regulate search by imposing caps on earnings from search, much as the Kingsbury Commitment imposed caps on AT&T's earnings. Recall that the Kingsbury Commitment capped earnings but left AT&T intact; breaking up the Bell System would have been bad for America, but untrammeled monopoly power would also have been bad.

Breaking up Google would not by itself lower the total real financial cost that society pays for "free search" or improve search quality. Indeed, as we have seen from our study of competing MP3PPs and reverse price wars, breaking up Google might make things worse, just as breaking up AT&T in 1913 would have done.

We need a modern form of the Kingsbury Commitment, since it appears that nothing is going to limit Google's market power, not even the eventual success of competitors like Bing. Google's profits would be capped. But Google would be free to design the best search algorithms it could, and indeed would be free to make the best business decisions, technology decisions, and strategy decisions it could, subject to an earnings cap.

The second thing I would do would be to regulate search to ensure quality and fairness in search results. There are numerous stories of intentional bias in the order of search results, for commercial reasons or to influence public opinion. There have been studies of Google's ability to influence public opinion sufficiently to affect the outcome of close elections in the USA and abroad. As colleagues have suggested, perhaps we need a Federal Search Commission, which would impose a modern form of the Fairness Doctrine that used to be applied to broadcast journalism.[7] Yes, there is an almost end-less source of diverse opinions on the net. But Google is a powerful arbiter of public opinion because Google determines what we can easily find. Most of us use Google search, and thus most of us learn what Google wants us to know about them.

The next thing I would do would be to prohibit vertical integration by a search engine, any search engine. That is, I would prohibit Google from expanding into products and services unrelated to search. Just as AT&T's control over long-distance communication gave them the ability to block competitors in broadcast radio, Google's control over search gives them an enormous ability to promote their own offerings and to hide the offerings of existing, high-quality competitors. Just as AT&T was forced to divest its ownership in WEAF, Google could be forced to divest its ownership in a range of other businesses, which would then have to compete on their own merits and without Google's support through search.

Yes, there are arguments that vertical integration can lead to greater effi-ciency in manufacturing and distribution of physical goods. There are arguments that a simpler distribution channel leads to lower prices in the absence of what's called *double marginalization*—a fancy term for saying that if the manufacturer sets its profit-maximizing price, and then the retailer sets its own profit-maximizing price, then prices may be higher and consumer purchases and consumer surplus may be reduced. That in turn is a fancy way of saying as consumers we'd like to pay less and buy more. However, there is no indication that efficiency would be harmed by having a regulated search company forced to stop competing with a wide range of retailers and of service providers. That is, search engines should not be retailers or service providers with unfair advantages due to their gateway role; search engines should provide consumers with the best possible access to retailers and ser-vice providers.

In other words, search would be behaving exactly as intended, and the Internet would be delivering exactly what we expected from it.

Breaking up Google into two companies would be the most controversial aspect of the most likely proposed forms of regulation. One company would keep the search business, and this business would be regulated. A separate company, not a separate division of the same holding company, would retain

---

[7]See "Federal Search Commission - Access, Fairness, and Accountability in the Law of Search", by Oren Bracha and Frank Pasquale, Cornell Law Review, Vol. 93, No. 6, September 2008, available online at http://scholarship.law.cornell.edu/clr/vol93/iss6/11.

some of the Android-related mobile businesses and would be only lightly regulated.

Breaking up Google would address many but not all of the problems with the current structure of the company. We might not need Google to divest itself of Gmail, Google Earth, Google Maps, and YouTube. We probably would need to take a careful look at the MADA to ensure that other companies could successfully compete in the market for the most popular mobile apps without being crushed by the power of an Android-centered platform envelopment strategy.

Finally, I would take action to protect users' privacy. This would limit Google's ability to data mine users' activities, and limit their ability to integrate data from search with data from e-mail, text, and GPS. This would limit Google's ability to monetize individuals' personal information. Monetizing personal information takes many forms. Google argues—correctly—that they never provide an individual's contact information to a company that wants to offer tailored services at a tailored price. They never provide information that directly identifies an individual as really needing to fly, and therefore willing to pay more. They never directly identify an individual as a poor driving risk or a poor health risk, who should be charged higher insurance premiums. They do, however, send messages to individuals characterized using whatever combination of information the advertiser wants to use. And of course, the advertiser knows exactly what combination of criteria was used to select consumers to target for each message. Consequently, as soon as the individual responds to any specific ad, the advertiser immediately knows which offers to make and which offers to withhold. The "*Myth of Anonymity*" suggests that users are never harmed by Google's revealing their individual identity, and it is demonstrably false. Often the information is valuable to advertisers precisely because it is harmful to consumers.

Restricting Google's ability to monetize personal information would affect Google's ability to provide a range of services that are subsidized by this monetizing of personal information. This is complicated and would also be highly controversial. The convenience of getting free services provides an obvious benefit to Google's users. The costs associated with violating their privacy are far less clear, making it hard for users to assess the relative costs and benefits of free services supported by monetizing private information. We will return to this subject in Chapter 11, when we discuss online business models, and in Chapter 12, when we discuss the future of technology, of regulation, and of the form of society we want to have.

9.9   A Final Cautionary Note on Regulation

First, "Do No Harm!" Only then can you start to solve the problems!

How do regulators and legislators ensure that they do no harm? I would suggest a short set of guidelines.

- Avoid imposing any more structure or any more rules on Google than were imposed by the Kingsbury Commitment. Cap Google's earnings, but leave management free to manage.
- Limit Google's ability to expand in lines of business unrelated to search, just as AT&T was forbidden to operate a broadcast radio network. Spin-off Android-related mobile businesses into a separate company.
- Avoid anything that looks like censorship of the net, while avoiding bias in the order of search results. This may be the true meaning of net neutrality. And it may be outside the expertise of existing regulatory agencies like the Federal Communications Commission.
- Block both the company created from Google search and the company created from Android and mobile businesses from vertical integration into sales or other online services.
- Provide transparency, so that users understand how the order of search results was determined.
- Prohibit a wide range of privacy violations. Prohibit all companies from sharing personal information that can affect what consumers are charged, or can affect which consumers are offered or denied access to individual products and services.

It will not be simple or easy to design a coherent regulatory policy that achieves all of these objectives without unintentional side effects that harm the market for online services.

However, I believe that we have shown that the potential for harm with the current obsolete regulatory policy is too great to be ignored. This includes harm to competitors of Google in its wide range of businesses, harm to companies that use search to be found, and to consumers. Moreover, it seems unlikely that the market will provide mechanisms for natural correction any time soon, and therefore the prospect of continued harm seems almost inevitable.

Regulations need to be carefully tuned to ensure that they have the desired effects and avoid harmful unintended consequences. However, some form of regulation will be essential.

9.10 Summary

Chapters 7 through this chapter complete our analysis of platforms, gateways, and MP3PPs. We explore their unique source of power and explore why normal forms of competition are not sufficient to restrain that power. We explore how they use that power, both to control the prices platforms charge for participation in search and to control who can and cannot be found. We show that this control allows them to enter a wide range of businesses unrelated to search and to dominate many of them. We show how their profits allow them to buy loyalty, as was the case with other, earlier forms of MP3PPs.

Finally, we conclude that market forces and normal sources of competition are not sufficient to limit the power of MP3PPs, and that as a result companies and consumers have been harmed and will continue to be harmed. Finally, we explored why regulation may be appropriate, and the forms that regulation might be expected to take. If you were the owner and operator of a successful MP3PP gateway, regulation might be the only thing that could end your competitive advantage; that's why Google spent more on lobbying in 2017 than any other corporation in America.

Appendix: Showing That There Is Monopoly Power in Search—How Would You Know?

There are standard measures of monopoly power. And it surely looks like monopoly power by those measures!

There are two measures that regulatory economists often use to determine if market power exists. In the USA, these tests are principally used to determine if mergers should be permitted or blocked, and they measure how much market power would be present if a merger occurred. By both measures, Google's market power in search is *way* above the redline used in these tests. At present, Google's market share in search globally is just over 90%.[8] The level for a *rebuttable presumption* of monopoly power is anything over 2/3.[9] While having 90% market share is not *proof* of monopoly power, it is

---

[8]http://gs.statcounter.com/search-engine-market-share, current as of 24 July 2018.

[9]Rebuttable presumption is a great phrase. It means basically "It sure looks like us to a monopoly! But we'll give you a chance to prove that you don't really have monopoly power." http://www.americanbar. org/groups/young_lawyers/publications/the_101_201_practice_series/monopoly_power_following_ the_doj_single-firm_conduct_report.html.

a strong indicator. There is a second, more complex metric, the Herfendahl Hirschman Index (HHI) used to determine industry concentration and power. This measure is the sum of the squares of individual companies' market share. If four companies each had an equal share of 25% the HHI would be 4 * (25 * 25) or 2500. If ten companies each had 10% the HHI would be 10 * (10 * 10) or 1000. The threshold used for monopoly power before a merger is to ensure that the HHI would not be over 1800.[10] The HHI for concentration in search worldwide is over 8,000. Both of these metrics—simple market share and the HHI—would suggest significant concentration and significant monopoly power exist in search.

An additional standard measure of monopoly power is the ability to use excess profits to cross-subsidize additional businesses, and thus to extend the original monopoly. The argument is simple: If you have lots of money left over from one business, and can invest it in another, perhaps you are able to earn too much in the first business. Perhaps you have monopoly power in the first business. And if you can invest *enough* in another business, perhaps you can create a second monopoly. Google's ability to create and subsidize Android, and to catapult it to a position of market dominance worldwide, could be taken as an indication that the market for search is not *contestable*, that is, no company can threaten to contest Google's market share in search, and thus no company can exert pressure on Google to reduce the price of key words in search.

And, of course, there is both the theory and the history presented in the previous two chapters. As we have seen, Apollo's 27% market share was sufficient for monopoly power in air travel search, and Google's market share is much higher. Google's profit margins provide clear indication that competition with Bing or DuckDuckGo is not limiting the prices of Google's key words. Indeed, the prices themselves may be an indication that there is only limited competition. The most expensive cost per click, as of this writing, is <<best mesothelioma lawyer>>, at $935.71 per click.[11] Clearly, that price is in no way determined by Google's costs to provide search, or by anything other than Google's ability to charge whatever it wants in the absence of competition from other search providers.

---

[10]https://www.justice.gov/atr/15-concentration-and-market-shares.

[11]https://searchenginewatch.com/2016/05/31/the-most-expensive-100-google-adwords-keywords-in-the-us/, current as of 21 October 2016.

Part III

I Got It! Learning to Work with These Patterns?

10

Scenario Analysis and Managing Strategic Ambiguity: How to Remember Future Events, Before They Actually Occur!

This chapter introduces scenario analysis, a technique for dealing with strategic uncertainty, and it introduces a new way of thinking about problems. Scenario analysis is based on *the power of question-driven planning to embrace uncertainty and strategic ambiguity*. We use scenario analysis when we don't know what will happen next. I don't mean that we use scenarios when we can't assign probabilities to a known set of possible outcomes, like predicting the outcome of a football game. I mean when we *really* don't know what will happen next. I mean when we are facing such strategic ambiguity that we don't even know what game we are playing.

Some aspects of digital transformation are like that. We don't immediately know what the rules are. If we're executives, we don't immediately know what the new technology can do yet. We don't know what our customers will want or what our regulators will permit. And we don't know what our opponents' strategies will be, or what strategies we should follow in response. If we're just consumers, we don't know what to buy, or how to choose, or what the *sharing economy* of Uber and Airbnb will do for us, or to our neighborhoods.

We need a systematic way to deal with strategic ambiguity. There is so much we just don't know how to incorporate in our planning. First and foremost, we need a way to figure out what the new rules will be, and what the new strategic choices will be. We need to know what game we are playing. Then, and only then, we can develop our strategies, for our businesses and for our lives. Scenario analysis enables all of this.

© The Author(s) 2019
E. K. Clemons, *New Patterns of Power and Profit*,
https://doi.org/10.1007/978-3-030-00443-9_10

Scenario Analysis: *Scenario analysis* deals with strategic ambiguity. We use scenario analysis when we *do not have* enough data and indeed *cannot get* enough data to analyze critical decisions. Scenario analysis starts by *asking what we need to know*, rather than by *examining what we already do know* or even by *examining what it is possible to know*. By asking what we need to know and then examining illustrative sets of possible future values for what we need to know, scenario analysis converts an unstructured and unsolvable problem into a small set of structured and solvable sub-problems. History and the decision-maker's expertise are then enormously powerful when applied to each of the structured and solvable sub-problems. We can apply each of our six information-based patterns to each of these sub-problems. Scenario analysis can prepare us for the uncertain futures so completely that I often claimed that it enabled me *to remember the future*, and to remember events and responses to them even when they had not yet happened and perhaps had never happened before.

Scenario analysis often doesn't start by gathering data and indeed often ignores the data that you already do have. Rather, the process starts by identifying the questions that will be important and then seeks to determine the data that you will wish you could have to answer those questions, rather than starting with the data that you can get. This sounds alien to scientists, engineers, and executives. I use it because it works, and it works better than any other method I have found for uncovering hidden patterns, early, before they become obvious.

Scenario planning is one of the best ways for learning about the structure of an industry quickly, for learning what about that structure is most important, and for determining which elements of that structure are vulnerable to disruptive change. It's one of the best methods for enabling professionals to anticipate changes in their own areas of expertise and to revise their own deeply held beliefs, and to do so early, before the necessary data are available to anyone using more traditional data-driven methodologies.

The sections in this chapter fit together to teach the scenario analysis process. I hope that by the end you will be converted from a skeptic to an enthusiastic user. More importantly, I trust that you will be able to use scenario analysis as an important element of your own strategic planning and risk management repertoire. I believe that scenario analysis is the best way to anticipate and manage the transformational effects of information.

10.1 Remembering the Future and Using Scenarios for Rapid Recognition and Rapid Response

Remembering the future can save your life! We use scenarios to take the surprise out of surprise and the danger out of danger!

This section uses a single personal experience to illustrate and then to motivate the use of scenarios to allow exploring the future. Exploration of the future can be so thorough that if and when the scenario occurs *for the first time* it's as if you are reliving the experience. It is about enabling you to remember something before it happens, what I call *remembering the future*, for rapid recognition and rapid response. It is about learning from experiences you have not yet had. Learning from experience can be painful, even fatal. We don't want our children to learn about hot stoves by burning themselves or to learn about the importance of traffic safety by having an accident.

It's better to learn from the experience of others. But how do you learn from an experience that no one else has had?

I'm about to provide the story of the time my car ran away with me. I was approaching a cliff at well over 100 miles per hour, with no obvious way to keep the car from continuing to run away, and no way to stop it from continuing to accelerate. The story captures all of the essential elements of scenario analysis:

- **It is driven by questions, rather than by data**. Long before I encountered the problem, I thought about the problem. Long before my car decided to take control of itself, I asked myself the relevant questions. I asked "*what would happen if the accelerator linkage failed*" rather than "*what do the data say about accelerator linkage failure?*" or even "*what do the data say I should I should worry about as the principal safety hazards in my car?*"
- **It's based onpatterns**. We all know that brake failure is a common enough problem, and that it can be catastrophic. But if brake failure is catastrophic, then so is its opposite. If I am going to worry about what to do when my brakes fail, in the *full off* position, then I should worry about what I would do if my accelerator failed in the *full on* position. If brake failure is catastrophic, then accelerator linkage failure might be catastrophic as well.

- **It is not based on data**. I had never heard of accelerator linkage failure in automobiles. If I had thought to look at the data, I would never have studied the problem because the data unambiguously suggested that the problem was not especially important. This was a long time ago, before complex fuel injection systems and computerized engine controls and I had never heard of cars just running wild, accelerating as fast as they could. There was no history to suggest that I needed to worry about accelerator failure.[1]

- **The problem really was important**. I studied an event that mattered to my future survival. My rapid recognition of the problem when it actually occurred and my immediate and informed response to the problem saved my life. If I had not performed this particular scenario analysis in advance, I would have died from the rare event of accelerator linkage failure. I would have approached a cliff, at about 140 miles an hour, failed to negotiate a 90-degree turn, and exploded upon impact with the face of the cliff.

- **The technique is not based on waiting until the critical problem arises!** The technique is not based on experience and does not require waiting for experience.

Years ago, a friend was seriously injured when the brakes failed in his car while he was driving at high speed. I thought through what I would have done if my brakes had failed.

But <<*brakes*>> are only one strategic uncertainty as a determinant of an automobile's velocity, and <<*failed / locked full off*>> is only one value that this strategic uncertainty can take. I decided that preparing mentally for potential driving disasters would require examining the most significant other strategic uncertainty, which was the exact opposite. I started worrying about <<*accelerator*>> and <<*failed / locked full on*>>. *How would I know* that my accelerator had locked full on? *How much time would I have to respond* if my accelerator had locked full on? *How would I respond?* I thought through my answers, and I filed the information away for future use, just in case.

---

[1]As I wrote the final draft of this chapter, I Googled <<"brake failure">> and <<"accelerator failure">>. The first returned 566,000 results, while the second returned 3530. When I Googled <<"brake failure" stop safely>>, there were still 270,000 results, and when I Googled <<"accelerator failure" stop safely>>, there were only 2800 results. Of the two, stopping safely after accelerator linkage failure accounted for only 1% of the total number of the results. If I merely looked at data, and indeed had done so in 1986, accelerator linkage failure would not appear to be a significant safety hazard.

Several years later, I was driving home to Philadelphia from Cornell. I was driving quite discreetly, although in a custom-modified, inter-cooler turbo Volvo. By the time I completed my modifications, I had what looked like a sedate middle-aged professor's commuting car, but with double the expected horsepower.

In order to avoid a minor traffic accident, I temporarily needed full acceleration, which I had never tried before in that car. I needed to accelerate and I did.

And then I went faster. I took my foot off the accelerator. And yet I went faster still.

The accelerator pedal was flopping freely. The accelerator was locked full on. And there was nothing I could do about it, nothing I could do to release the accelerator, and nothing I could do to stop my speed from continuing to increase. I was going to continue to accelerate until the engine exploded, or until *something worse* happened.

And then I discovered what the *something worse* was going to be. By now I was going maybe 135 miles an hour, continuing to accelerate, and approaching a 90-degree right turn in the road. I had maybe 20 seconds to do something *right now* to avert the deadly impact.

At this point, I interrupt the story and ask my class for suggestions. The following usually come up, in the following order:

1. *Try the emergency brake*—No luck. This won't help. The brake will stop the car from starting to slide down a hill, but won't do anything against a couple of hundred horsepower of a runaway turbo-charged engine.
2. *Kick in the clutch*—This should definitely be a last resort. I've seen videos of this. With 200 or more horsepower suddenly no longer connected to any load, the engine reaches maybe 10,000 RPM instantly and then explodes through the hood. Tie rods, even cylinders, can come flying through the windshield. This is definitely not good for the car and is potentially fatal for the driver as well.
3. *Jump out,* tuck and roll, *and pray*—This is also not a great alternative.
4. *The only solution that works is ...*—By now, of course, you have thought too long before acting, and you and your passengers are dead, but if you had thought of this in time ... you would ... *carefully turn off the engine.* This is the only thing that works. You don't want to do anything that locks the steering wheel! You hold as straight as you can, stomp as hard as you can on the brake, and hold down the brake until you come to a complete stop.

Because of my previous analyses of accelerator linkages, I was prepared for the problem. I instantly knew what had happened and I instantly knew what to do. I implemented option 4. The car stopped with maybe a couple of thousand feet to spare. I was glad to be alive.

And I was alive because of scenario analysis. I had *remembered* this scenario, and I had *remembered* the necessary response, even though the scenario had not happened yet.

I call this *"remembering the future!"* It definitely was not learning from my own experience or from anyone else's.

Life throws a lot of problems at us. The first part of solving a problem is figuring what the problem is. It's useful to think of this figuring out what game you've just been dropped into. I had just been dropped into *deal with the runaway car game.*

The rest of this chapter provides a more formal introduction to the role of scenario analysis. It also highlights the use of patterns and reasoning from the patterns that we covered in the first nine chapters of this book.

10.2   Learn to Ask the Right Questions, Even If You Can't Answer Them

It takes courage to ask the right questions publicly, especially if you know you can't answer them!

Suppose you were a senior member of Sears Roebuck's management team in 1996. You're trying to figure out what your eCommerce strategy should be. Is eCommerce going to be important? Do you need to prepare for it at all, or can you ignore it for now? If you do need to prepare, *how* should you prepare? Will eCommerce replace your catalog sales or build on it? Should you get rid of your catalog division because it is unprofitable now and likely to become even less profitable if current trends continue? Or should you expand it, knowing that online sales will grow out of your catalog division and ultimately replace catalog sales, and knowing that the logistics systems you built for catalog sales are going to provide a major source of competitive advantage? Your new catalog division, now called *Distance Shopping*, will be even larger and even more important than it had been, even if you never print the catalog again. What will eCommerce look like, and how should it best be folded into your existing portfolio of business activities?

Suppose you were a senior member of the executive team of the London Stock Exchange a few years earlier. Should you prepare for online securities trading or can you ignore it? If you do need to prepare, *how* should you prepare? Will online trading strategies create enormous new opportunities for investors to interact with the Exchange, requiring new telecommunications hardware, new trading systems, and possibly even new trading rules for the Exchange and for the London market? Or will online trading strategies replace the Exchange as investors' principal place for trading? Is online trading a threat, an opportunity, or both? Can regulators help position the Exchange to exploit new opportunities? Can regulators help protect the Exchange from new risks? What do you and your team want to do to prepare for the future of online trading?

I was lucky enough to work with the management team of both Sears Roebuck and the London Stock Exchange to examine these questions and to help them begin to prepare their strategies. It was clear that neither group had enough information to answer their questions yet. They did not have the data they needed to begin their planning. And yet, they could not wait for the data that they needed, because by the time the data were available it would be too late to begin planning, and too late to begin coordinating with other actors in their market or their marketplace. And yet, both teams *did* wait for the data to be clear. And both teams paid a heavy price for waiting.

As with my runaway car, identifying the right questions—identifying what you would need to know in order to decide—was almost as helpful as having the data in advance.

10.3   When "Good Data Goes Bad," or What to Do When "Convincing Data Actually Lies to Us"!

Sometimes we have to ignore our data. The data may still be an accurate record of what happened, but they provide no information on what will happen next!

Why does scenario analysis start with questions? Why doesn't it start with data and drawing lines and making inferences about the continuation of existing trends? A manager can usually rely upon data. Managers do spend a great deal of time making routine operational decisions based on historical experience. Usually, having data helps, and having lots of data, decades of data, helps even more. But executives are also called upon to make strategic decisions, often in the absence of some or all of the necessary data.

Leadership sometimes requires making decisions without data, even when it appears that the firm has decades of data, conclusive data, data that all points in the same direction. Sometimes data can lie, and in those cases, using data can be dangerous. Prior to problems with runaway acceleration in some Toyota models, which occurred years after my problem with my Volvo, there was little available data, and certainly no data in my life, to suggest that I ever needed to think about my car running away with me. Had I let that guide my analysis, I would have died.

Sometimes we need to ignore data. From time to time, life throws a *discontinuity* at us, which changes the world in ways that mean future data are going to look very different from comfortable and familiar historical data.

Still, it takes real courage for an executive team to ignore decades of data, simply because they are guessing that the data sets are no longer *"relevant."* Sometimes the importance of ignoring all available data is obvious after the decisions are made, but it is seldom clear at the time. It takes courage to run a strategy meeting for your most senior team without relying on data, without regression analyses and without any of the techniques which we teach so intensively in MBA programs around the world.

At least some of the time, your data are *wrong*. They're even *dangerously wrong*. Let's see why.

The strange story of ZapMail provides a useful example of the dangers of relying on a long and convincing set of data. The story is also old enough that its implications are unambiguous; we now know with certainty that ZapMail management made the worst possible decisions using the best available data.

In 1984, Federal Express understood that overnight delivery was just not going to be fast enough to compete with immediate electronic messaging—e-mail and text—in the near future. FedEx attempted to preempt future adoption of e-mail by making it unnecessary. They launched *facilitated fax*, the transfer of virtual copies of complete, signed documents. FedEx would pick up physical documents from the sending customer, fax them to the FedEx office closest to the intended recipient, and then deliver the faxes later the same day with a traditional FedEx truck. These virtual copies could be delivered much more quickly than actually transporting the hard copy of the documents. They based their new service offering on a concept that seems bizarre today but seemed brilliant at the time: door-to-door delivery of faxes to provide greater speed for customers who were currently relying upon FedEx overnight delivery of hard copies of letters and short documents.

The fax machine was first invented in the middle 1840s. Yes, that is correct and not a typo. Technology has steadily improved from the clumsy fax machines of the nineteenth century. Fax machines began to see at least limited use as the technology got better. But for almost 100 years, the fax machine was largely ignored. Sales data for fax machines for the 50 years leading up to ZapMail would have been a flat line hovering around zero. The data were unambiguous. Clearly, ZapMail was not going to get significant competition from FedEx's clients' own fax machines! Consequently, the market for same day cross-country delivery of letters was wide open. FedEx saw an enormous opportunity, and one they believed that could capture immediately, without waiting for connectivity like what we now call the Internet.

Fed Ex introduced ZapMail to seize that market. With ZapMail, a FedEx vehicle would pick up your document, bring it to a local FedEx office, and immediately fax it to another FedEx location near your intended recipient. The receiving FedEx location would in turn deliver your document to its final destination. In many cities across America, ZapMail offered door-to-door fax delivery within a few hours, and it worked even if neither the sender nor the receiver owned a fax machine.

The initial adoption of ZapMail was overwhelming, and the senior team at FedEx began to plan to develop infrastructure to support the continued expansion of ZapMail usage. Their analysis looked at their current extraordinary rates of growth and considered the future rates of demand that might develop over time. They probably did what most of us do when we have data we trust and need to consider whether current trends will continue or not. They probably considered three crude scenarios, *high growth / low growth / medium growth*. The use of High / Low / Medium estimates is nearly universal in corporate planning, and it's an acceptable way of dealing with traditional uncertainty. Assume the game isn't changing, but that perhaps the values of data elements might change. Prices might go up or down a little, growth might speed up or slow down a little. Of course management believed that the half century of customers not purchasing their own fax machines would continue. The game wasn't going to change.

High / Low / Medium estimates can be useful and help us to avoid acting with too much certainty when data can change. It can also be catastrophically misleading when the game changes, not just some values for some estimates.

Imagine that the FedEx team thought that demand for their services might continue to grow at its current pace, or slow down, or even flatten out. Based on their estimates of future demand, they invested hundreds of millions of dollars in proprietary satellite capacity, sufficient for their anticipated middle rate of growth.

And yet the initial rapid success of ZapMail did not signal future success. It signaled complete and total future failure. Demand for ZapMail totally collapsed.

ZapMail led directly to a dramatic increase in the sales of fax machines. Although the fax machine had been around for almost a century, no one bought a fax because no one else had a fax. Like the first phone, or the first e-mail account, which were both useless until there was someone to call or some to e-mail, there was no reason to own the first fax machine because there was no one to receive your faxes, and no one to send faxes to you. This is yet another example of a positive network effect, which is critical in the launch of so many communications systems, from the telephone in the early 1900s to Facebook today. However, once FedEx provided ZapMail, ZapMail's customers could send faxes even to correspondents who did not own a fax. ZapMail customers could send a fax to FedEx, and FedEx would deliver it to the final recipient even if the recipient organization did not have its own fax machine. More and more ZapMail customers bought fax machines, since it was faster and cheaper to use ZapMail with your own fax machine rather than relying on FedEx to send a truck to pick up your document.

Ultimately, so many organizations had their own fax machines that they began to notice that most of their intended recipients also owned machines. ZapMail customers started sending faxes directly to each other, with no need for FedEx trucks or FedEx fax machines as intermediaries. And this is what caused the collapse of ZapMail.

So, yes, sometimes data lie. The historical data on the adoption of fax machines, and FedEx's own data on the growth trends for ZapMail usage, were both dangerously misleading. Scenario analysis forces us to *accept and embrace uncertainty*, even when historical data seem to be quite compelling.

Because of advances in information technology, data lie more often than we expect. Nothing in Nokia or Blackberry's history alerted them to how quickly smartphones would destroy both companies. Nothing in the 100-year history of Sears Roebuck or the 200-year history of the London Stock Exchange prepared them for the profound changes in behavior that would drive so many consumers online and so many fund managers off the Exchange. Nothing in the 100-year histories of the New York Times and the Washington Post prepared their editors for the challenge from Google, Twitter, and Facebook, and nothing in these papers' histories prepared traditional politicians for the impact of social media, reality show candidates, or fake news.

10.4 Learn to Ask the Right Questions, Even If You Can't Answer Them: Lessons from the Future of Chinese Consumer Behavior

Ask the right questions. Sometimes the most important questions are the ones you can't answer!

So, rather than starting with the data we have and the questions we know we can answer, we start with the data we wish we could have, and the questions we wish could answer.

Knowing which questions to ask is always useful. If we knew which questions to ask, we could convert our ambiguity about the future into a set of known problems. Each possible set of answers to the questions creates a unique scenario. Each scenario describes a plausible future world, and we can then plan for each of those worlds, one at a time, as if we knew with certainty that it was the one true future that would occur.

Knowing which questions to ask is very important. Indeed, it's often the best we can do. Unfortunately, it's often quite difficult.

Assume that you're trying to do strategic planning for Walmart, contemplating its first major expansion into grocery sales in China. You realize this entails momentous decisions, and you approach planning the way emperors in China did for millennia; you consult a local fortune teller. You find a reader of *oracle bones*.

Your oracle bones reader does everything according to tradition. He places a ram's shoulder bone in an open flame, waits for the heat to shatter the bone, and then reads the messages revealed by the cracks. He momentarily looks baffled. Then, his face clears and he says *"Shopping will become more Western, but with Chinese characteristics."*

Chinese will consume products selected to delight themselves, not to impress their neighbors and colleagues. No more keeping up with the Zhangs next door.

Chinese consumers will stop believing that western goods are cleaner and safer, more prestigious, with fewer harmful additives. Western goods will be seen as alien. Why drink expensive French wines with traditional Chinese cuisine when local brown wine is so much more suitable, and why have Starbucks with donuts for breakfast, when a pot of Chinese tea and noodles is so much more wholesome?

So, basically, your fortune teller has just told you that everything you thought you knew about Chinese consumer behavior and all of your market research are both wrong. You need to toss out your plans and plan for the opposite of everything you thought you knew. OK. You know how to plan for that, too.

But what if he's wrong? You don't want to change everything if he's wrong.

1. So what else do we know about our fortune teller? First, he never picks unimportant questions. As always, he's talking about the most important questions you need to answer.
2. Unfortunately, sometimes his answers are dreadfully wrong.
3. But fortunately, your fortune teller is never just slightly wrong. If he's wrong he's dead wrong, 100% wrong, as wrong as it's possible to be wrong.

Since he *always* picks the right things to worry about, he always provides valuable insight into what you need to consider, even if you can't trust his answers. And since his answers are either entirely right or entirely wrong, he's given more than just insight into what to consider. While he hasn't really told you what to do, he has told you what questions to ask!

1. *"How will Chinese consumption patterns change?"*, rather than *"Chinese consumption will be for personal delight."*
2. *"How will Chinese perception of domestic and foreign brands change?"*, rather than *"Chinese will stop preferring Western brands."*

He thinks he's given you the right answer to these two questions, and he thinks that he's told you exactly what the future will be. We know that he's actually given you two answers to each of his questions. The first answer he's given you is the exact right answer if he is right. But he's also given you the exact wrong answer if he's wrong, which means that the exact opposite of what he told you would be perfect. This is *almost* as useful as always being right, although it is *not quite* as useful. Instead of defining *the one true future*, he's laid out *the four possible alternative futures*. The one true future is described by both of the answers he believes. The other futures come from flipping one or both of his answers to their direct opposites. Figure 10.1 shows the two questions, the set of four answers, and the four possible alternative futures.

Why is that useful? Obviously, we'd all like to know the future so that we could plan for it. He didn't give us that. But we no longer have to consider *all possible futures*. That would be impossible. We only need to consider the four possible futures implied by the answers to his two questions, and that's a lot easier to do than to plan for everything and for anything.

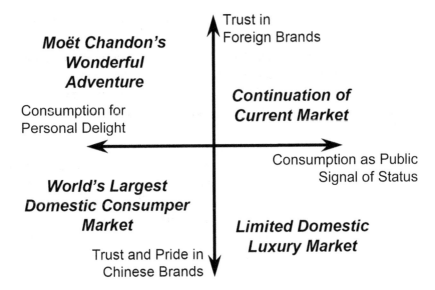

Fig. 10.1 Four scenarios illustrating four different futures for the future of Chinese consumer behavior and for the future of the Chinese economy

Scenario analysis allows us to take an ambiguous future and convert it into a set of potential, uncertain, but unambiguous alternatives. We can then take each of the *possible* alternatives one at a time and act as if each were *certain* to occur. We sequentially believe a set of inconsistent and incompatible alternatives, one at a time. However, once we suspend disbelief and act as if one of the alternatives was the true, correct, and inevitable alternative, we can examine it using our traditional tools for strategic analysis to understand that alternative. We do this until we have understood the entire set of alternatives.

10.5 Working with Questions If All You Have Is Questions: Remember What They Say About Making Lemonade If Life Gives You Nothing but Lemons

If life gives you lemons, make lemonade! If life gives you questions, guess the answers and work from there!

Your fortune teller has given you the right questions about the future of Chinese consumer behavior and helped you enumerate the possible answers. We can define a set of four scenarios.

In this section, we study those four scenarios in detail. We use them to examine the future of China's economy, analyzing the implications for consumers' shopping. That in turn has implications for domestic and foreign manufacturers, service providers like restaurant operators and retailers. The magic of the scenario process is done; we restructured strategic ambiguity and reduced a shapeless future into a set of well-understood alternatives. What's left is just strategic planning. We can use any and all of the tools for strategic analysis that seem most natural to us; in this section, I will principally rely upon resonance marketing (from Chapters 4 and 5) and secondarily on resource-based competitive advantage (from Chapter 6, Sect. 6.2).

Let's agree to assume that China's economy will continue to move forward, but the rate of growth, the industries with the fastest growth, and the industries with the highest profit margins cannot yet be predicted with sufficient accuracy. And yet, these are vitally important questions to answer, for policy-makers in China, for industrial leaders and investors in China, and for anyone who wants to export to China. These questions are equally important to investors and business leaders in the developed world, who want to know where to invest within the Chinese market, or how to prepare for exports to and for competition from China. These questions are important for anyone who wants to understand the economic and the political future of China.

No one is able to answer these questions or to predict the future of the Chinese economy at this time. This suggests the importance of preparing a set of scenario analyses on the future of the Chinese economy. That in turn requires identifying the right questions to ask that will provide the keys to our question-driven planning. These will provide us with the key uncertainties that form the framework for the creation of our scenarios, which will help us determine the possible paths for the future of the Chinese economy.

We usually don't have access to a fortune teller to provide us with a set of questions. How would we have done this if we didn't meet our oracle bones reader in the previous section?

We can ignore technology as the source of our critical uncertainties, since there is very little uncertainty about the direction of technological change. For the near future, technological factors all move in the same direction and will not determine which scenario emerges. The number of web sites in China, the number of Internet users in China, and total value of eCommerce purchases are all increasing and will continue to increase. Processor speed, the number of people with smartphones, the capability of smartphones, and the number of wireless hot spots will all continue to increase. We can be certain that mobile computing and mobile shopping will become even easier and even more convenient.

In contrast, the future of Chinese consumer behavior is uncertain, like human behavior everywhere. That makes consumer behavior much more interesting to a scenario planner than technology, unless the scenario planner is specifically studying technology. After considerable study in China, I selected the following two uncertainties in consumer behavior as key to the scenarios for the future of the Chinese market.

- **Will consumption be used as public signal of status or for personal delight?** At present, there is a puzzling distinction between the ways Chinese people consume status goods in the privacy of their own homes and the ways they consume these goods in public places like restaurants. Most Americans drink the same wine and beer at home that they drink in public. Most of the Chinese participants in the focus groups my colleagues and I conducted described drinking better brands in public, when they could be seen and observed. They described wanting to be seen drinking coffee at Starbucks and the importance of large glass windows facing the street so they could be seen when they were in Starbucks. We make the distinction here between consumption of luxury goods that is largely in *public* and used to signal *status*, as opposed to consumption that focuses on private enjoyment and *personal delight*. An increase in consumption for personal delight would lead to a larger market for high-end goods within China and a larger domestic market for consumer products generally. A great deal has been written about changing consumption patterns in the USA and the conspicuous consumption that followed the economic shortages of World War II. A great deal has been written about changing consumption patterns in Japan and South Korea in the postwar years, as younger workers rejected the austere lifestyles and self-sacrifice of their parents' generations. Both may help us predict the future of consumption in China. Scenario analysis does *not* require that you forget everything that you already know, and what we know about changes in consumer behavior elsewhere may be useful to our understanding of China! It does require that you accept that Chinese historical data may not accurately predict the future of Chinese behavior. Moreover, although we know what happened to consumption patterns in the USA and many other countries, we really do not know what will happen next in China. Scenario analysis *demands* humility and it *demands* an acknowledgment of critical ignorance. We believe we know the transformations that have occurred in consumption elsewhere, around the globe. They may occur in China. However, the data don't yet tell us if similar trends are underway in China, or when these changes might emerge.

- **Will Chinese consumers exhibit trust and pride in Chinese brands or trust foreign brands?** Will Chinese consumers continue to view foreign brands as more prestigious than their own domestic brands? Will Chinese consumers continue to view foreign brands as higher quality than domestic brands, or safer, or less likely to have been subject to contamination through the use of substandard ingredients or forbidden additives? China has suffered from highly visible scandals involving melamine contamination in milk products, hormones in pork, or rotten beef and chicken being repacked and sold as wholesome and safe. If this problem continues, and if the awareness of it creates the perception that Chinese products are inferior, it will severely limit the development of Chinese brands that sell to consumers, both in China and in export markets around the world. Alternatively, if Chinese consumers come to trust domestic companies and domestic products, the market for Chinese products and even for Chinese high-end and luxury products may grow rapidly. It is even possible that over time Chinese consumers may come to prefer domestic companies and domestic products, much as American consumers have come to embrace California wines as fully equal to many of the best wines from France and Italy and to accept American craft beers as the equal of the best beers from Belgium, Germany, and Britain. If the Chinese population develops trust in its own consumer products, this drives a much larger market for Chinese brands and for Chinese-branded consumer products. In contrast, the fear that Chinese products have low quality and may even be unsafe will limit the growth of Chinese brands and leave China as the world's low-cost, low-margin workshop for foreign companies and for brands owned by foreign companies.

The answers to these questions could completely change your plans for retailing in China. What would you sell? How would you sell it? How large would your market be? And who will be your major competitors?

These questions are what scenario planners call the *key drivers*. They determine your full set of alternative scenarios.

These are the things that you ***can't*** know …	[*They remain uncertain.*]
but that if you ***could*** know …	[*But if they were not uncertain …*]
then you ***would*** know …	[*Note the* all-important *conditional here.*]
exactly what you ***needed*** to know	[*They are so important that they would resolve your strategic uncertainty.*]

As we will see in the next section, having the right questions is almost as helpful as having the right answers. And it is a lot easier to ask the right questions than it is to provide answers to them without data!

10.6 The Future of Consumer Behavior in China

Isn't this exciting! With question-driven planning you can look like an expert, even in a country where you don't yet know anything yet!

We have our drivers. In this section, we will develop a set of scenarios and use them to start the strategic analysis of a business problem.

Choosing the two extreme endpoints for the two questions yields four different future worlds, each with its own story or its own strategic scenarios. These are shown in Fig. 10.1.

Remember why we focus on the end points and on the extremes. Examining the end points helps bring future changes into the sharpest possible focus. If I said that the role of consumption in China will be a *little more* like the role of consumption in the USA or Japan, I might not be able to figure out what that means. If I said that the level of trust Chinese consumers have in their domestic brands will become a little more like the nature of trust in domestic brands in the USA or in France, once again I might not be able to figure out what that means. But when I examine the extremes, the implications become much more clear and much more obvious.

Scenarios on the left side are based in large measure upon resonance marketing. Consumers increasingly make their purchases in pursuit of personal delight. Scenarios on the top are based in large part upon resource-based competitive advantage, in which trust in the manufacturing integrity of a nation becomes a significant determinant of consumer behavior and thus a critical resource in consumer-focused marketing strategy. In the top scenarios, foreign firms that enjoy strong reputations for integrity and quality, and that have the equipment, skill base, monitoring, and experience producing superior products, have advantages that are not easily overtaken by domestic firms. Each of the scenarios tells a different story, with different strategic implications.

- **Continuation of current market**: This scenario results from the combination of a majority of Chinese consumers continuing to focus on consumption that is largely directed at providing public symbols of status, along with Chinese consumers continuing to place greater trust in foreign companies and foreign brands. This results in relatively limited consumption of luxury goods compared to scenarios in which consumers choose products because the products delight them, and in which they consume these products whether or not their behavior is being observed by others. This is the "current market" faced by most retailers and therefore by most manufacturers. In this scenario, any growth in the consumption of imported luxury goods would be driven by the continuing increase in the size of the Chinese middle class rather than by any changes in consumer behavior. Individual purchasers of milk, baby formula, fresh meat, and vegetables rely on reputation when selecting products, especially products that they intend to eat or drink or expect to serve to their children. They are unlikely to change their behavior until the quality and the reputation of Chinese brands improve. Those Chinese industrial products that still rely on consumer trust will not do well in this scenario. For example, a Chinese producer of jet aircraft might be able to convince a foreign international airline that their products were of sufficiently high quality to be safe, but the operator of the aircraft would have difficulty convincing their passengers that the Chinese aircraft were sufficiently well made and sufficiently safe. No matter how good the aircraft actually were, they would be difficult to sell. Note that in this instance our "more of the same" scenario, in the upper right, is the worst scenario for Chinese retailers, Chinese manufacturers, and Chinese consumers. Although the scenario closest to the current situation is usually shown in green, in this case it would be shown in red.

- **Moët Chandon's wonderful adventure**: This scenario results from the combination of Chinese consumers adopting patterns of consumption for personal delight along with their continuing to have greater trust in foreign companies and foreign brands. In this scenario, the market for high-quality products becomes considerably larger than it is at present, but this growing market continues to be dominated by foreign firms. This is the "official future" of most foreign manufacturers, including automobile companies like BMW and General Motors, wines and spirits companies like Johnny Walker and Remy Martin, and status product companies like Gucci and Louis Vuitton. It would lead to an enormous increase in Chinese demand for foreign luxury goods. But it is not the best for Chinese producers or for Chinese workers; even when the products are manufactured in China, most of the profits are still retained by the foreign owners of the brands, and the workers continue to be paid low wages associated with piecework manufacturing. It would be shown in cautionary amber.
- **Limited domestic luxury market**: This scenario results from the combination of two factors. Consumption of luxury goods continues to be mostly public and is mostly a signal of status, and thus is relatively

limited. Additionally, Chinese consumers have developed greater trust in their own domestic companies and their own domestic brands. This would result in a shift in demand away from American, German, French, Japanese, and Korean products, and toward demand for products from domestic Chinese brands. This would occur in a wide range of product categories, including clothing, food and beverages, cameras and consumer electronics, and wines, whiskey, and cognacs. It would lead to a dramatic shift in the source of luxury products consumed in China, but not in a dramatic increase in the size of the market. Once again, any growth in the consumption of domestic luxury goods would be driven by the continuing increase in the size of the Chinese middle class rather than by any changes in consumer behavior. This is not the best scenario for Chinese producers or consumers, and is again shown in amber.

- **World's largest domestic market**: This scenario results from the combination of Chinese consumers adopting patterns of consumption for personal delight and from their now having greater trust in and greater pride in domestic companies and domestic brands. They consume more of "the good stuff" and more of it is made in China by Chinese firms with Chinese brands. In this scenario, the market for high-quality products becomes considerably larger than it is at present, and this growing market begins to be dominated by domestic firms. This is the best possible outcome for China and for Chinese brands. A strong local market, with strong local demand, was the basis of American and British economic strength, both domestically and as dominant exporters, and it can serve as the foundation for greater Chinese economic strength. Having strong domestic brands will allow China to earn far more from its exports than being the source of basic commodities, or being the workshop that pro-duces branded goods for other companies to sell. It is the best scenario for Chinese producers, consumers, and retailers, and it would be shown in green.

10.7 Working with the Scenarios for the Future of Consumer Behavior in China

With question-driven planning and information-based patterns you really can be an expert, even in a country where you didn't think you knew anything!

Each of these four scenarios can be analyzed in as much detail as necessary. I have worked with Chinese executives to examine the scenarios in more detail by having them answer the following questions for each of the four scenarios:

- What sort of *manufacturer* succeeds best in this scenario? What sort of manufacturer does poorly in this scenario? What are the implications of the scenario for manufacturers of goods intended for Chinese consumers? What are the implications of the scenario for consumer goods intended for export? What are the implications of the scenario for heavy manufacturing, both for domestic consumption and for export?
- What sort of *retailer* does best in this scenario? What product mix do retailers need to carry, including the range of product offerings within a category? Does country of origin for the brand matter? Does country of manufacture matter?
- What sort of *service provider*, excluding retailers, does best in this scenario?
- How does this scenario feel to Chinese *consumers*?
- Is this a scenario that should be advanced by the Chinese government? If so, what actions might the Chinese government take to advance this scenario?

The Chinese government has not explicitly picked a single scenario among the four, but it has taken actions that might influence the outcome. A recent crackdown on corruption has greatly diminished consumption as public displays of wealth and status. More importantly, the Made in China 2025 initiative[2] suggests that the Chinese government is acting in ways that would accelerate the move to stronger, more trusted, and more profitable brands.

All of the executives had studied the six patterns for understanding information-based strategies with me. What follows summarized our analysis of one scenario, seen through the perspective of these patterns.

In **Continuation of the Current Market**, the future is very much like the present. Most consumption of status brands in China is publicly visible, intended to send a public signal of wealth, rather than in private, intended to deliver personal enjoyment and delight. And, whenever possible, consumers prefer to purchase foreign products for their displays of status. French wines, German beer, Japanese and German and American cars are all seen as higher status than Chinese products. They are also seen as safer, because they are less prone to tampering, spoilage, unsanitary production conditions, or contamination. This scenario explicitly addresses the prevalence of

---

[2]See https://www.cfr.org/blog/why-does-everyone-hate-made-china-2025.

the compromise discount and the uncertainty discount as barriers to domestic Chinese firms. It addresses the fact that consumers have ready access to information, but that resonance marketing has not yet become a dominant driver of Chinese consumer behavior.

What sort of manufacturing firm in China does best in this scenario? Obviously, foreign-owned and foreign-branded manufacturers enjoy a strong reputation for quality in China. Their products can still be manufactured in China without sacrificing their reputation; most mid-market and luxury cars sold in China are from foreign brands, but most are manufactured in China. Manufacturers who produce foreign-labeled products for export are succeeding at the moment, but price competition among them is brutal. Virtually, all titanium golf clubs sold in the USA have famous Western names, but virtually all are made in China. The attractive margins on the newest clubs are kept by Western firms that sell them to consumers and own the brands, and not by Chinese firms that are the actual manufacturers. The cost pressure on Chinese manufacturers remains extreme. Nowhere is this more clear than in consumer electronics. Approximately half of the selling price of the newest iPhone or iPad goes to Apple in Cupertino. Perhaps 3% remains in China, where the actual product is made. This explains the brutal working conditions of manufacturers in China who produce for export, like Apple's supplier Foxconn. It would be hard to argue that these China-based manufacturing firms or their employees are doing well, at least by Western standards. So, foreign-owned firms with trusted foreign brands do well, even when they manufacture in China. Coca-Cola and Paulaner, Buick and Audi are all visible examples. Firms that manufacture in China for foreign brands are being squeezed; Foxconn is merely the most publicized example.

Heavy manufacturing, like making off-shore drilling platforms, rail cars, container ships, or other industrial equipment, shows how Chinese brands with a reputation for quality can succeed. Industrial buyers perform due diligence, whether they are buying from Siemens in Germany, Asea Brown Boveri in Sweden or Switzerland, or from Huawei or from a newer firm in China. If the buyer inspects products before buying, and if the Chinese seller actually has quality products, then the Chinese seller can successfully enter these markets for industrial equipment. Consumers cannot perform intensive chemical testing for quality and for contaminants before purchasing baby formula or canned tuna fish, in the USA, Europe, or China, which makes it harder for Chinese-branded consumer products to succeed in this scenario.

At least three kinds of retailers will do well in this scenario.

- Foreign retailers who can protect their reputations do well, especially because of the lack of trust that plagues many Chinese firms. Protecting reputations in China is not always easy. Apple found to its surprise that there were almost two dozen counterfeit Apple stores operating illegally in China; in some instances, even employees did not know that they were working for a fraudulent operation and were not Apple employees.
- Domestic retailers who sell trusted products do well.
- Domestic retailers with impeccable reputations for quality do well. Yihaodian has been growing at rates as high as 20% a month. The secret to their success is the strictest quality inspections and the strictest quality enforcement policy in their industry. They inspect every shipment they receive from every supplier. And if there is even one counterfeit item, one contaminated item, or one older than its sell-by date, the entire shipment is refused. The supplier replaces it at his own expense. And if the supplier wants to continue to work with Yihaodian, the supplier also pays a penalty of ten times the total value of the entire shipment that contained the defective item. At the beginning of Yihaodian's operations, before suppliers actually understood the implications of their contracts with Yihaodian, there were occasional problems. Yihaodian was relentless in their pursuit of violators. With Yihaodian's rapid growth, suppliers were unwilling to lose their contracts with Yihaodian, and with penalties, these high suppliers don't take unnecessary risks. The quality of items they ship to Yihaodian is now as close to perfect as they can manage. Yihaodian shoppers know this, and Yihaodian's quality has been essential to their growth strategy since the firm's creation. Their growth and their reputation were both so extraordinary that Walmart acquired them in 2015 as the cornerstone of their eCommerce strategy in China. The following year Walmart sold them to JD.com, the largest online retailer in China, for a 5% stake in JD.com.

Eating in a restaurant is usually a shared and a public experience. This suggests that in this scenario restaurants should do well because they are a form of public consumption. Foreign-owned restaurants have done especially well. Interestingly, even eating in restaurants that are considered fast food budget restaurants in the West, like McDonald's and Yum Brands' Pizza Hut, Taco Bell, or KFC (Kentucky Fried Chicken), was considered a public display of status. However, just as with retailers, restaurants must vigorously protect their supply chains in order to preserve their reputations. Recent scandals with tainted chicken and beef supplies in China have significantly damaged the reputation and standing of these brands.

The Chinese government did what it could to advance the current economic scenario for decades. By working to support this scenario, the Chinese government achieved the fastest economic growth of any nation in history. This scenario led to a rapid increase in employment and a rapid increase in the quantity of food and other goods available to Chinese consumers. But this scenario should no longer be a priority for the Chinese government. Recent sessions of the People's Congress suggest that the government is now focused on higher-quality goods and services, higher margin products, higher margin exports, higher wages, and a higher standard of living for all Chinese citizens.

Similar analysis can be done for each of the other three scenarios. Once we select a scenario to study, we agree to ignore much of the strategic ambiguity we will face in the future. We agree, at least temporarily, to decide which of the games we will be playing and we agree, at least temporarily, to ignore the others. This is not cheating! We perform the analysis, step by step, for *each* of the games and for *all* of the games. We are not deciding in advance which game we will play, or which future we will encounter. We are not making a single prediction. We are, rather, examining each of the futures, agreeing to act for the moment as if this scenario would occur. It is possible to do the analysis for each. That way it is possible to play for all of the possible futures.

There are occasionally exceptions to the idea that the flow between scenarios cannot be controlled or even influenced. Often governments can control at least some aspects of their own futures. In this case, scenario analysis can go beyond recommending how to respond to a scenario, and can focus additionally on how to influence which scenario actually emerges.

10.8 What's So Special About Four Scenarios?

Why do we work with exactly four scenarios? Is that important? Is that necessary? Or is that an accident?

Interestingly, almost all scenario diagrams start out as 2×2 grids. And yet, the world *never* forces us to face *exactly* two decisions. So why are scenario analyses so often structured around 2×2 grids? I think there are three reasons.

First, most of us have difficulty thinking through 8, 16, or 32 interrelated possibilities, all of them partly overlapping and most of them partly contradictory. It's just not useful to expand the number of questions initially, because that degree of complexity defeats the structured analysis that scenarios were intended to support.

Second, it's usually not necessary to consider more than two questions at a time. Start by identifying and focusing on the two most important questions. Then, you will find that there are subsidiary questions that are useful for analyzing one or more of the scenarios. Once I have decided to analyze one particular scenario or one part of the scenario matrix further, *then* I can decide how to divide up that portion of the matrix. If I want to focus on online shopping in China, then I need to consider the role of consumers' trust of online merchants: Will Chinese consumers continue to trust Walmart online the way they do offline, or might they prefer a different player, a pure Internet player, like Amazon in the USA or Yihaodian in China? I may also need to focus on the potential role of new entrants, either as competitors or as targets of opportunity for acquisitions. As necessary, I can subdivide my scenarios, and inside each scenario, I can stack sub-scenarios like nested Russian dolls. But I almost always start with two questions and with four scenarios.

Finally, these subsidiary questions are just not useful at the same level of analysis as the two most important questions are. While these subsidiary questions are useful for analyzing one or more of the scenarios, they are almost never useful for examining all of the scenarios. When considering a lack of trust in Chinese brands, it might be useful to consider the levels of consumers' trust separately from levels of trust of corporate customers. As we have seen, consumers cannot afford the careful quality assessment that commercial customers conduct when performing due diligence inspections.[3]

10.9   Summary

Scenarios are used to impose structure on an ambiguous future. They allow you to work within the data you have, by focusing on the data you wish you had. This is especially important when addressing digital transformation, in which anything and everything may have to change.

---

[3]However, as we learn more about trap doors, Trojan horses, and the mechanisms hidden with some Chinese corporate electronics products, we understand that even for corporate customers thorough quality inspections may not be possible. Trap doors are deliberate defects placed in code to enable the author to gain control over the program or the device later. Trojan horses are pretty much the same thing, but usually are built into chips. Both have been problems with Chinese high-tech imports.

Scenario analysis does not enable you to predict the future, but it does enable you to delimit the set of possible futures. The structure and the structured set of futures allow you to move forward with planning activities, without waiting for the phone call from God, or from your reader of oracle bones, or your favorite source of supernatural intervention.

Again, scenario analysis is not the same as making a prediction. Scenarios provide us both with a set of competing potential predictions and with a mechanism for recognizing which element of the set is going to emerge next. Since each scenario is defined by a specific set of drivers, we are able to receive and observe reliable early warnings of the single future that is about to unfold. We know the factors that would create a specific scenario, and we can tell when those factors are starting to change, even before the scenario arrives. Scenario analysis lets us know what to look for. Scenario analysis helps us to recognize the signals sooner, when they are still weak signals, still imprecise, and still easy to miss unless we are already looking for them.

Scenario analysis also allows us to prepare. Scenario analysis allows us to make plans for each of the scenarios. It allows us to practice our plans for each scenario, so that we can respond quickly if and when the scenario arises. This is most useful if we believe that some scenarios will require an immediate response, with the greatest rewards received by the first player to act.

Since scenario analysis allows us to prepare first, and to act first, it is often a source of superior strategies and a source of competitive advantage. Scenario analysis also allows us to prepare a detailed strategy and a detailed sequence of actions, since it allows us to anticipate how the initial scenario will evolve. Thus, we can use scenario analysis both to capture and to sustain competitive advantage.

We use scenarios so that we can recognize a situation instantly and know how to respond almost instinctively, even if we had never encountered it before. I called this "*remembering the future.*" Remembering the future allows rapid recognition and rapid response, instead of eventual recognition and eventual regret. Paradoxically, although the scenario process uses very little data, it is often the best way of learning about the transformational impacts of information.

11

Examining the Wide Range of Business Models Currently in Use in Online Businesses: How to Understand a New Business Using Existing Frameworks

Over time, the net has indeed facilitated the digital transformation of everything. Not surprisingly, since most human needs have not changed dramatically over the past twenty-five years, most of the activities transformed by the net have been the activities that humans have pursued since the beginning of time. With a few significant exceptions like online social networks, the net has not created entirely new classes of activities, or entirely new classes of human needs. We still eat, protect our families, seek shelter, make purchases, travel, read, and need entertainment and diversion. Our desire for these activities has not changed much in the few short years since the development of information technology.

We use the net to facilitate the same things we always did. The net has allowed online retailing to augment and even replace many traditional retailers; look at the growth of Amazon, in all its departments. The net has transformed reservations and selling of tickets, for everything from travel to movies and live theater. The net has transformed traditional media; I have subscriptions to numerous magazines and newspapers, but I cannot remember the last time I actually held a newspaper in my hands except on an airplane. Netflix and movies on demand have altered watching movies and television. But I'm still doing the same things, even if I purchase them differently or select them differently or access them differently. The digital transformation of everything has not resulted in the digital *elimination* or even the digital *replacement* of everything.

© The Author(s) 2019
E. K. Clemons, *New Patterns of Power and Profit*,
https://doi.org/10.1007/978-3-030-00443-9_11

Still, are there entirely new online businesses? Does the net allow us to do anything we couldn't do previously, rather than simply making it easier for us to do what we always did before? Yes and yes.

This chapter introduces the concept of *Digitally Transformed Business Models and Fully Digital Business Models.* We assess each using the patterns that were introduced in Part I and Part II.

Digitally Transformed Business Models and Fully Digital Business Models: Most online business models involve starting with a traditional set of business functions and transform them, doing them better, often much better, by moving them online. Other online businesses are truly new and fully digital. They are more than the transformation of existing physical businesses and more than the transformation of business models that have existed for decades.

Both offer significant opportunities to earn profits and to improve customers' experiences.

11.1 Fully Digital Business Models and Partly Digital Business Models

When is an online business a fully digital business and when is it a digital version of a physical business?

Online social networks are new, although there is nothing new about the idea of forming clubs, teams, and social networks in general. We have always needed clubs, lodges, and ways to indicate who was part of our group and who was not, whom to like and trust, and whom to view with a touch of suspicion until we got to know them better. Prehistoric Fred Flintstone had his Order of the Water Buffalo, postwar New York bus driver Ralph Kramden had his Raccoon Lodge. Even the aristocracy of the British Empire, which has long trusted in its specialness, has its orders of chivalry to show that some are more special than others. But online social networks, and the ability to remain in touch with friends, semi-friends, and pseudo-friends, are indeed new.

Games are not new. In some sense, even a kids' game like capture the flag can be viewed as a competition between teams on a quest. But shared virtual experiences in massive online virtual realities have to be seen as something new. World of Warcraft is new. And selling virtual accessories to enhance a virtual experience must be seen as new as well.

Control of retailing gateways existed long before Google. Walmart and other major physical store retailers are essential to most consumer packaged goods companies; many of us are now more loyal to Walmart or Costco, or to Whole Foods or Trader Joe's, than we are to Kraft, Unilever, or P&G. Walmart has enormous power over retail distribution. But no single traditional retailer has nearly the power to direct customers' purchases that Google now enjoys. Retailers sometimes are able to charge slotting allowances, a fee for including a company's product in their inventory, but mostly traditional retailers earn their profits by actually selling products to consumers. Google earns its profits by directing traffic and by deciding which products get seen first, which products get seen later, and which products entirely disappear from view. In some critically important sense, control of an online gateway must be seen as a new digital business, and not merely as an extension of the gateway function of traditional retailers.

The net is the most powerful and the most personally empowering tool to be introduced in decades. It has brought us resonance marketing, streaming video, and online all-day global news coverage. It has transformed all aspects of existing businesses, from music to higher education, and from grocery shopping and drinking beer to selecting international travel destinations. It has already improved the lives of everyone with online access.

And yet, it would be surprising and disappointing to think that this powerful and empowering tool cannot have more interesting uses than the ones we've found today. It would be disappointing if the net could not be used for anything more interesting than the transformation of existing services or for the faster delivery of existing content.

And again, it would be surprising if the net needed to be funded solely through advertising or the abuse of gateways. My students think nothing of paying telecommunications bills between $100 and $200 a month; they are willing to pay for cell phone, unlimited texting plans, mobile surfing data plans, basic cable TV, premium cable TV, and high-speed Internet. However, they expect all of their online activities to be free, which in reality means they expect all of their online activities to be funded by revenues obtained through advertising. In fact, I would be surprised if the ethical forms of advertising over the net continue to be effective. I would be equally surprised if the effective forms of advertising, and of monetizing private information, continue to be legal.

So, in the end, corporations will need to deploy a wider range of online business models. If information indeed is as transformational as we believe, it will change more than the sale of existing goods and services, and our access to information will be funded by something more appropriate than the centuries-old business models of embedding ads in our content and updating it for online media.

11.2   The Full Range of Online Business Models

Learn the eleven basic models for online businesses.

The following are the most common online business models today:

1. **Actually selling real stuff, both goods and services**—using the net for the digital transformation of retailing.
2. **Using ads to sell real stuff**—using the net for the digital transformation of advertising, including much finer targeting of messages and promotions to individual consumers.
3. **Selling content online**—using the net for the digital transformation of media, including newspapers, magazines, television, and video. This is a digital version of a business that is largely traditional and that has existed for centuries in a physical form.
4. **Selling online education**—replacing traditional four-year colleges, one course at a time.
5. **Selling online services**—using the net to select a physician or a repair person, or to get training and education. This is similar to finding a service provider through the telephone yellow pages, or to learning through a paper-based correspondence course. And yet, the digital selection of services based on a curated list of service providers and online customer reviews represents a significant improvement, and online education is enormously more powerful than any correspondence course could ever be. In many ways, this is a new and largely digital business.
6. **Creating exchanges for business-to-consumer and direct consumer-to-consumer interactions**—using the net to create online marketplaces, rather than traditional stores, where businesses and even other consumers can interact directly with consumers. eBay was the first dramatically successful consumer-to-consumer (C2C) marketplace. The entire sharing economy, like Airbnb and VRBO, Uber and Lyft, and an ever-increasing number of other examples, is based on online exchanges.
7. **Control of gateways and charging for customer access**—using control over a gateway to decide who does and who does not get to see

customers. This can involve being paid by Party-3 to direct a customer to its website. Sometimes this involves charging for misdirection, sending a customer to a website, he would not prefer and would not otherwise have visited. This can also involve charging for avoiding mis-direction, and charging Party-3 a fee simply to avoid having poten-tial customers sent away from Party-3's website and sent instead to a competitor willing to pay more for customer access. This is a new and entirely digital business, using the net for the digital transformation of sellers' access to customers.

8. **Providing virtual experiences and associated virtual stuff**—using the net for the digital transformation of entertainment, focusing primarily on user-created or co-created experiences. This includes self-produced entertainment, which at present includes Facebook, gaming, and virtual reality experiences.

9. **Harnessing social networks for something other than advertising**—using the net for the digital transformation of product promotion and search. This is a new and entirely digital business,

10. **Selling contextual referrals based on data mining and exploiting individual in-depth profiling**—using the net for the systematic gather-ing and integrating of personal information to create accurate individual profiles that are valuable for sales and marketing. In a real sense, this is also an entirely new business, using the net to monetize privacy viola-tions. Probably, the most extreme form of this is tailored fake news, as described in Chapter 12. Data mining allows analysts to develop deep profiles on all of us and to identify which voters can be manipulated, and what to say to each subgroup to manipulate them most effectively.

11. **Selling contextual referrals to enable ads to be directed to mobile users**—using the net to get messages to mobile users for last minute purchase decisions, and for time-sensitive purchase decisions. Again, this is a new business model, entirely online, although it is most often used to sell traditional products.

We'll discuss each of them in turn.

There are three important things to remember about this chapter. First, the net truly is transformational. Almost everything we used to do can now be done better, faster, cheaper, and with more customization. Second, the net is truly liberating. We can do things we could never do before and do some things we never even imagined doing before. Finally, the effects of any previous profound transformation have never been fully understood before they occurred or controlled while they occurred. The agricultural revolution gave us civilization, along with writing, literature, art, music, organized religion, and education. It also gave us mass warfare, urban diseases and diseases transmitted from our domestic livestock, enormous wealth inequality, and a lifestyle and a diet that reduced life expectancy and quality of life for most of the planet's inhabitants for centuries.

Likewise, the industrial revolution and the associated progress in all the sciences greatly increased the quantity of goods and services available to most of the world's population, dramatically improved medical care, and provided telecommunications and transportation that made the world a single community. It also brought mechanized warfare and pollution on scales that could not have been imagined before.

And, since we believe the net is transformational, it too is going to surprise. We need to understand the net. We need to control the net. And to do that we need to understand the business models employed on the net.

11.3   Selling Real Stuff

Selling stuff is one of the oldest business models, online and off.

The net can be used to sell real stuff. Some of the largest online businesses in the world, like Amazon and Walmart in the USA and Yihaodian and 360Buy in China, sell real products. We are all familiar with online retailing, and only a few points are worth mentioning.

We can find anything. This is resonance marketing, selling us things we really want, even if we cannot find them locally.

Prices can be very competitive online, since sellers have to compete with everyone else and with everywhere else. The competition discount will continue to be real for everything but resonance products.

11.4   Using Ads to Sell Real Stuff

Using ads to sell stuff may be the oldest online business model. But we probably will continue to distrust ads.

I'm still not sure about the future of advertising on the Internet. Some of you may hope to make a fortune with the next killer app, which provides horoscopes based on the exact time, date, and geographical location of your birth, and earns revenue by surrounding the horoscope with ads. Before you invest too much of your own money in developing the app, consider the following:

- **Mostly, ads don't work very well because mostly we don't trust them**. Firms are exploring more inventive ways of getting us to pay attention to ads, including having them appear to come from our friends. Recommendations from experts or from community content websites are more effective than ads in influencing consumers' opinions. This will become even more true over time.
- **Mostly, we hate ads when we can't just ignore them**. I know that some of us love Super Bowl ads. I know that some of us love ads in the special editions of some of our favorite magazines. If we didn't hate ads, and if we didn't want to avoid them, television stations would not work so hard to make sure we see them. All of your regular network news shows broadcast ads at exactly the same time. Why? So you cannot channel surf to escape the ads. If the stations thought we loved the ads, they would show them at different times so that we could channel surf and make sure to see all of them. If you loved the ads, you wouldn't fast forward past them when watching recordings.
- **Mostly, we have to be trapped for ads to work**. If all the TV stations are showing ads at the same time, we can still leave the room to skip the ads. Mostly, we have to be trapped for ads to reach us. If we are not trapped, we can skip the ads. One of the problems with ads online is that online we are never really trapped.

That does not mean that ads cannot work. Ads that appear to be personal recommendations from friends are probably very effective, especially when targeting juveniles. I suspect that these will soon be illegal, at least for children's products.

Ongoing research is exploring how to manipulate ads where companies pay people to send recommendations to their friends, and where the companies can then choose what text to place in the recommendation to achieve maximum impact. I would be really displeased to find a friend accepted payment to recommend something to me that he would not buy for himself. I would be displeased to learn that my friend was paid to let the company send me an ad that looked like he actually wrote it, where the text was actually personalized by the company to have the greatest impact on me. I remain unconvinced that this form of advertising will remain effective when we are better informed about what these ads really are.

11.5   Selling Content Online

Providing online content works very well. We can provide any content to anyone who wants it. The trick has been getting anyone to pay for it!

Charging for online content has proven very difficult every time a paid service initially replaces, competes with, or even augments existing free services. In turn, I resisted the move to basic cable, HBO and other premium services, and then pay per view movies and events. I now pay more than $200 a month to Comcast, and I appreciate the value of the services I get. I have hundreds of movies. I can watch a wider range of sporting events. I can compare network news from Fox, CNN, Al Jazeera, and BBC News.

My students currently have the same attitudes toward paying for any and all online content, including software, that I originally had about paying for TV. Many of the grand old names among American newspapers have been in and out of bankruptcy. Young readers get their news online, and do not believe that they should have to pay for news or for any Internet content.

Charging for online content has proven very difficult, especially in the USA. There are companies that have succeeded, like Netflix for online movies and series, or the *New York Times* and the *Wall Street Journal* for news, but these are the rare successes.

What should we expect going forward? A free press is fundamental to any form of participatory democracy. We will probably find a way to protect professional news content. The major democracies will figure out that they cannot allow search engines to plunder from mainstream journalism or destroy investigative journalism.

I am less certain about how much protection is appropriate for creative content, and what limitations are appropriate for the reuse of creative content. Copyright laws were developed to benefit society by increasing the total amount of creative content available to society. If artists are not able to receive payment for their work, the incentive to create is greatly reduced. Copyright laws were developed because of the belief that creativity was hard work and that creative talent was rare. If that's true, then without hardworking and creative people there would be no new art, no new music, no new books and screenplays, and thus no new movies or videos. If those creative people are motived in large part by the rewards they receive, then copyright protection is an essential part of ensuring new artistic content for society.

But historical assumptions about creative content may no longer be true, and the justification for copyright protection may have been diminished.

With mashups and reuse of creative artistic content itself now considered art forms and a major source of new artistic content, the public would be better served by changing copyright laws in ways that permitted and even encouraged reuse. Reuse requires original creative content to reuse, and we need to provide incentives for the creative artists whose original work is being reused. But changes to copyright law will shorten periods of absolute protection and permit creative value-adding reuse when that reuse represents more than theft of protected intellectual property.

11.6 The Digital Transformation of Higher Education

Do we really need four-year colleges? Is that the most effective way to train future generations?

Sometimes online content comes with advice or with other functions that are themselves so valuable that the combination of content and advice needs to be considered an online service, rather than simply content. The net has transformed many of the ways in which we acquire short-term services, like a single home repair, or long-term services, like finding a dentist or a pediatrician. It's transformed the way we get a ride; we hail a stranger with a car. As importantly, the net may transform the entire business of education. These are in some ways entirely new digital businesses, rather than the digital transformation of existing businesses.

Distance learning and online education may become one of the largest online industries, although it is at present really only in the preliminary stages of development. Colleges and universities perform many functions, of which education is only one.

- They provide education in areas of directly measurable competence, like mathematics, engineering, or foreign language studies.
- They provide education for judgment, which is the principal role of a liberal arts education, and increasingly is a role for business schools as well.
- They provide education for professional skills, like medicine, nursing, law, or dentistry.
- They provide formal certification of competence, which remains critical for lawyers, doctors, and many other professionals who cannot get their official state certification without first obtaining university certification.

- They provide informal screening and certify a student as a member of the educated classes.
- They socialize students so that they learn to behave as members of the educated classes.

The cost of a four-year college education at a top-tier private institution and the cost of a professional school education at a top university are becoming prohibitive for students who do not get significant financial aid. Many students are graduating with crippling debt. As importantly, many students are discovering that their undergraduate education has not prepared them for a career that will enable them to repay their debt.

It seems a near certainty that over the coming decade online alternatives will evolve for a large number of the functions currently performed by colleges and universities. Some changes may result in more efficient and less expensive delivery of university services. For example, distance learning and massive open online courses (MOOCs) may not replace the core curriculum of the world's top universities, but smaller online closed courses (SOCCs?) may be the most effective way to deliver a lot of what is now taught through lectures, allowing class time to focus on students' interaction with faculty and with each other, and on exploration of deeper learning than is possible in lectures or in MOOCs. Other changes may result in some services moving away from universities and toward stand-alone online service providers. Many colleges and universities may fail and close. Others may become much smaller and much more focused institutions.

11.7   Selling Online Services

Selling online services is a business model that is rapidly growing. It's still a challenge to get consumers to pay for some services, at least in the US.

Charging for online services has been quite difficult in the USA. Apple, Microsoft, and Google make so many services available without charge that consumers expect even essential online services like e-mail, search, and mapping to be available free.

Charging for services is not nearly as difficult outside the USA. Tencent is an online services company and China's largest and most used Internet services portal. Baidu is the major search engine company in China and the local equivalent of Google for search. Baidu's revenues from search are less than Tencent's revenues from digital services like e-mail, online storage, photo sharing, instant messaging, and gaming. Most of Tencent's fee-based services are services that would be free in the USA. And apparently, the business model works in China; Tencent's market capitalization is greater than Baidu. I must confess, I have no idea why China is so different, and I do not yet know enough to speculate. Some aspects of the market for Internet services are universal, across cultural differences. Others are not.

In brief, purely online services do exist. Most of them, like education, recommendations, or matchmaking, represent the digital transformation of existing services.

11.8   Creating Exchanges for Business-to-Consumer and Direct Consumer-to-Consumer Interactions

The sharing economy is one of the most dramatic forms of online businesses.

Exchanges, in the form of markets, have existed for millennia. When you need to buy something, it's helpful to know where the sellers are. When you want to sell something, it's helpful to know where the buyers are. Permanent markets, souqs, bazaars, and temporary fairs have existed for as long as humanity. More specialized commercial exchanges have existed for centuries. Lloyd's, the world's largest market for specialized insurance, originated in Edward Lloyd's coffee house more than 325 years ago, where ship captains and wealthy individuals could meet to negotiate insurance. The organization now known as the New York Stock Exchange started with the Buttonwood Tree Agreement, which was signed by twenty-four of New York's most important stockbrokers, and was named after the Buttonwood Tree where they initially met. Buyers and sellers have always needed to know where to find each other, and they have always needed rules to govern their trading. This was true long before online trading of any kind.

Online exchanges for businesses are not new either. Foreign exchange dealers traded electronically, long before the existence of the net. Instinet was created as an electronic exchange for institutional investors in 1969, again long before the Internet. All provided a means for buyers and sellers to interact, without actually requiring them to meet physically. The scale of business through commercial B2B markets and the small number of participants made online business markets practical before the introduction and widespread adoption of the net.

There are many more individual consumers in the USA or China than there are manufacturers or suppliers to the automotive industry. Creating a trading network for institutional investors trading stocks and bonds was relatively easy. Creating a trading network for C2C consumers to trade baseball cards, watches, sports memorabilia, and indeed anything else you might want to get or to get rid of, really was not possible before the net. Probably, the best-known C2C online markets in the world are eBay in the USA and Taobao in China. Purists may wish to think of these as principally business-to-consumer markets, because most of the selling is now dominated by a few corporate sellers. Still, they originated as online exchanges where anyone could sell, and anyone can still sell there today.

The *Sharing Economy*[1] truly has grown exponentially. From a small start with B2C companies like Zipcar and a few guest apartment rental services, we now have global car service companies like Uber and Lyft, and the global short-term apartment rental market Airbnb. These truly are consumer-to-consumer exchanges. Individuals with a car, a license, and free time can drive others who need transportation. This is great for drivers who need a little extra money, and it's great for travelers who either don't want to wait for a taxi or didn't think to book a limo service in advance. Airbnb allows apartment dwellers who are traveling to rent out their apartment and earn a little extra money. It also allows travelers who don't want to stay in a hotel much greater freedom in choosing their accommodations.

Of course, there are complaints, from both sides of the transactions. Traditional taxi owners complain of unfair competition. Apartment rentals lack some of the services and amenities of hotels, and they lack many of the regulations that ensure safety, cleanliness, and consistency. There have been complaints that companies are buying up apartments and converting them into Airbnb rental units, forcing out tenants and changing the character of entire neighborhoods, and complaints that commercial Airbnb operators are competing unfairly with existing hotels. But there have always been complaints as new markets grow and impinge on existing ones. I am quite certain that we will learn how to ensure quality and reliability in the sharing economy without interfering with its growth.

There is an entire generation emerging in the west that wants to be served, even wants to be envied for their experiences, but doesn't value owning stuff and doesn't want to be envied for what they own. The sharing

---

[1] The *Sharing Economy* is the term used to describe online services that match people who own property but are not using it with people who want to use it briefly, for a fee. The best-known *sharing services* involve automobiles and apartments.

economy, with Zipcar and Uber, is dramatically altering the automobile industry. When I bought my first Infiniti, it was an aspirational car. No one needed an Infiniti when Nissan also offered an equivalent Nissan model that was physically and functionally almost identical. Yes, the service and maintenance with Infiniti was almost effortless. But with Uber and Lyft, I don't ever have to think about service or maintenance. I might buy an Infiniti, a BMW 700-Series or a Mercedes 6-Series S Class sedan if I were thinking in terms of *Pride of Ownership*. If I'm thinking solely of cost-effective and comfortable transportation, I may rely on Uber Select and Uber Black. The transformation—from *Pride of Ownership* as a business driver to *Effortless Transportation* as a business driver—is going to give executives many sleepless nights at BMW, Mercedes, Infiniti, and Lexus. In the 1990s, I called this *the end of stuffism*, but I never expected to see it emerge this quickly.

11.9 If the Sharing Economy Is Transformational, Maybe We Should Say a Bit More About Building Sharing Economy Websites

Form follows function, and structure follows strategy!

Louis Sullivan famously said *"form follows function."* The shape and structure of an item, from a home or an office building to a teapot or smartphone, should be determined by its use. Why do smartphones have cameras on both sides? Because we need to see what we're shooting, whether it's a selfie (us) or a sunset for Instagram (in front of us). Why do teapots and kettles have spouts on only one side, the side away from the handle? Because we need to be able to pour hot tea, or even hotter water, into a glass without pouring it on our hands at the same time.

Just as form follows function in good product design, *"structure follows strategy"* in good website design for online consumer-focused markets. Again, what does that mean?

Uber doesn't promise to delight me with personalized service. They offer me a driver, a car, and an expected arrival time. I can take it. I can refuse it. But I can't negotiate with them for a different car or a different driver. Their website provides almost no information and offers me no choice. They are efficiently matching supply and demand. They are not providing a resonance ride service. The nature of their service is reflected in their website design. Form follows function and structure follows strategy.

In contrast, Airbnb does promise to delight me. They allow me to travel and live like a local resident, not like an executive on a business trip staying in an industrial hotel. I specify the city and the neighborhood where I want to stay. I check out a range of alternatives. I can apply some more filters to focus my search. Eventually, I can choose a couple of apartments to examine in more detail, check out their distance to the nearest Métro or U-bahn station, and look at a dozen photographs of the bedroom furniture, the stereo, and the view from the balcony overlooking the Seine or the Embarcadero, or whatever else interests me. Living like a local is indeed a resonance service, and the amount of information I need to make a choice is reflected in their website design. Once again, form follows function and structure follows strategy.

My colleagues explored several dozen websites with me, and we found this pattern repeats. Does the platform appear to match supply and demand efficiently? Then, the website designers seek simplicity, provide limited information, and offer little or no choice. Does the platform promise delight, pursuing a resonance strategy? Then, the website designers need to accept some complexity, because they need to offer me not just choice but control, and this requires *informedness*.

11.10   Control of Search and Charging for Customer Access

Online gateways, especially the MP3PP versions, are among the most successful and among the most powerful businesses in the world today. Can you create an MP3PP business?

Platforms that control search and or control online gateways follow a purely digital business model. This can entail charging sellers for access to their customers, who otherwise might not find them and might end up buying from other sellers. It can involve developing additional new online businesses and promoting them through their own gateway, reducing or even effectively eliminating competitors' ability to find new customers. This is more than transformation of retailing. This is controlling who gets to sell and who does not, and this is an entirely new digital business.

We discussed gateways in Chapters 7–9, when we discussed the Mandatory Participation Third Party Payer Pattern and the Online

Gateways Pattern. The online gateways business model can be based on misdirection or on the threat of misdirection. If a website is not as good as the one that the consumer is trying to find, the search engine can charge its operators and can redirect and misdirect consumers to the inferior website, for a fee. If a website *is* the one the consumer is trying to find, the search engine can still charge that website, in this case for *not* sending the consumer elsewhere.

This business model is effective. It's enormously profitable. I am certain that it is harmful to consumers, for the reasons, we have discussed previously: It increases the prices they pay, and it increases the likelihood that they are deliberately sent to inferior websites, and therefore it increases the likelihood that they make inferior purchasing decisions. It's also harmful to competition generally, since the platform operator can use it to harm competitors and limit consumer choice.

Many entrepreneurs envy Google and want to replicate their business model. The inability of Bing to make much headway, despite pouring billions of dollars into software and marketing, suggests encroaching on search is going to be very difficult. Moreover, it should be clear how few opportunities exist for MP3PP variants of Google's business model when we consider how few MP3PP businesses we can list. So, we may envy Google, but we can't easily find opportunities to be like them.

Still, hope springs eternal, and if you can find a new market segment for a gateway or new opportunity for an MP3PP, it's worth a try. The business models are not illegal, and current evidence suggests that it's hard to be so greedy or so successful that you get into regulatory difficulty in the USA!

11.11 Selling Virtual Experiences and Virtual Stuff

Who needs drugs? If you don't like your real life, make up a new one online.

Selling virtual experiences is different from selling content. If I watch a movie online through streaming video, I am viewing online content. But virtual experience goes well beyond content. If I play a video game, especially a video game that involves full immersion in a virtual world, and interaction with that world and with other players in it, that's a virtual experience. Virtual experiences can be very intense. I've had Wharton MBA students who felt stronger bonds with members of their World of Warcraft guild than they felt toward members of their Wharton study teams.

Virtual experiences, or virtual worlds, currently have two sources of revenue. The first is revenues from the experience itself, and the second is revenue from the purchase of experience-related add-ons. As an example of the first revenue source, World of Warcraft charges a monthly fee for participation.[2]

An alternative business model is based on paying for stuff that you use during virtual experiences. The best-known example of a virtual experience that was not based on gaming was Second Life. In 2009, there were actually discussions at the World Economic Forum in Davos about whether the Forum would continue to meet in person, or whether our Avatars would conduct future sessions without the need for travel. Second Life has not replaced travel or any other major aspects of our First Lives; indeed, 2017 revenues were estimated at about half of those in 2009. It is not entirely clear to me why any of us would value virtual skydiving, or sitting in a virtual hot tub counting virtual stars. It is not clear why any of us would purchase a virtual sailboat or rent a virtual island.

Even after saying that, I realize that virtual reality technology is getting better all the time. Virtual sailing, virtual skydiving, and virtual hot tub experiences may be a bit much, given how many senses need to be fully engaged. Virtual sightseeing, like touring the Taj Mahal or the Great Wall, but without the crowds and the jet lag, may be only a few years off.

I can't judge the future of this. I admit to being surprised by the flash success of Zynga in March 2014, when its Farmville game soared in popularity and its share price surged. In February 2014, there were more search results returned for "Farmville" (6,430,000) than for "Jesus Saves" (551,000) or "Nuclear Nonproliferation" (294,000). I failed to see the attraction of playing a pseudo-farming game, or of paying to improve the quality of my pseudo-farm. I remember one of my students telling me her ex-boyfriend continued to "gift" her Zynga Farmville pseudo-sheep and asking me what I thought that signified. And I remember not being surprised at all when Zynga's share price collapsed by 61% over the next seven months. And yet, there are almost twice as many search results returned for "Farmville" today (13,100,000). Zynga's share price has rebounded somewhat, and 2017 revenues were the best in the company's history. Perhaps it is too soon to write Zynga off completely yet.

There are games, like World of Warcraft, in which paying for stuff of any kind is strongly discouraged. You would not pay someone else to enter tournaments and play chess for you just in order to get yourself a higher rating,

---

[2]This monthly fee is waived for the starter edition, which can be used until the player reaches level 20. See, https://us.battle.net/account/creation/wow/signup/.

nor would you expect to be allowed to pay your opponents to play badly just so that you could have a higher ranking. True ladies and gentlemen just don't do that. So true fans of World of Warcraft take a very dim view of *gold farming*, in which you pay someone else to play the game long enough to develop a fully empowered avatar for you. Likewise, true fans take a dim view of paying someone to acquire *in-game* stuff for you, like weapons, jewels, or other forms of power and wealth.

And yet, no nineteenth-century big game hunter, whether an English lord or American President Teddy Roosevelt, would have set off on safari without all of the latest equipment, comforts, and porters. Today's gamers are often willing to pay for in-game equipment. As a result, gold farming is alive and well. Increasingly, games are designed to allow users to buy in-game accessories and capabilities and to pay for these upgrades through out-of-game hard currency.

Paying for in-game stuff has developed into a big business, and game designers increasingly are capturing this revenue source for themselves, rather than allowing gold famers to capture it. At the time that I am writing this, the current market leader for in-game purchases may be *Game of War: Fire Age* from Machine Zone. Game of War is free to download and free to play, but if you want to play well, you need to be well-equipped, and equipment is not free. You can purchase what you need, but you need to pay for it with real-world currency. Equipment may be quite expensive, depending on what you intend to do. The record for individual purchases from Game of War was $46,000 when I first drafted this chapter in November 2017; by now, the record for Game of War appears to be approximately $1 million.[3]

So can we sell virtual stuff? Absolutely. The market for this definitely is larger than I thought. And it appears to be growing.

11.12 Harnessing Social Networks the Right Way

I'll have what my friend just ordered, online, all day, around the world.

Community content can have great value in resonance marketing, as we saw in Chapter 4. Hotel reservations systems piggybacked off TripAdvisor, and the Beer Yard piggybacked off RateBeer. It's fair to say that the online travel

---

[3]See "California man spent $1 million playing Game of War—Mobile game described as 'like gambling, but with no possibility of winning.'" https://arstechnica.com/tech-policy/2016/12/california-man-spent-1-million-playing-game-of-war/.

industry, and a wide range of resonance consumer products, were enabled by community-generated online content. The essence of community content as the basis for marketing is that it is sincere, genuine, authentic, fair, informed, and unbiased. There are so many words that can be used here, and so few of them can also be used to describe paid search.

A few companies have found a way to monetize the use of social content to guide consumers' choices of products and services. TripAdvisor was initially monetized by providing credibility to InterActive's online travel sites. The online version of Zagat's restaurant rating service was initially monetized by its relationships with OpenTable.

Social Search uses community content to generate search results, but in a traditional search setting rather than in stand-alone applications like the Beer Yard's. This would probably be extremely valuable to consumers. Social Search generates its list of search results based on what an individual's friends have tried and liked. It is tailored search, harnessed to the reviews from a population that is likely to be relevant in determining an appropriate set of guiding opinions. Imagine that you asked *"Where do my friends stay in Chicago? Which hotel is most popular with my friends? Which hotel gets the highest reviews from my friends?"* As long as you have a large enough network of friends who stay in Chicago, this does not need to involve invasion of privacy, since it is based on reviews from several friends, not the review from a single friend. Since recommendation is based on reviews from several friends, I cannot single out any individual as the source, and no one's privacy is compromised. This is not spam, since it is information I trust, that I get only when I ask for it. It is not information an advertiser wants to send me, when that advertiser wants to pay for sending it.

Social Search based on community content shows great future promise, as an alternative to the distortions and the high costs of paid search. This will eventually be done correctly.

And yet, most approaches to monetize social networks so far are just silly.

Most social encounters have codes of behavior that are not designed for selling:

- Have you given a speech as best man, or father of the bride?
- Did you try to sell anything during the speech?
- Have you ever recommended a product or service to your friend?
- Have you ever recommended a product or service because you were paid to do so?
- Have you ever included an advertisement of any kind, for any product, as part of a holiday card or wedding announcement?

And yet, at the moment my views on the use of social networks for advertising are not widely held. Many of my faculty colleagues believe that paid recommendations are the future of advertising. Several Ph.D. students are currently studying the "optimal" way to manipulate online referrals. That is, they are studying how to start with a referral from a friend, and what text to add to it to maximize the likelihood that it will successfully manipulate the recipient to make a purchase. I find the idea of paying someone to refer a product to a friend, and then modifying the referral before it is sent, ethically suspect at best. I believe that many people will agree. But the net is new, and we are still figuring out what works. I expect this practice ultimately will fade away, but not before several more Ph.D. degrees are awarded.

Ultimately, behavior in online social networks will be similar to behavior in any other social setting. Social content and friendship are not easily hijacked and used as part of a manipulative and deceptive promotional strategy. Social Search will succeed. Manipulated social network referrals may not.

11.13 Selling Referrals Based on Snooping or Context

Homeland Security needs a warrant. The Department of Justice needs a warrant. Why can so many companies do whatever they want with your data, whenever they want, millions of times a day, without a warrant?

Contextual referrals are even more invasive than manipulation of search, which was described in Sect. 11.10. With the manipulation of referrals, there is no need for companies to wait for you to search. All you need to do is appear to be getting ready to search, and your device stops communicating *for* you and starts communicating *to* you. You text to a friend that you're hungry. The friend texts back that he is too. Google knows where you both are because of the GPS on your Android devices. Google knows that you both like Thai food. The next thing you know, you get a text or an e-mail from Google suggesting a Thai restaurant that's close to where you are, even before you decided to invite your friend to lunch and before you decided to search for a restaurant.[4]

---

[4]And why are the examples always about Google? Because no one else in the Western World can do this yet. No one else reads your Gmail and your Android texts and tracks them with your Android GPS location, your use of Android Google Maps, and your search history. No other firm in North America has the information. No firm in Europe can legally do this. Facebook knows an enormous amount about you. But it knows only what you and your friends choose to post. Facebook is getting more intrusive, but it does not have full access to your GPS information, your search history, or your texts and e-mails. Major platform operators now consider it acceptable to data mine your calendar and your list of contacts.

I call targeted ads *contextual referral* because the process is based on where you are, what you have just said, and to whom you said it, and so much more. I call it contextual referral based on snooping because the context is learned by snooping on you and your friends, tracking your search history, your e-mail history, your text history, your GPS history. I know that the term contextual snooping sounds so much more judgmental than contextual advertising. This is an even more effective form of misdirection than manipulation of search. And it is even more effective in allowing sellers to manipulate prices based on your current needs and your current willingness to pay for any item, any product, or any service.

Of course, Google loves this idea. No one can compete with them, because no one else has so much information about you.[5] If you are like the rest of us, they have your search history. If you have a friend with a Gmail account (and who among us does not!), they know a lot about the e-mail you send and receive. If you have an Android device (and a significant fraction of the world's population now does), they have your text history and your GPS location history as well.

But why should Google stop with just a targeted e-mail for the Thai restaurant? Why not include a 10% off coupon? Then, these targeted messages will be even more effective, and owning a Google phone will be even more valuable, and Google's market share and power will increase. Now, this looks good for users and for Google.

How will it work out for restaurants? Who will pay for the 10% discount? The search engine isn't going to contribute the 10% that you are no longer going to be charged. Obviously, the restaurant is going to fund the 10% discount. But will it actually cost the restaurant only 10%? Over time, when directed contextual promotions become an essential source of customers, Google will demand a fee for providing the customer flow. That could easily add another 10% to the restaurant's costs. Many restaurants will become dependent upon purchasing the flow of diners, just as many hotels have become dependent upon hotels.com, and many other businesses have become dependent upon paid search for their survival. This is just another mandatory participation third-party payer online gateway system. But restaurant margins are too tight to allow restaurants to give up 20% on a substantial fraction of their customers' bills. Prices will have go up, and we will

---

[5]Facebook and other online service providers love the idea as well. Ultimately, no one will be able to do this as well as Google. First, no one else has as much information. Second, no one else is really in the business of making recommendations. Most users go to Google to find a restaurant or book a flight. Most users do not go to Facebook to find a restaurant or book a flight.

all pay higher prices to eat out. Once again, another Internet facilitation application will become a wealth harvesting mechanism, transferring money from consumers and restaurants to Google.

What will the economic future be for search based on contextual referrals and snooping? I see two alternative paths for search.

1. Google can change the way it views search. In that case, when I do a search, or when I appear ready to perform a search for something, my search engine will give me what I really want. The search engine will base its decisions on my search history, my current location, and my recent communications with my friends. That is, my search results will still be based on deep profiling, but now they will be designed to serve my needs at that place and time. Only Google will be able to do this. No other search engine and indeed no other Internet company will know enough about me to be able to do this. This would have enormous benefits to Google. It would actually be foolish and counter-productive for an individual to carry a phone that was not Android, to use any e-mail program other than Gmail, and to use any search engine other than Google's. The market-share implications for Google would be enormous; everyone, even I, might be a loyal Google user. The revenue implications would be more complex. Google would have to stop charging for keywords and for preferred positioning within search, since it was going to provide perfect search results every time, without payments for keywords altering the order of search results. Google might start charging users a small monthly fee for search. Or Google might increase its reliance on other revenue sources, like the revenue from targeted ads.
2. Google can continue to operate search largely as it does now. This is spectacularly profitable. There have been issues about Google's abuse of monopoly power and over-charging merchants for keywords, which we have discussed elsewhere. There have been related issues about the abuse of monopoly power and the inappropriate promotion of the firm's products and services above those of competitors. There are emerging concerns about the firm's ability to use the profits from search to cross-subsidize a range of other monopoly and near-monopoly services. But there has been no lasting damage to the company's reputation. If the business model still works the way Google wants, why should they change anything?

Likewise, I see two alternative paths for contextually based targeted ads pushed through Gmail. This is a separate business from search, which is based on deeper profiling and more complete integration of information from numerous sources. And it is potentially far more profitable than search.

1. Google will continue to do whatever they want. They will continue to earn enormous amounts of money doing by whatever they want. They will continue to engage in deep profiling, learning more and more about you, and getting more and more accurate in their profiling. They will continue to invade your privacy by allowing companies to learn about you through targeted ads. Companies will routinely invade your privacy to send you targeted ads, if for no other reason than their competitors will do so. Companies that do not use the best available information about you, learned when you click on targeted ads, will suffer as a result of their ignorance. Sometimes these ads will be to sell you things you want, at prices that are fair and even attractive. Sometimes these ads will be more to learn about you than to actually sell you anything. They will be a quasi-legal form of phishing. And they can be used to overcharge you for some purchases, or even to deny you access to some services at any price. Again, eventually all sellers will be forced to engage in this form of phishing, because any company that did not do this would be operating in an information vacuum compared to its competitors. Google would earn an enormous amount selling information that you or I would rather not have sold. This will be even more profitable for Google than its current reliance upon search, and this will be even more expensive for consumers. And still, their services will all appear to be free.
2. Regulation will prohibit the most abusive practices within data mining and deep profiling. Targeted ads will not be based on aspects of profiling that represent deep invasion of privacy. Targeted ads will not be based on aspects of profiling that signal your willingness to pay for a product, your riskiness, or the cost to serve you as a customer.

Frankly, I am not sure which outcome I should expect for the future of search. Likewise, I am not sure which outcome I should expect for the future of targeted ads. I remain a Digital Optimist, but I am now a *Reformed* Digital Optimist, not a *Pure* Digital Optimist. That is, I believe that we will figure out how to regulate the net in the public interest, just as we figured out how to regulate telephony, telecommunications, railroads, and food and drug manufacturers. Of course, I expect resistance, both from the giant Internet companies that benefit the most from the current lack of regulation and from consumers who do not yet understand the implications of the giants' current online business models. But we will get there.

11.14 Using Contextual Referrals to Direct Ads to Mobile Users

Trying to sell to us, no matter where we are and no matter what we are doing. Trying to get us to buy something, right now!

Mobile promotions sent directly to users' mobile devices initially seemed intrusive, but we are coming to accept them. At some point, they may be the only ads we will want.

Consider the following scenario. You're in New York. Clark Terry is playing at the Blue Note that night, and the 8 p.m. set is not sold out! It's Louis Armstrong's 100th birthday, and Jon Faddis is in from the West Coast as a mystery guest. You get a text or an e-mail inviting you to grab the last two seats. This sounds great.

It sounds great because it satisfies *The Big Three of Mobile Computing*:

1. It's *Contextually Relevant*—I care, because of who I am and where I am
2. It's *Actionable*—I can do something with it
3. It's *Time Sensitive*—I care now; I don't want to wait until I am back at my desk tomorrow before I learn about this.

Once I received a promotional e-mail message from Nikon, telling me that the company had just introduced a new Coolpix digital zoom camera. The timing of the e-mail was perfect. My daughter had just left for the summer with my Coolpix, and I was leaving for Singapore the next evening without a compact digital camera. I stopped at my favorite camera shop on the way home and bought the new Nikon. Mobile messages can be great, if and when they are perfectly timed. Of course, the timing of this message was largely coincidental; Nikon didn't know that my daughter took my camera.

How is this going to work out for consumers? Will mobile computing be used to deliver perfectly targeted messages that help the consumer? Or will mobile computing be an even more effective form of direction and of misdirection? I really don't know. Perfectly designed mobile messages could be effective, and if they were fair, honest, unbiased, and delivered without great cost to the seller, this would be an effective alternative to manipulation of search. But it is not immediately clear how this can be monetized, except as a variant of paid search. Nikon doesn't know enough about me to send perfectly timed ads to me. Only Google does, and their incentives do not align perfectly with mine or with Nikon's.

11.15 Summary

We have all this great new technology. It would be a pity to pretend it's no more than a new way to deliver television, newspapers, or one-to-one marketing messages. It would be a pity to think it's just about ads. It's going to enable online communities, with social customs and behavioral norms like any other community. It's going to be voluntary, dynamic, and participatory, like a medieval fair, not passive with the trapped audiences we find at the theater, at movies, and to a lesser extent even with television.

We do all need to understand current online business models. We need to understand the costs and the benefits to each of us. And we need to figure out how to regulate the net to make it work for all of us, and not just for the giant corporations that control it now. I remain a Digital Optimist. But I no longer believe that the net will regulate itself in the best of all possible ways, any more than the *robber barons* of the 1880s regulated themselves. Over the next half century, we needed agencies like the ICC, the FDA (Food and Drug Administration), the FTC, and the FCC. I believe that we are going to need to make some informed decisions, as a society, on how the net should be used and on how the value it creates should be shared. And we are going to have to enforce them.

12

Information Changes Everything: Implications for Society

Like the other chapters in Part III of the book, this chapter does not introduce a new pattern. Instead, it explores in more detail the social implications of the patterns that were introduced in the first two parts of the book. Yes, it's great that Capital One and Uber have introduced business models that enhance efficiency in pricing and efficiency in the allocation of scarce resources. That means more of us get what we really want, more of the time. That is unambiguously *a good thing*. However, this efficiency comes with a price. It has dramatically reduced what we traditionally call fairness, and will continue to do this more and more. We are *not* all equal to companies, and they will increasingly be able to treat us differently. They will have the information, and the internal information systems, to dramatically reduce fairness. Should we accept this? Should we change our definition of fairness? Or do we need new social policies?

In our new online world, every text you send, every search you make, every step you take, they'll be watching you. Yes, it's great to be connected and to be able to send and receive texts and e-mails. It's great to be connected and to be able to search for anything and everything, from anywhere and everywhere. And it's great to be safe and to know that surveillance cameras are everywhere, with face recognition and pattern recognition software behind them, to protect our security. But where do we draw the line? God may indeed note every sparrow that falls. Indeed, the proverb assures us that it pains Him; it does not suggest that He sells this information. Big data aggregators note the equivalent of every sparrow that falls, and we can be less certain that their use of the information is benign. Should we care? Should

© The Author(s) 2019
E. K. Clemons, *New Patterns of Power and Profit*,
https://doi.org/10.1007/978-3-030-00443-9_12

we take measures to protect ourselves from the integration, reuse, and sale of personal information? The European Union has already taken some steps to protect their citizens, through stronger regulations. The most recent step, the General Data Protection Regulation (GDPR), enacted in May 2018, may represent the most comprehensive attempt to protect individual privacy. The GDPR goes far beyond any protections available in the USA. This chapter and the next end the book with some suggestions for privacy regulation that might be desirable everywhere and proposes a few simple measures we can take to protect our own privacy and the privacy of our families.

12.1   Let's Just Do the Right Thing

Let's just do what's fair! How hard could that be?

OK, so the digital transformation of everything makes everything faster, more efficient, and more personal. Why isn't that always a good thing?

As we saw in Chapter 9, old regulations may not be appropriate for managing the digital transformation of our society. Why can't we all agree on what to do next? Because we can't even agree on what's fair. Let's take the case of insurance. Remember, insurance is based on symmetric ignorance. I don't know when I am going to get sick, or have an accident, and neither does my insurance company. I'm betting I will have a claim and will need the insurance, and the company is betting that I won't have a claim and that they can keep the insurance premium I paid to them. As long as both sides are equally informed, or both possess symmetric ignorance, people with claims get paid and insurance companies avoid bankruptcy.

But symmetric ignorance is no longer enough. With modern DNA testing and data mining, both insurance companies and their applicants have a very good idea of how risky they are. Symmetric ignorance is now actually very well informed, more so than at any time in the history of insurance. This changes the behavior of insurance companies.

- Low-risk individuals will be offered very low rates, because both they and the companies know that on average these applicants won't have claims. Insurance companies know that these individuals can safely be offered low rates. They also know that these individuals know they are low risk and that they will not willingly accept policies that charge them more than the price based on their expected cost to serve.

- High-risk individuals, the ones who really need the insurance, will be charged much higher rates because both they and the insurance companies know that on average these applicants will be very expensive to serve. The insurance companies don't want to lose money serving these high-risk individuals. And, as long as they can afford their premiums, these high-risk individuals will purchase insurance to protect themselves from the not-unlikely possibility of catastrophic losses.

Is it fair to charge low premiums for people lucky enough to be young and healthy? Is it fair to charge much higher premiums for people who are old, or who lost a genetic lottery and are high risk for cancer or other medical disasters? Is it fair that some people may not be able to afford their insurance? Is it fair when people who cannot afford insurance still receive medical treatment, and the rest of society has to pay their expenses?

Economists can't answer those questions, because economists can't tell you what's fair, or what your morality should be.

Economists can tell you what is, or is not, efficient.

Suppose you decide that everyone should pay the same premium, set as the average for healthy people in their age group. Insurance in the USA today is sold by companies, designed to earn a profit where possible and to avoid bankruptcy. A fully informed and fully rational insurance company would understand consumer behavior. Consumers who were extraordinarily healthy for their age group might conclude that the insurance is too expensive and refuse to buy it. Consumers who were really sick would cost too much money for the insurance company to serve. So fully rational insurance companies would offer the one price for each age group but would *deny coverage* for those who were too sick. The really healthy would choose not to purchase insurance. The really sick wouldn't have access to insurance. The insurance company would survive, but more people would be uninsured. That cannot be efficient.

Suppose you still believe that everyone should pay the same premium, set to the average for healthy people in their age group. Now you want to ensure that no one could be denied coverage because of preexisting conditions or genetic tendencies toward acquiring expensive conditions in the future. The extraordinarily healthy would still choose not to purchase insurance. The truly sick would be provided insurance with premiums that were not high enough to cover their expected costs. Insurance companies would face bankruptcy, and then no one would have insurance. Surely that can't be efficient.

Suppose you decide that everyone should pay a premium based on their own precise expected average cost to serve, and that no one could be denied coverage because of preexisting conditions. Insurance companies would charge everyone premiums based on each individual's expected costs, so healthy applicants would have low prices and really sick applicants would have high prices. Some people might not be able to afford their insurance. Is that efficient? Actually, it is. Is it fair? That depends on what you believe. If you believe that health insurance is a basic right, like the right to a basic education, then it's not fair. If you believe that, hey, some people can't afford a boat, or can't afford the house they want, and hey, some people can't afford medical care, and if you believe that those are all the same, then you probably believe they're all fair. Economists can't tell you what to accept as fair.

OK, so let's design an insurance market for maximum efficiency, where I arbitrarily define that to mean that the most people have insurance coverage. What would that look like?

- First, I would charge everyone a premium based on the expected cost to serve people of average health in their age bracket.
- Then I would require that coverage could not be denied because of expensive preexisting conditions, or genetic predisposition to develop those conditions, which I consider lurking future preexisting conditions.
- Then I would require that everyone buys insurance that was priced for their age group. This is called the *Individual Mandate* in the Affordable Care Act. I would have to do this to avoid hyper-rational consumers from avoiding insurance until they developed expensive conditions and then opportunistically jumping into the market. Buying insurance only when you really need it is not consistent with the idea of symmetric ignorance. It's also not insurance. It's getting medical care without paying for it. It's the equivalent of being allowed to buy automobile insurance only after you've had an expensive accident, but at the same price you would have paid before the accident, while still requiring the insurance company to pay your expenses from the accident.
- Then I would add Federal subsidies as soon as I realized that this design is still going to be too expensive for some age brackets. In particular, the elderly, who all have a preexisting condition called *aging*, are going to suffer from demographically adjusted fair pricing. The current system is breaking down because in some healthcare markets, like Arizona, almost everyone is suffering from aging, and the fair price for health insurance in Arizona is still quite high.
- Finally, I would openly and honestly add taxes to support the Federal subsidies. I wouldn't do sneaky things like overcharge the younger and healthier groups for their insurance, because they are rationally going to avoid insurance and encounter the hated rule that they buy insurance

anyway, even though it is not priced accurately for them. Of course, new taxes mean that some people will be paying into the system now, to support others. However, since we all get old eventually, these people will benefit from the system when they get older.

That's efficient. It provides affordable care for all, without bankrupting either sick individuals or the companies that serve them. It would work. It's pretty much how the Affordable Care Act eventually got designed. And we cannot implement it because Congress cannot agree on whether it's fair or not and because Congress is seeking a simpler solution. All simpler solutions will lack one or more of the elements critical for a stable efficient market for insurance that covers everyone.

It turns out most of us have very clear ideas of what is fair, and are strongly committed to them. Most of us have much less understanding of economics, and even less interest in it. The problems facing society are going to require balancing very different concepts of fairness and will require doing so in ways that are also consistent with economics.

12.2   Fake News: Is This Really a Big Deal? Isn't This Just Bigger, Faster, More Personal, and Efficient?

Yeah. Let's talk about how big, fast, personal, and efficient fake news can be! Let's talk about why it's different from fake news in the past.

Fake news is not new.[1] Governments always lie, at least some of the time. That's one reason why democracies have freedom of the press, so that investigative journalism keeps governments honest. Individual politicians and individual political campaigns have lied since the beginning of politics.

Some governments lie more than others. Fascism depends on finding a lie that enough people can believe, to get them to suspend judgment, to allow leaders to subvert their societies' democratic processes. Here I'm not talking about *nouveaux* liars, like President Trump's Press Secretaries. I'm talking about traditional fascists, like Hitler and Goebbels, or Mussolini. But under

---

[1]While fake news is not new, the term is being used in a new way. Fake news is fabricated news, disseminated to influence behavior, beliefs, and the outcome of elections. Fake news is not the same as carefully researched journalism that does not support your beliefs, no matter how strongly you disagree with it.

normal circumstances, it's tough to find a single lie that can deceive enough Germans, or enough Italians, to sweep a fascist into power.

Modern lying does not require a single lie that we can all believe. Modern lying tailors its lies for separate groups. Ultimately, modern lying may tailor its lying for separate individuals. And a well-designed lie is hard to refute.

Well-designed lies are more convincing and better engineered than the truth. Suppose I wanted to convince an audience of coal miners that Global Warming was a hoax. And suppose I knew that only coal miners would read my carefully targeted fake news report, distributed through personalized media like Facebook feeds. So, first I tell my readers that the Chinese made up the whole fraudulent idea of Global Warming in order to improve Chinese businesses, by making the coal-powered Chinese economy more cost-effective than the US economy. Then I tell them that the entire science used to explain Global Warming is based on lies. I tell them that climate always changes, but there is no indication that any human activity involving fossil fuel has affected climate. I summarize by noting that although climate always changes, there is no proof that any human activity of any kind has ever affected the Earth's climate.

Then I make it personal and powerful. I tell them that they lost their jobs because of US environmental regulations, designed to protect Americans from a climate change problem that will never occur. I never mention the impact of automation on mine employment. I tell them that the Chinese know Global Warming is nonsense, so they know that it's environmentally safe for them to cheat and still rely heavily on cheap coal, which gives the Chinese competitive advantage.

When we're done it's clear to the miners they've been harmed by environmental regulations, and it's just as clear that no one will benefit from the regulations that harmed them.

Finally, we promise that they can all get their jobs back when the US economy returns to its reliance on coal, and that we can accomplish this without harming anyone but the liars in China.

That all sounds pretty convincing. It would sound even more convincing if you were one of its intended recipients, since it was designed to resonate with you. Remember, trolls pushing fake news do not send the same message to everyone, although all the messages are designed to lead readers to the same conclusion. The message is a designer lie, and it's designed to deceive its readers into believing that Global Warming is a hoax.

How do I refute that lie? Actually, it's quite difficult to defeat simple lies with the complex truth.

Let's start with the science, simplified. Molecules have resonant frequencies. Microwave ovens are able to heat food because their microwave generators are tuned to the exact frequency of water molecules. Water molecules get excited, and then they dance around. Food—meat and vegetables—contain a lot of water, while plates do not. And that's what heat is, increased molecular activity. So, microwave ovens make the water molecules dance, heating our food, while leaving our plates untouched.

When light strikes the Earth, the Earth heats up, but it doesn't get infinitely hot. Some of that heat bounces up into space. And some of that heat is radiation of exactly the right frequency to make carbon dioxide molecules get excited. This is by chance, not by design like in a microwave oven! But it has the same effect. The CO_2 in the atmosphere gets hotter. The air gets hotter.

Of course, the air doesn't get infinitely hotter either. When you put on a blanket, you get warmer but you don't melt. Eventually, the blanket radiates heat. That's why when it's colder you need more blankets. Blankets leak heat.

More CO_2 in the Earth's atmosphere has always resulted in higher temperatures. That's not a guess; we have records based on CO_2 levels in arctic ice cores and in other records that allow us to say with certainty that CO_2 levels and temperature have been closely correlated for millions of years.

Human industrial activity, especially the burning of fossil fuels, releases carbon dioxide. Fossil fuels are, well, fossilized life. Coal is fossilized plant life, which is carbon based, so coal is mostly carbon. Oil is fossilized ocean animal life, which is more complex; oil is mostly hydrocarbons. Burning coal and oil releases the carbon back into the atmosphere.

And CO_2 levels have never increased this quickly, at least never in the 65 million years since the extinction of the dinosaurs. That's not a guess either. And we know that when CO_2 levels increase quickly, temperature increases quickly, since CO_2 levels are correlated with temperature. And again, that's not a guess, although we don't know exactly how fast temperature will increase.

When temperatures increase, wind patterns change, rainfall changes, and some farmland will become more productive and some will become less productive. Some nations may become richer over time, when they figure out what crops to plant. Other nations will become poorer immediately, when their current crops start to die.

Human societies have built up around oceans, ocean ports, and rivers. Sea levels rise when temperatures rise, which happens when CO_2 levels rise. These are not guesses either. When sea levels rise many cities, like New York and Miami, are going to disappear. Other cities, like London and New Orleans, are going to be at risk when once-in-a-century storm surges become once in a decade, or even annual events. Bangladesh is going to disappear. So will the Netherlands. So will most of Florida.

India, Pakistan, and China all depend on water that flows from the melting of Himalayan glaciers. Global Warming will make all three nations happier, briefly. And then all three nations will need to scramble to protect their "fair share" of the river water. And they will not agree on what is fair. They are all nuclear powers. It won't be pretty if they go to war over water or anything else.

So, when scientists call for expensive activities to limit Global Warming, they're not trying to save the planet. They're trying to avoid mass extinction events, which occur when environmental changes are so fast that they are lethal to many species on Earth. They're trying to keep Earth comfortable for us. Other species fill in the gaps after mass extinction events. They always have. The Earth isn't empty now that the dinosaurs are gone. The Earth wouldn't be empty if humans are gone. The planet will survive. It's us that scientists are worried about.

OK, quick. Let's have a quiz. If you were a coal miner, could you repeat the explanation for why Global Warming is a Chinese hoax? If you were a coal miner, could you repeat the scientific explanation of why Global Warming occurs when CO_2 levels get higher from the burning of fossil fuel, and would you believe the list of disasters I provided? Could *you* repeat the scientific explanation of why Global Warming occurs when CO_2 levels get higher from the burning of fossil fuel?

But what if you're not a coal miner? What if you don't believe that Global Warming is a Chinese hoax designed to steal American jobs? What if you have noticed that the weather around you actually has changed? Fake news trolls use different lies for different folks, with different beliefs and different fears. That's what's so great about modern fake news. If I really understand you, I can target your fake news so that you will believe it.

Suppose I know that you are skeptical of scientists and experts of all kinds. Suppose I also know that you are concerned that *something* seems to be happening to the weather. More storms. Warmer temperatures. What do I tell you? First, I tell you that of course, it looks like things are getting warmer, but that's only because you remember years with storms or floods more clearly than years without. And, I remind you that of course, summers have gotten hotter where you live in the USA. But winters are colder. How can you call that Global Warming?

Then I tell you that of course, we may have warming right now, but it doesn't mean anything. There are so many factors other than CO_2 levels. What about sunspot activity? What about solar winds? What about twitches in the angle of the Earth's axis?

And, I remind you that we've always had short-term climate change. The 1600s, the middle of the Little Ice Age, were brutally cold, which eliminated the Norse settlements on Greenland. Then things warmed up. Human activity had nothing to do with either the cold or the warming, since the Industrial Revolution had not yet begun at the time and humans were not yet burning fossil fuel. And human activity had nothing to do with last year's hurricanes either.

That's all pretty simple and easy to remember.

How do I refute that? A different lie requires a different response. This requires that we talk about statistics. Random events are not entirely predictable, and you can have runs of "good luck" or "bad luck." A basketball player might shoot 85% from the free throw line. That doesn't mean he misses every seventh shot. He might make 24 in a row. He might miss 4 in a row. He might even miss 14 in a row. But on average he misses about every seventh shot.

And temperature "shoots" at random also, or at least short-term weather changes are so complicated that they look random. Some decades are warmer than average. Some decades are colder than average. So, let's assume that 85% of the winters in Europe are warmer than some temperature, which I don't know exactly, and 15% are colder. But just like the basketball player can miss 14 foul shots in a row, European temperatures could just by chance be colder than average 14 decades in a row. That's not Global Warming. That's chance.

So, even in the absence of changes to the underlying average temperature distributions, mini heat waves and mini ice ages will happen.

But science says that the underlying distribution of weather events is tied to atmospheric levels of CO_2. And CO_2 levels are higher now. So the weather will "shoot" above previous averages more frequently and now will pass the former 85% threshold more than 85% of the time. We can do statistical analysis and demonstrate that average temperatures have changed, and that the frequency of what had been above average temperatures has changed as well. Not every year will be warmer than average now, just as some years were warmer than average before CO_2 levels increased. But warmer years are indeed more frequent than they were.

Finally, I suggest that if you give me another century of data I will surely convince you. Come back in 100 years and we'll both be certain.

Let's have another quick quiz. Assume that you're a climate change skeptic and you're not a statistician. Could you repeat the argument about why you don't need to worry, because there are always environmental changes? Could you repeat the argument about why you should worry, because although there are always environmental changes, there is an underlying trend line here, based on millions of years of data, which will become undeniably clear even to skeptics in another hundred years? Which is easier to remember? If you're not a statistician or a climate scientist, which argument will resonate with you?

And resonance is the key concept here. Resonance is what enables fake news to go beyond being credible and to go viral, earning likes and retweets. I can tailor my fake news to anything you already believe, to increase the likelihood that you end up agreeing with what I want you to accept. I just need to tailor my falsehoods to sound plausible to you, based on what you believe. I also need to tailor my falsehoods so that I avoid making false claims directly in your areas of expertise.

But we said politicians always lie. Why is modern fake news different? Why is it even interesting? Because campaigns can now have designer lies, as easily as we can have any other designer products. We can have resonance lies, as easily as we can have resonance beer or resonance denims or any other resonance product. And this is different from previous mass-market lies because these designer lies are much more effective. Over time, as trolls gain experience with tailoring designer lies to their intended audience, they may become more convincing than the truth.

Candidate Trump lost the popular election, but won the electoral vote by the thinnest of margins in three closely contested states. The Brexit Referendum passed, with the thinnest of possible margins.

Both the Trump campaign and the Brexit campaign were the beneficiaries of coordinated fake news campaigns. Would they have won without the fake news campaigns? We'll never know if the winning margins were the result of Cambridge Analytica's exploitation of fake news. But we do know that the margins that determined the electoral outcomes were small, and we do know that both the Trump campaign and the Brexit campaign benefited from well-designed fake news and well-executed fake news campaigns.

Why do we need to do anything? Why won't the market just shut the trolls down? If users can't detect fake news, then users are not going to shut fake news down or make it less effective.

And Facebook won't voluntarily stop fake news, because it's just too profitable for Facebook to permit it as just another form of advertising. We know that Facebook knowingly allowed information on millions of users to be harvested for years, for a price. And we also know that Facebook knowingly allowed this information to be used for the targeting of fake news directed to its users, also for years, also for a price.

Facebook Chair Mark Zuckerberg promised to be more proactive about limiting the abuse of private information, but he pointed out that we need to be patient, because fixing the problem will take three years. That's not quite true. Fixing the problem while coming up with alternative revenue sources might take three years. And, proactive or not, Mr. Zuckerberg does not want to do anything that would limit Facebook's revenues. Some of us remember the medical disaster caused by Thalidomide. And those of us who remember can only imagine the backlash against the company and against its regulators if their Chair had suggested that it would take three years to get Thalidomide off the market.

Many of us continue to use Facebook, despite the dangers resulting from misuse of our private information. The market has not yet indicated that competition can control Facebook. This may represent an additional area where some form of regulation is required.

12.3 How Price Discrimination Affects Fairness for All of Us

Sometimes it's hard to know what fairness is!

We noted when we talked about newly vulnerable markets that they are based on price efficiency. They are based on surfing the customer profitability gradient. Some customers cost Capital One less to serve so Capital One chooses to charge them less; that's *price efficiency*. Other customers are willing to pay more for a ride right now, so Uber chooses to charge them more to make certain they get a car even when there are not enough drivers to serve the entire market; that's called *allocative efficiency*. Efficiency is great in markets. All economists agree. But is it *fair*?

Sometimes efficiency and fairness may be in direct conflict. We agreed that maybe it might be fair to try to protect people whose preexisting medical conditions are the result of a genetic condition, even if it's not efficient. What if the illness is due to lifestyle choices, like smoking and drinking, and in some sense is the result of decisions and actions that person took? Would our conception of fairness change? Would it now be fair to charge him more? What about something in between, like getting injured playing basketball in your fifties or sixties, when the chance of a knee or ankle injury is greater than when you were younger? Big data aggregators know enough to charge each of us efficient prices. But that just makes fairness more complicated than it's ever been before.

If information changes everything, and if the Internet changes all aspects of access to information, then we are going to have a lot of new fairness questions to examine. The digital transformation of everything is going to include the digital transformation of *the social contract*. It will change the implicit agreement among individuals in society, and the agreement between those individuals and the marketplace, and the agreement between those individuals and their government.

12.4   How Much Should We Value Efficiency? How Much Should We Value Fairness?

Fairness usually isn't free. How much fairness do we want? Who pays for it? And how do we balance fairness against efficiency?

Why do we praise price efficiency? With operating efficiency we use less energy, or we waste less food and water, or whatever. There is more stuff for everyone. With greater price efficiency, there is more participation in the market. If I am willing to pay $50 for software that costs only $5 to produce, and the price is set at $100, I won't buy the product. That's *deadweight loss*; if the company could set my price at $49.99, I would have the product for less than my valuation *and* the company would earn an extra $44.99.

There are potential problems with efficient pricing. If every consumer is charged a price close to the value he places on a product, we observe a reduction in consumer surplus and a reduction in one form of fairness.

- **Consumer surplus**. If I know what you are willing to pay for something, and if I can find a way to charge you *exactly* that amount, there is no consumer surplus. Consumer surplus is a fancy sounding economist's term for the joy that is left over after you pay for something. If you think a bottle of beer is worth $6 or a bottle of Chardonnay is worth $65, and that's exactly what you have to pay, that's fine, but there is no leftover joy. If the bottles are priced at $5 and $45, you might buy the Chardonnay, just to *keep* the extra $20's worth of joy. That's consumer surplus.
- **Fairness**. We've already discussed what happens when some people are charged much, much more than others for insurance, and with perfect information that is going to happen. But with perfect information, we will end up paying different prices for airplane tickets and hotel rooms, books and CDs, credit cards, and potentially everything else. Many of us

would agree that this is less fair, and a society that is less fair may also be less stable and less tolerant.

Why is efficient pricing interesting now? Now is the first time in human history that sellers can have nearly perfect information. This information is integrated from the widest possible range of sources, your searches, your texts and e-mails, your friends' texts and e-mails, your GPS information, what you read, what your friends read, and who knows what predictive analytics and algorithms this information is fed into! Sellers know what you want and how much you want it. They know what you will cost to serve and how much they should want you. They know exactly what to charge you.

With perfect information in the hands of the seller, we can expect a reduction in both consumer surplus and fairness. This is happening already and will continue and accelerate. There are numerous examples, like basing your insurance rates on monitoring how much you exercise or on how fast you drive. This seems like it's voluntary, at least in cases where the consumer agrees to wear a smart watch for behavioral monitoring or to attach monitoring equipment to his car. It isn't really voluntary. Ultimately, those of us who should have lower prices will have financial incentives to prove it. Those who don't provide the information will look like they have something to hide, and will be charged higher prices.

12.5   Why Is Fairness a Social Policy Issue?

If fairness isn't free, who decides how much fairness is enough? If fairness isn't free, who decides how the costs are divided? If fairness reduces efficiency, is seeking too much fairness possibly even unfair as well?

Why is price efficiency or allocative efficiency a social policy issue? Because we never addressed information-enabled efficiency as a society. We never gave the data harvesters, and the data analyzers, and the data repackagers, and the data sellers, permission for their activities. We never even thought about these activities. And if we don't address this and set a policy, it will become the new norm by default. This is true, just like abusive child labor practices, air and water pollution, and all of the problems of crowded slum living became the new norm in Britain after the industrial revolution. We're still wrestling with whether human-driven climate change is real two centuries after the start of the industrial revolution, and if so, what to do about it. I don't want us to be dealing with issues of privacy, data integration, and pricing decades from now, because their impacts on society may have become much more harmful and irreversible.

So we need a policy on privacy, data integration, and their implications for pricing. What should the policy be? That's certainly way beyond my ability to decide! This is a societal issue. We all need to become fully informed about the issues. And then we need to decide what we, as a society, actually believe. And this is complicated. The more the EU improves privacy protection, the more American tech giants mock them for stifling innovation.

There are some constraints on any policy we want to design. First, whatever society decides, it cannot suspend laws of economics. We cannot require that some people get *better than average* prices, but that no one gets punished by paying *worse than average prices*. We can share the pain equally, and all pay the same prices. Or we can share the pain only slightly, and let some have slightly better than average prices while others pay slightly worse than average prices. Or we can let pricing and allocation be entirely determined by informed economic actors, and let the pain fall where it may. But the pain has to be borne by someone.

We don't want or need a fairness policy for everything. We probably cannot ban companies from placing different values on customers and for charging different prices for hotel rooms, air travel, credit cards, and other banking services. We probably shouldn't.

However, we probably cannot safely tinker with insurance markets without causing their collapse. They were based on *symmetric ignorance*, and ignorance no longer exists. So if we think it is fair for everyone to have affordable health care, we need some coupling of price efficiency with external support for those who are *medically disadvantaged*. As we've seen, this is complicated and cannot be achieved simply by tinkering.

12.6 Privacy in the Online World

Privacy is complicated! We're all hurt by data mining, but not in the same ways. We all benefit from data mining, but not in the same ways.

The GDPR makes privacy the default. Companies cannot use your data without your permission. EU citizens have automatically *opted out* of most forms of online tracking and targeted advertising. Major advertisers have effectively blocked opt out as the default in the USA, and in their defense they have argued that 85% of Americans prefer free Internet services supported by advertising to retaining their privacy and paying for services. I suspect that these estimates are indeed correct.

And yet, my own research is that most people view Internet ads as essentially the same as reading an ad in a print newspaper or watching an ad on broadcast television. Most people do not understand just how much the operators of giant platforms know about them, and how much these platform operators share with other companies. Most people do not understand that this information can and is being used to alter the prices they pay and the services they are or are not able to receive.

Not all of us are desperately ill, at least not all of the time. And not all of us urgently need to fly, again, at least not all of the time. But most of us do get sick. And most of us do have urgent needs. And as a result, most of us can expect to pay a surcharge imposed by sellers, as a result of online tracking and deep profiling, at least some of the time.

Should we care? A devout economist would argue that this makes markets more efficient, and indeed that's true. A devout economist would argue that efficient pricing is fair, and as we've seen in at least one sense that is true. However, we've also seen that in other senses having us all pay different prices can be profoundly unfair.

What should the US policy be on deep profiling? Should a new American privacy law resemble the GDPR and require that opting out of all forms of tracking and profiling becomes the default setting for all browsers, search engines, and social networks? Use of the net would no longer be funded by revenues from targeted ads and deep profiling, and the cost of using the net would be visible and paid by users. That would be massively unpopular. On the other hand, the total cost of using the net would actually be significantly lower, since funding the net through revenues from targeted ads and deep profiling ads significant costs to all businesses, and is the most expensive way to fund the net.

No one yet knows what the US privacy policy should be. But design of our national privacy policy is certainly too important to be left entirely to Google, Facebook, and data aggregators who profit from the current lack of policy in the USA.

12.7   Fairness Considerations in Platforms and the Sharing Economy

There are so many ways to trade off efficiency and fairness!

We all want to keep the Internet as open, as flexible, as innovative, and as valuable as possible. And many of us assume that this means the net should be subject to no regulation at all. This argues for letting innovators, entrepreneurs, and investors try as many things as possible, as quickly as possible. It argues for letting markets sort things out. In its most orthodox form, this argues that any attempt to outthink and outsmart the markets is unnecessary. Worse, it argues that any attempt to outthink the markets will create significant delay in innovation, perhaps allowing the economic benefits of innovation to shift to looser regulatory environments overseas, while adding no meaningful or necessary forms of protection for local consumers.

And yet most of us can agree that some form of regulation of online platforms is appropriate. Imagine a hypothetical firm Hootel, a sort of X-rated version of a platform for hotel and apartment search and rental. In Hootel, you not only acquire a room in a foreign city for a couple of nights, but a sexual companion as well. It gives whole new meanings to the idea that you don't just *visit* Paris, or New York, or any other cosmopolitan city, you actually *live* there like a local. Most countries, most states and provinces, and most cities would agree that they have a legal and moral right to regulate such platforms in the interest of public safety, and to slow the spread of diseases such as HIV/AIDS. When I suggested Hootel as a business opportunity at a conference on platform-based competition, my academic colleagues were suitably outraged.

OK. So most of us can now agree that there is a line that platforms should not cross. But where do we draw the line? Where do we set the boundary for what online platforms are and are not permitted to do? The fact that we can agree on one or two extreme examples where regulation is appropriate does not suggest that we can agree on much else in the regulation of platforms.

Should we as a society permit Airbnb to flourish because it is efficient to allow the owners of properties to find their most economically valuable use? If it is more profitable for building owners to refuse to renew the leases for some apartment residents in San Francisco and to convert their properties into full-time Airbnb rentals, should we permit it without question? If the residents object to being evicted from their apartments rather than having their leases renewed, or their neighbors object to having strangers and transients in an apartment building so that their home feels like a hotel, should we protect residents instead of property owners? What should we do when hotel operators argue that apartment owners and apartment tenants who rent out their space through Airbnb have an unfair advantage because they pay fewer taxes, have fewer safety regulations, or can locate in residential neighborhoods where hotels cannot? Should we impose greater restrictions on Airbnb simply to level the playing field and help hotels compete? When cities object that they are losing hotel occupancy tax receipts as a result of Airbnb, should we care? Who would really benefit from these additional laws and regulations and how do you balance competing interests? How would you decide on the appropriate guidelines for regulators to follow? Yes, these were interesting questions *before* the arrival of Airbnb, but Airbnb resulted in an enormous increase, probably a thousand-fold increase, in the size of the market for unregulated short-term residential rentals.

If taxi and limo drivers object to Uber should we care? If Uber X has created more operating efficiency than a limo company because of its technology, is that enough reason to endorse Uber? If Uber Black and Uber X both can deliver cars to the customers who really want them the most because they are unregulated and can change prices to match supply to demand at all times, is that enough reason to let Uber operate in competition with taxi companies? Is there any legitimate basis for an objection to Uber Black, which is more of a luxury car service and does not really compete with taxis? What about the other forms of Uber, which compete more directly with taxis throughout the day? Should Uber's taxi services be subject to all of the same regulations as traditional taxi drivers? Who would really benefit from these additional laws and regulations and how do you balance competing interests? How would you decide on the appropriate guidelines for regulators to follow?

12.8   Why Is It so Hard to Agree on Fairness?

If we can't even agree on what's fair in competition between businesses, how can we hope to agree on what's fair to us? Fairness to us is much more personal!

Is it even necessary or appropriate to try to protect consumers from harm they might potentially suffer online? Clearly, we protect kids from smoking and drinking, partly to protect them from harm they cannot yet fully evaluate for themselves, and partly to protect ourselves from the externalities that intoxicated teenage drivers impose upon their friends and other drivers. We agree that teenagers can't always judge the long-term impacts of smoking or of other potentially harmful activities, and we feel that society has the right to protect them. We use similar arguments to justify at least some restrictions on the online activities of children and teenagers. Perhaps we need more regulations to protect what can and cannot be done with their data, if we believe that they cannot judge long-term risks and cannot give fully informed consent to future violations of their privacy.

But is it appropriate to regulate the online activities of adults or of companies that provide services that consumers really value? Is it really even possible that some consumers cannot judge the impacts of their online activities, both on themselves and on others? Isn't this the age of the Internet, of online access to everything, and of perfectly informed consumers? Is it possible that some consumers don't know how Google and Facebook use their information, or how big data integrators merge their transaction histories from all of their online activities? Is it possible that some consumers really don't know how this information can lead to their paying higher prices, or even being denied employment or being denied access to some services?

Yes. It seems obvious that we don't fully understand the impacts our online activities have on our own lives. And it seems even more clear that we don't understand the impacts these activities have on the lives of others. And yes, many individuals were surprised to see how Facebook cooperated with foreign trolls, permitting them to attempt to influence elections in the USA and the Brexit Referendum in the UK.

Maybe we need more transparency, so companies are required to explain all the ways they use our data and let others use our data. Perhaps we need restrictions on what can be done with consumers' data, how it can be shared, how it can be moved across borders, and how it can be integrated with and without consumers' explicit permission. The new EU GDPR attempts to address both. The USA places far fewer restrictions on the companies' use of their customers' data, arguing that this is an essential element of the First Amendment's protection of freedom of speech. Which model, tight controls or freedom of innovation, is better for society? How should we decide?

12.9   So Where Should We Draw the Line?

If there are so many ways to trade off efficiency and fairness, how should regulators attempt to balance them?

OK, so how should regulators choose where to draw the line when regulating online platforms or other online services? Honestly, we don't yet know. The community of Internet innovators and entrepreneurs want no regulation at all, and it is hard to blame them. It is not clear what should be regulated or how it should be regulated, and until we know more, the foremost regulatory guideline should still be *"Do no harm!"* It would clearly be inappropriate if overly restrictive regulation were to reduce consumers' choices and their access to new products. We all want to avoid that. It is clear that consumers are more likely to embrace the potential benefits of information technology innovations and downplay the risk.[2] And it is also clear that regulation of any kind will cost innovators and entrepreneurs significant amounts of money by reducing investment opportunities. Innovators and entrepreneurs are going to be too generous in what they permit, and too reluctant to impose restrictions of any kind.

So what kind of regulations would entrepreneurs and consumers accept? The legal and regulatory community is trying to use the same frameworks that have been used to regulate interstate and international commerce for decades. They have achieved only mixed results, because traditional guidelines do not always apply in the online world.

There are two reasons why it may be critical to reexamine and redesign regulation today.

- *Current mechanisms for privacy protection no longer work.* Online anonymity is a myth. It's clear that the amount of information available for targeted advertising today is not just greater than before, but qualitatively different from anything we've seen in the past. Privacy regulation based on primary identifiers is not adequate in an era of big data, when we can identify almost anyone uniquely from his or her transaction history without relying on name, tax id, or street address.
- *Privacy violations are far more serious today.* The implications of online privacy violations are also different from the implications in more traditional businesses, since targeted marketing online does not just mean sending unsolicited ads, but also means price discrimination. A well-informed seller can charge higher prices to travelers based on their need to travel and can charge higher prices to anyone, in any market, in ways that we have never debated as a free society.

And there are many reasons why existing regulations don't really fit. Mostly, this is because companies do not fit neatly into traditional categories or traditional business models anymore, meaning they don't fit into traditional regulatory categories anymore either.

---

[2]I find this a little puzzling. Consumers seem terrified of genetically modified crops, although virtually every agricultural product we eat today, anywhere on Earth, has been genetically modified slowly, by centuries of selective breeding by farmers. Consumers trust anything they see on Google Play or the Apple App Store. My guess is we trust innovation unless we put it in our mouths or feed it to our kids.

- Uber claims, rightly, that it is not a taxi company. But does that mean it is not providing transportation services and cannot be regulated in any way? Uber claims that its drivers are not employees. That seems to be true. Does that mean they have no rights? Does that mean that Uber does not need to screen them and train them as rigorously as if they were employees? How should Uber and its employees be managed?
- Airbnb claims, rightly, that it is not a hotel company or a real estate management company. Does that mean its properties are not subject to any zoning restrictions? That it does not need to implement the same safety regulations that a hotel does? How should Airbnb properties, owned by private individuals, be inspected and rated for safety and cleanliness? Are the implicit biases of renters the responsibility of Airbnb? Do they need to protect the rights of minority property owners, to ensure equal rental profits in the presence of biases among their potential guests?
- Google claims that it is not a media company, that it does not compete with media companies, and that it can take at least limited amounts of the content of media companies and make them available to their users immediately without charge. Newspapers can't do that with the content of other newspapers.
- Google claims that it is a search company, not a ticket agency or a retailer, and obsolete rules developed in the era of telephone service cannot be used to compel it to make competitors' products as easy to find as its own.
- Google also claims that it *is* a media company, and that it can use search order to advance or hinder the interests of an individual, a politician, or a company. They claim it's their right under the First Amendment to express their opinions through the order they impose on search results, and they can use it just like *The New York Times* can use their first amendment rights to express an opinion in an editorial.
- Facebook claims that it is not a media company, and they have no obligation to police the content that others place on their Web sites, other than the obvious restrictions on hate speech and calls for violence or other criminal acts.

I propose the following topics for future consideration by all of society, not just by regulators, lawyers, or entrepreneurs and investors.

- *Does the platform create value or merely exploit a regulatory loophole?* Uber Black provides a new service, a real-time market for cars and drivers during periods of peak demand when traditional taxi service is inadequate.

Uber Taxi may simply be competing with traditional taxis, offering lower fares because they are subject to fewer regulations. If so, should Uber Taxi face stricter regulations, or should the regulations on taxis be relaxed? When is a platform creating value and when is it merely harvesting value that was previously available to others?

- *Does the platform create an environment in which market competition cannot effectively determine prices, requiring regulatory attention?* As we have discussed previously, there are categories of systems where the user does not pay for platform use; this does not mean that the platform is free, merely that the costs are imposed on parties in ways that competition does not control.

- *Does the platform create negative externalities that might disadvantage some consumers?* Negative externalities occur any time any of us engages in activities that harm others. Negative externalities have been discussed by economists since the beginning of economics as a discipline. Zoning laws suggest that I cannot operate a hog farm in my backyard in a Philadelphia suburb or operate a large medical clinic in my apartment. Does Airbnb harm anyone? It survived the referendum on Proposition F in San Francisco, but an informed debate on the externalities of rental platforms is still necessary. The *dark side of the sharing economy* does indeed need to be understood, as well as the obvious benefits.

- *Does the platform exploit an environment in which some parties can take advantage of differences in regulation across borders?* Google and Facebook earn their revenues in large measure through the value of the private information they are able to collect on their billions of users every day. These revenue sources are not available to European firms, which must adhere to stricter European privacy regulations. Google and Facebook can use these revenues to offer goods and services free, or at least at prices that home-grown European competitors cannot match. Should Google and Facebook be forced to follow the same privacy rules that European firms must follow, at least when Google and Facebook are operating in Europe? Is this simple self-protection, or a form of illegal non-tariff-based protectionism?

- *Can consumers really judge the benefits and rewards, costs and risks, of using a platform?* Would warnings on Internet software sites be sufficient, the way warning labels are supposed to be sufficient in limiting tobacco smoking? Or are stronger restrictions required, at least for young Internet users, the way society uses more than just warnings to limit teen drinking and smoking?

Answering those questions won't tell us what to do. But it will tell us a great deal about whether or not we need to do anything.

12.10   And, Finally, What Should We Do Now?

It's a complicated world out there, and it's getting more complicated. It's always been dangerous, but it's getting more dangerous. How do we protect ourselves and our kids?

Most of us don't have to worry about the digital transformations of our firms because most of us are not executives and will not be charged with designing the transformation of our organizations. But the rest of us have lives, and the digital transformation of everything is causing some profound changes in our lives. What do the rest of us need to do now?

First, manage your digital footprint and think about the digital history you are creating. This is going to be as important to you as your credit rating. And most kids are as totally uninterested in their digital footprints as they are uninterested in their credit rating. Most of us are not terrorists. Most of us don't need to worry about doing things that are illegal, or about arousing the interest of responsible authorities, because most of us just don't do these things. Most of us are not *persons of interest*. Yeah, if you repeatedly Google the design of an explosive trigger device for a low yield tactical atom bomb just because you are curious about how hard it would be for a terrorist to create one and you changed planes in Turkey on your way to a vacation on Cyprus, you might get a phone call. But mostly we don't need to worry about anyone studying what we do online.

But a lot of us don't understand that whatever we do online is there forever, and the net neither forgives nor forgets. My students are certain that everything they do now will in the end be judged by people *just like themselves*, and that nothing they do online could ever be offensive to people *just like themselves*. But forever is a very long time. At a friend's 25th college reunion, I noticed three things that I could never have imagined seeing, if I had been asked about them 25 years earlier. One of my friends wanted to bring his gay lover into the house and live as a threesome with his wife and their kids and she refused; his friends were horrified at how parochial she was. Our attitudes toward gays and gay rights have made enormous progress. Someone else celebrated 25 good years by snorting some cocaine in public, and no one seemed to care. No one seemed to worry that *the man* was everywhere, and a drug bust was just one small mistake away from all of us. And someone else wanted to smoke a cigar in public, and he was informed that tobacco was an immoral drug. I am not judging whether my friends behaved well at the reunion or not. I am not commenting on whether sexual threesomes in the privacy of their own bedrooms should be acceptable to everyone else or not. I am neither praising nor condemning a good Havana cigar. I am simply commenting on how surprised we all would have been, 25 years earlier, if we had been told what would and would not be the new norms for our friends 25 years after graduation. I do feel the need to say something to my students, and to my young family members, when they confidently assure me that all online records of all behavior will be totally acceptable when people *just like them* are in charge 25 years from now.

And my graduate students and my young family members assume that they know so much more than we do. A young friend worked for Homeland Security. When she first applied for the job her mom said, "*Make sure there is nothing stupid on your Facebook page when you submit your application, sweetie.*" The friend replied said, "*What do you think about what's on my wall now, Mom?*" Mom responded by saying she had no idea what was on her wall, and the friend "*Of course not. It's private. Nobody can see my wall without my permission!*" That's nonsense! If the FBI, the CIA, Homeland Security, or a really experienced hacker somewhere in Asia want to read something badly enough, he or she will read it. Most of us truly are not interesting enough to justify the effort of hacking our friends' Facebook accounts. But if someone wants your information badly enough, as when you apply for a job in some Federal agencies, you should act as if your information will be read.

So private isn't always private, and something that is acceptable to you and your friends now doesn't mean that the record of it is really going to be acceptable to everyone, forever. If you're not sure, don't do it, and don't post it, and don't text or chat about it. Our research showed that a surprising number of kids are comfortable posting about, texting about, or e-mailing about underage binge drinking and about sexual activities, including texting nude photographs of their sexual partners. An even larger number of them were comfortable forwarding texts and e-mails about their friends' activities, including texts with nude photographs.

And likewise, free isn't always free. The fact that the provider didn't charge you directly for a service doesn't mean you didn't pay for it. If online merchants have to pay enough to participate in sponsored search, and if they raise their prices as a result of the cost of online keywords, then you pay for free search every time you buy something. There may not be an explicit, clearly marked line on your bill that corresponds to the increased price you paid because of the merchant's higher costs, but the price increase is there. For some services, like free search, "free" may actually be the most expensive way to provide the service.

And getting something free isn't always a big deal. One company's free search or free e-mail program may look attractive, but you may be able to get the same service without charge elsewhere, perhaps with better protection of your privacy. Alternatively, you may be able to get the same service elsewhere, for a small charge, and with much better privacy protection. The value of the free service you are getting may be much less than you think, when you consider the alternatives available to you.

Why should you care about privacy protection? Because as we saw in Chapter 11, there are entire business models that are based on earning their enormous profits by violating your privacy, and by giving companies enough information about you to allow them to charge you higher prices or to deny you services or to refuse to hire you. Moreover, even if you don't care about your own privacy protection, the people you interact with may have reason to care about their privacy, and your choice of free software affects the privacy of everyone you interact with. If you have an Android phone or a Gmail account, you may or may not have read the various privacy policies that come with your device and your software before you agreed to them, but at least you agreed to them. People who interact with you have no choice. If you use an Android device, texts you receive can be scanned. If you have a Gmail account, messages that you receive can be scanned. When you accept Google's services, you are signing away the privacy rights of everyone who interacts with you.[3]

My own experience is that getting students to protect themselves by protecting their privacy and getting students to respect the privacy of others are both almost impossible. I have had students say in class, "*I understand everything you say, and maybe Google abuses your privacy. Google gives me* **so much** *free stuff, they* **must** *like me. Google is my friend!*"

How do you protect people who refuse to protect themselves? Partly, you protect them by increasing their awareness of the costs of privacy violation. We found the vast majority of people surveyed were either unaware of current practices by software vendors, or disapproved of those practices. In most cases, like data mining text, e-mail, or social networks, the percentage of

---

[3]This really is true. If you agree to Google's privacy policies on Gmail you give Google rights to the contents of e-mail sent to your Gmail account, without the senders' consent. Canadians seem to worry about this more than Americans do. See http://techcrunch.com/2012/10/08/google-email-privacy-lawsuit-canada/. The courts in the USA appear much more sympathetic to Google. http://techcrunch.com/2012/10/08/google-email-privacy-lawsuit-canada/.

users that were *both* aware of the practice *and* approved of the practice was between 1 and 2%. This is not informed consent.

And partly you protect them through public policy. Ignorance is not informed consent. If transparency doesn't work something more proactive may be required from regulators. Big American platform operators are going to continue to do anything that is not illegal. Perhaps they will continue to do anything that is illegal, as long as the penalties when getting caught are still far less than the profits from the violations. In the USA, most violations have led to minimal punishment, or to no punishment at all. Perhaps we need a clear and unambiguous policy on data mining and deep profiling of kids. Perhaps we need a clear and unambiguous policy on data mining and deep profiling of the rest of us. Perhaps the authors of the EU's General Data Protection Regulation were correct, and that a clear and unambiguous policy needs to be backed up by the possibility of appropriately staggering penalties for sufficiently egregious violations. Soccer players are aware of how a Red Card ejection affects their teams and American football players know that a multi-game suspension harms them as well as their teams. Maybe the penalties for data privacy violations need to be set high enough that executives, boards of directors, and shareholders all take them seriously.

And what should you do now? First and foremost, enjoy the transformation! The net is a wonderful thing. Although I want it to be better, and I want firms to behave better, I surely would not want to give up anything I now enjoy! With everything from CNN to Fox News, and everything from the BBC to Al Jazeera News, available online, there is no reason for any of us to be uninformed, ever again. With online reviews, online content, and resonance marketing, there is no reason for any of us to make an uninformed purchase ever again. With everything from Masterpiece Theatre to forty-year-old sitcoms available as streaming video, there is no need for any of us to be unable to find something to watch. With smartphones with 512 GB of storage, we can carry all of our music, a dozen videos, and a couple of hundred great books with us everywhere we go; there is no need for any of us be bored, ever again. Life has never been better. It will be better still when we learn how to obtain the full value of the net. But it is great already.

And, yes, the *digital transformation of everything is* a wonderful thing as well. It will be better still when we learn how to obtain its full value and to manage its downside. But it is great already.

12.11 Summary

We need to decide, all of us, as a society, how much efficiency we want and how much fairness we are going to sacrifice. We need to decide, all of us, as individuals and as families, how we are going to protect ourselves, and how much efficiency we are going to sacrifice, and how much free software we are going to walk away from, to preserve our privacy. This chapter is not about gaining competitive advantage for a company, but about achieving the greatest gains for society as a whole.

However, if we understand the new patterns of power and profit, we are far better prepared to make decisions, fully informed, in the information age.

And I remain a reformed Digital Optimist. With a small amount of planning, we're going to do just fine.

13

Epilog: What Could Go Really, Really, Wrong?

First, a disclaimer. I originally wrote this book in 2015 and I kept updating it to reflect every major change in the online world. But the changes never stopped occurring. I had to freeze the book and stop revising chapters or it would never be released. So there are some very interesting developments that are not reflected in the previous chapters. Yes, Mark Zuckerberg acknowledged that it will be expensive to hire humans, tens of thousands of them, to check news feeds, but Facebook's fundamental business model hasn't changed. Fake news works, and Facebook's revenue went up, even though the share price temporarily dropped almost 20% when the Cambridge Analytica scandal first broke. Yes, Amazon is creating its own delivery service, taking over functions it previously contracted from the US Postal Service. But Google and Facebook have not yet replaced journalism. And Google and Amazon do not yet provide private security or private police forces as part of their platform envelopment strategies.

Despite my declaring myself a professional paranoid, paid to worry for clients in business and in government, the previous twelve chapters have been seriously optimistic. Yes, Google may impose very high costs on all of society, even if mostly they are well hidden. Yes, Facebook may be able to manipulate elections at the moment. Yes, the digital transformation of everything may radically alter many industries, like health care. And yes, the digital transformation of everything may require that societies think long and hard about fairness and the new social contract.

But regulation catches up, and societies solve their problems. They always have.

© The Author(s) 2019
E. K. Clemons, *New Patterns of Power and Profit*,
https://doi.org/10.1007/978-3-030-00443-9_13

But what if this time they don't? AT&T cooperated with the government and avoided abuse of monopoly power. Railroads were tamed, in the USA and abroad. Food standards were maintained, in the USA and abroad. The power of robber barons and mega-financiers was controlled.

What if this time is different?

Like a true professional paranoid, I made a list of things I don't know, indeed that I can't know, but that I really need to know. I then narrowed the list down to this paranoid's two favorites:

1. Does the west, and principally the USA, continue to dominate technology and the net? Or does *Made in China 2025* achieve its objectives, allowing China to dominate the technical world? That would lead to an end of American control of the net, possibly with shared control, and in its most extreme form a shift to Chinese dominance of technology and the net.
2. Do nation-states as we know them continue to dominate the post-war World Order, with capitalism and democracy protected to varying degrees by independent nation-states? Mostly, in the west, we find that democracy, capitalism, respect for human dignity, and an absence of military conflict within the west, have all been the new normal since 1945. But technology has transformed the role of the nation-state in the past. What will the digital transformation of geopolitics look like?

My European colleagues and executive contacts see many reasons for the current US domination of the net. Venture capital was available in the USA, even for many ventures that seemed unlikely to succeed, as long as there was the possibility of an enormous upside. EU investors seemed less willing to accept the prospect of total losses. The USA had the largest single market in the developed world. The EU was a larger market, but national differences in areas like privacy limited European development. And European entrepreneurs were more concerned with focusing on what actions were *explicitly permitted,* while US entrepreneurs were focused on what opportunities they could exploit for which *no individual, or no firm had yet been convicted of any crime.* The American advantage online may now be too great for any effective European response.

The situation in China is different and it may not be too late for a Chinese response to American technological domination. Surely China could someday become the single largest market for online technology and for online applications and services. Although the USA does have an enormous advantage now, China has a plan for redressing America's advantage. China has launched *The Made in China 2025* initiative (China 2025). *China*

2025 has government backing. That means it has unlimited funding and is unlikely to be encumbered by antitrust complaints, privacy complaints, or government impediments of any kind. Their objectives go beyond ending their dependency on Western technology. Their objectives go beyond seeking parity with Western technology firms. They seek to dominate technology in a number of key sectors with the greatest economic and military significance.

Will American firms continue to dominate? Or will *China 2025* succeed? I don't know. So, in the spirit of scenario analysis, I consider both extremes.

The concept of nation-state, with its monopoly on armies and the use of force, seems like it has existed forever, but the concept of nation-state as we see it today was formalized in 1648 with the Peace of Westphalia. That's recent, almost 150 years more recent than Bavaria's formal rules on what ingredients could and could not be used in beer! The boundaries of Europe have frequently been changed by technological developments. The use of mass armies by Napoleon redrew the map of Europe. Modern technologies led to the consolidation of Germany and Italy as nations rather than as collections of small states. Modern technology allowed European nations to colonize much of Asia and Africa, and draw new maps yet again.

Does modern technology make the nation-state obsolete? I can't claim to have invented the idea. Science fiction writers have explored the idea of our current world order and its reliance upon nations being replaced by a collection of translational mega-corporations governed only by the agreements among them. Bruce Sterling's *Islands in the Net* and Neal Stephenson's *Snow Crash* both describe worlds where everything is controlled by corporations. Everything is dictated by what you can afford to buy. If you feel the need for enhanced security you purchase Singaporean citizenship, which allows you access to a franchised network of safe houses. Not surprisingly, this is a corporate offering, with no actual affiliation with the government of Singapore. Is Amazon's new move into home delivery just the first unilateral step toward subsuming the functions of government and other corporations? Will Google become a dominant telecommunications provider? Will Facebook replace traditional media, and help to render governments irrelevant by cooperating with other global mega-corporations to decide how the shells of former nations are governed? Will Baidu and Tencent provide 24/7 security monitoring of the entire planet, keeping us safe and compliant? I don't know. I didn't imagine this world, Sterling and Stephenson did. Again, in the spirit of scenario analysis, I consider both extremes.

These two extremes yield the following four scenarios, as shown in Fig. 13.1.

Fig. 13.1 Four scenarios for the future shape of the digital transformation of everything

I've named each of these scenarios after a movie, a book, or a publication that I thought was striking and would provide an easy way to remember each scenario.

- **Groundhog Day**—This scenario closely resembles the world as we know it today. The future is like the present, only more evolved in some beneficial ways. Progress has been made in the directions where I hope to see change. We understand this world, we understand how to cooperate with the EU and how to compete with China. We deal with groups that reject the Westphalian world order, like North Korea or Hezbollah and ISIS. We know how to regulate global mega-corporations, and we have updated antitrust law and privacy law. The social contract endures and America continues to dominate the net.

- **Thucydides Trap**—The *Thucydides Trap* is an article published by Harvard Professor Graham Allison, who notes that when an existing dominant power faces competition from a rising power that may supplant it, war usually ensues. When China dominates technology, the Chinese economy will supplant the US economy as the largest in the world. China's army will not only be the largest but the best equipped in the world. If nation-states remain the dominant form of global governance, war between the two largest superpowers in history becomes a terrifying possibility. Not much else matters except avoiding Armageddon.
- **Islands in the Net**—In the dystopian novel *Islands in the Net*, corporations have replaced governments. World war is unlikely. But the social contract between citizens and their government is gone as well. It is unlikely that Western governments would willingly accept a transition to this scenario, assuming that they saw it coming in time to act and to restrict the behavior of net-based global companies while they still can.
- **Made in China 2025**—As I envision this scenario, it is very similar to the world we encounter in *Islands in the Net* or *Snow Crash*, except that Chinese firms dominate. Chinese dominance means that at least initially the social values of the Chinese government will dictate many aspects of the behavior of the giant corporations that control our world. Without a doubt, this is the worst of the four scenarios for human rights, democracy, and human dignity, at least as we perceive them in the west. As noted in the discussion of the previous scenario, it is unlikely that Western governments would willingly accept a transition to this scenario, assuming that they saw it coming in time to act and to regulate internet platform operators. However, if the dominant corporations are Chinese, Western governments may be unable to control their behavior, much as the EU has had only limited success controlling the behavior of giant American firms.

What would I *like* to see? I'd like to avoid the dystopian futures, described so well by Stephenson and Sterling. As imperfect as the nation-state regime of governance has been, control by millions of voters is usually more focused on democratic rights, human dignity, and creating rule of law than boards of directors are or should be. So, I'd like to see global platform operators regulated *now*, while it is still possible to do so. I'd like to stay on the right side of the scenario grid. Likewise, I'd like to avoid the Thucydides Trap and overt military conflict with China. I'd like to see technical parity, not Chinese domination, and trade, not war.

What do I *expect* to see? If I *knew* what regulators would do, planning for the future would be simpler. I would not have needed to draw both sides of the grid. If I knew how Chinese development of their own intellectual property would proceed, and if I knew how much of Western IP China would continue to acquire by means fair or foul, I would not have needed to draw both the top and the bottom of the grid. Both alternatives to the questions I ask remain viable in my mind, with both alternative answers still possible.

These are the most important questions facing governments, citizens, and corporations today. The actions they take in responses are critical.

What kind world will we live in? And will we act to protect that world now, while the choice is still ours? Again, this chapter is not about gaining and defending competitive advantage for a single company. This chapter is about achieving and defending the greatest value for society as a whole, and about avoiding the worst outcomes for all of us.

Related Works

Chapter 1—Introduction: You Get Control When You Recognize the Patterns

For more on newly vulnerable markets and the competitive advantage of new entrants, see my chapter "Technology-Driven Environmental Shifts and the Sustainable Competitive Advantage of Previously Dominant Service Companies" in *Wharton on Dynamic Competitive Strategies*, edited by my colleagues George Day and David Reibstein, from Wiley.

I love Nobel acceptance speeches. Perhaps the best source for Herb Simon's theory of bounded rationality is "Theories of bounded rationality", in Decision and organization: A volume in honor of *Jacob Marschak* (Chapter 8) from North-Holland. But there is so much more about economic behavior more generally in his Nobel Prize paper, "Rational Decision-Making in Business Organizations", which can be found at http://www.nobelprize.org/nobel_prizes/economic-sciences/laureates/1978/simon-lecture.pdf.

For an earlier review of patterns in the deployment of innovative information systems, see my paper in JMIS, "The Power of Patterns and Pattern Recognition When Developing Information-Based Strategy", *Journal of Management Information Systems*, Vol. 27, No. 1 (2010), pp. 69–95.

© The Editor(s) (if applicable) and The Author(s),
under exclusive licence to Springer Nature Switzerland AG 2019
E. K. Clemons, *New Patterns of Power and Profit*,
https://doi.org/10.1007/978-3-030-00443-9

Chapter 2—Information Changes Everything: It's Not What You Know, It's What You Know Before Everyone Else!

Again, Nobel Lectures can be especially interesting. George Akerlof, Michael Spence, and Joseph Stiglitz shared the 2001 Nobel Prize in Economics for their work on information asymmetry. Akerlof described how information asymmetry could lead to market collapse (see "Behavioral Macroeconomics and Macroeconomic Behavior", http://www.nobelprize.org/nobel_prizes/ economic-sciences/laureates/2001/akerlof-lecture.pdf). Spence described how individuals used behavior to send signals about the quality and type (see, "Signaling in Retrospect and the Informational Structure of Markets", http://www.nobelprize.org/nobel_prizes/economic-sciences/laureates/2001/ spence-lecture.pdf). Stiglitz discussed how screening mechanisms could induce individuals to accu-rately and correctly reveal their own types (see, "Information and the Change in the Para-digm in Economics", http://www. nobelprize.org/nobel_prizes/economic-sciences/laureates/2001/stiglitz-lec-ture.pdf).

For more on information asymmetry, see *The Armchair Economist: Economics and Everyday Life*, by Steven E. Landsburg. His humor is strikingly irreverent. He has a chapter on how smoking lowers our insur-ance premiums by providing a mechanism that insurance companies can use to set prices for the rest of us. He explained, long before the data were in, that seatbelts *kill* rather than saving lives, because they shift so much of the risk away from the driver and onto helpless pedestrians. This is an extraordinarily approachable book that uses recent work in economics to address many puzzles in modern life. *The Armchair Economist* is of course available on Amazon, https://www.amazon.com/ Armchair-Economist-revised-updated-2012-ebook/dp/B00120953U/ ref=sr_1_1?ie=UTF8&qid=1532817267&sr=8-1&keywords=the+armchair+economist.

The essay "*Winners Curse*" by Richard Thaler describes the winners curse, or how parties with insufficient information may end up wishing they were not the high bidder, or wishing they had not won the rights to a customer's account, or a building site, or anything else. See https://www.amazon.com/ Winners-Curse-Paradoxes-Anomalies-Economic-ebook/dp/B007QUY3GO/ ref=sr_1_1?s=digital-text&ie=UTF8&qid=1532817365&sr=1-1& keywords=winners+curse+thaler.

Chapter 3—The Power of Framing: If You Can't Answer the Question, Turn It into a Question You Can Answer

How to Solve It: A New Aspect of Mathematical Method by George Polya is probably the granddaddy of most modern work on reframing. I can't think of a better way to motivate this book than by cribbing a couple of sentences from Polya himself. *"If you can't solve a problem, then there is an easier problem you can solve: find it."* Or consider the following: *"If you cannot solve the proposed problem, try to solve first some related problem. Could you imagine a more accessible related problem?"* There are numerous publishers for this book now, see, https://www.amazon.com/How-Solve-Aspect-Mathematical-Method-ebook/dp/B0073X0IOA/ref=sr_1_1?s=digital-text&ie=UTF8&qid=1532817463&sr=1-1&keywords=how+to+solve+it.

The Chicken from Minsk: And 99 Other Infuriatingly Challenging Brain Teasers from the Great Rus-sian Tradition of Math and Science Paperback was written by Yuri Chernyak and my friend and undergraduate advisor Robert M. Rose. Bob was the sort of advisor who liked to have students figure things out for themselves, within reason. Once when I was rewiring my car he did not exactly tell me that I was about to make a *really* serious mistake, nor did he want to interfere with my self-discovery. He simply requested a few minutes to remove his car and everything flammable from the garage. I stopped and thought for a few more minutes, found my mistake, and avoided disaster. This book is in his teaching tradition. He describes it as *"A collection of puzzles and brainteasers ranging from tricky but solvable, to excruciatingly difficult. Every problem comes with a clue or two; most are illustrated; all have answers and many include background as to how and where they originated. This book should show you how much you have forgotten since school, animate dinner parties, infuriate friends and generally bring health, wealth and a feeling of well-being to all who possess it."* Well, no. That's going a bit far. See, https://www.amazon.com/Chicken-Minsk-Infuriatingly-Challenging-Tradition/dp/B011SJE08E.

The Mathematical Recreations of Lewis Carroll: Pillow Problems and a Tangled Tale is an interesting set of mathematical exercises written by the author of *Alice in Wonderland* and *Through the Looking Glass*. That would be by Lewis Carroll, also known as C. L. Dodgson, lecturer of mathematics at Oxford. The author thought that the problems could be solved relatively easily, without pencil or paper, in the few minutes before falling asleep. The publisher calls it whimsical and amusing. I found it amusing, instructive, and much more difficult than the name implied. See, https://www.amazon.com/Mathematical-Recreations-Lewis-Carroll-Recreational/dp/0486204936/ref=sr_1_1?s=digital-text&ie=UTF8&qid=1532818888&sr=8-1&keywords=lewis+carroll+pillow+problems.

The Art of Insight in Science and Engineering: Mastering Complexity also seeks to teach reframing and problem solving. The author, Sanjoy Mahajan, does not focus on business or strategy, but his approach to reframing and mastering complexity matches nicely what we introduce in Unit 3. See, https://www.amazon.com/Art-Insight-Science-Engineering-Complexity/dp/0262526549/ref=sr_1_1?s=books&ie=UTF8&qid=1532819413&sr=1-1&keywords=The+Art+of+Insight+in+Science+and+Engineering%3A++Mastering+Complexity.

Chapter 4—Resonance Marketing in the Age of the Truly Informed Consumer: Creating Profits Through Differentiation and Delight

This is certainly not the first text to notice that consumer behavior has changed. In *Trading Up: Why Consumers Want New Luxury Goods—And How Companies Create Them*, Silverstein, Fiske, and Butman attribute the change to a pursuit of luxury, what they call *"trading up"*. See, https://www.amazon.com/Trading-Up-Consumers-Goods-Companies/dp/1591840708.

In *The Long Tail: Why the Future of Business Is Selling Less of More*, Chris Anderson describes *trading out*, which he calls the long tail. He notes that it is now possible to stock almost everything. See, https://www.amazon.com/Long-Tail-Future-Business-Selling-ebook/dp/B000JMKSE2/ref=sr_1_1?s=books&ie=UTF8&qid=1532824089&sr=1-1&keywords=long+tail. If you want an approachable academic study, see "From Niches to Riches: Anatomy of the Long Tail", by Brynjolfsson, Yu, and Smith, in *Sloan Management Review*, available at, https://sloanreview.mit.edu/article/from-niches-to-riches-anatomy-of-the-long-tail/.

For a more complete explanation of the theory of resonance marketing, see my paper in *JMIS*, "How Information Changes Consumer Behavior and How Consumer Behavior Determines Corporate Strategy", *Journal of Management Information Systems*, Vol. 25, No. 2 (2008), pp. 13–40. For indications that it actually works, see my paper with my colleagues Lorin Hitt and

Guodong Gao, "When Online Reviews Meet Hyperdifferentiation: A Study of the Craft Beer Industry", *Journal of Management Information Systems*, Vol. 23, No. 2 (2006), pp. 149–171.

You can now get a definition of *astroturfing* from almost any dictionary. If you want to get a sense of why it is a problem, see, https://www.businessinsider.com/astroturfing-grassroots-movements-2011-9.

Chapter 5—Online Brand Ambassadors and Online Brand Assassins: Master the New Role of the Chief Perception Officer

The term Chief Perception Officer has been used since at least 2011, but in the more restrictive context of contemplating the public relations implications of decisions before they are enacted. See for example, the article in *Fortune*, http://archive.fortune.com/galleries/2011/fortune/1106/gallery.csuite_executives_future.fortune/9.html. Online search reveals dozens of firms offering to help the new CPO. The concept is now mainstream, but comprehension and implementation have both lagged the explosion of online community content.

Chapter 6—Resources, Platforms, and Sustainable Competitive Advantage: How to Win and Keep on Winning

To get a thorough grounding in competitive advantage, the classic text is Michael Porter. See, https://www.amazon.com/Competitive-Advantage-Creating-Sustaining-Performance/dp/0684841460.

David Teece is the senior scholar in research on the role of resources in protecting the competitive advantage from innovation; see "Profiting from Technological Innovation: Implications for Integration, Collaboration, Licensing, and Public Policy", in *The Competitive Challenge: Strategies for Industrial Innovation and Renewal*, https://www.amazon.com/Competitive-Challenge-Strategies-Industrial-Innovation/dp/0887304028/ref=sr_1_fkmr1_1?s=books&ie=UTF8&qid=1532895675&sr=1-1-fkmr1&keywords=The+Competitive+Challenge%2C+Cambridge.

Jay Barney was another early contributor to our understanding of the role of resources in achieving and protecting competitive advantage. See "Strategic Factor Markets: Expectations, Luck and Business Strategy", *Management Science*, Vol. 32, No. 11, "Firm Resources and Sustained Competitive Advantage", *Journal of Management*, Vol. 17, No. 1, and "The Resource Based View of Strategy: Origins, Implications, and Prospects", *Special Theory Forum,* Vol. 17, No. 1. My own paper with Michael Row was an early study of the role of differences among firms as a source of sustainable competitive advantage in the deployment of information technology; see "Sustaining IT Advantage: The Role of Structural Differences", *MIS Quarterly*, Vol. 15, No. 3.

For more on platform competition in two sided markets you can read the work of two serious economists, Rochet and Tirole (2003). "Platform Competition in Two-Sided Markets", *Journal of the European Economic Association*, Vol. 1, No. 4, and "Two-Sided Markets: A Progress Report", *The RAND Journal of Economics*, Vol. 37, No. 3.

Work by Eisenmann, Parker, and Van Alstyne focuses more on strategy and is more accessible; see "Platform Envelopment", *Strategic Management Journal*, Vol. 32, No. 12 and "Opening Platforms: How, When and Why?", *Platforms, Markets and Innovation.* Parker and Van Alstyne also address platform effects in information product design, "Two-Sided Network Effects: A Theory of Information Product Design", *Management Science*, Vol. 51, No. 10.

Chapter 7—Understanding the Power of Third Party Payer Businesses and Online Gateways

An approachable, non-technical analyses of MP3PPs and abuse of power, and the continued relevance today even in an online environment, can be found in two articles I wrote for the *Huffington Post.* "Third Party Payer Systems: The Most Significant Regulatory Problem in the Online World?", http://www.huffingtonpost.com/eric-k-clemons/post_2164_b_888842. html and "Why Is There Still Litigation in Third Party Payer Distribution Systems in Air Travel", http://www.huffingtonpost.com/eric-k-clemons/ why-is-there-still-litiga_b_887252.html. For early papers on the dangers of search engines engaging in platform envelopment strategy, which predates any formal complaints, see "The Real and Inevitable Harm From

Vertical Integration of Search Engine Providers into Sales and Distribution", http://www.huffingtonpost.com/eric-k-clemons/the-department-of-justice_b_851079.html. A For an early analysis of MP3PPs and Google's claim that there is adequate competition, see "One Click Away? Maybe and Maybe Not", http://www.huffingtonpost.com/eric-k-clemons/google-one-click-away_b_928009.html.

Chapter 8—The Continuing Power of Third Party Payer Businesses

An approachable, non-technical analyses of MP3PPs and abuse of power, and the continued relevance today even in an online environment, can be found in two articles I wrote for the *Huffington Post*. "Third Party Payer Systems: The Most Significant Regulatory Problem in the Online World?", http://www.huffingtonpost.com/eric-k-clemons/post_2164_b_888842.html and "Why Is There Still Litigation in Third Party Payer Distribution Systems in Air Travel", http://www.huffingtonpost.com/eric-k-clemons/why-is-there-still-litiga_b_887252.html.

Chapter 9—Power and the Potential for the Abuse of Power in Online Gateway Systems: An Analysis of Google

Readers interested in the history of business regulation in America are referred to *Prophets of Regulation,* by Thomas K. McCraw, https://www.amazon.com/Prophets-Regulation-Charles-Francis-Brandeis/dp/0674716086. Readers interested in the regulation of telecommunications and high tech more generally, from AT&T to the present, are referred to *The Master Switch*, by Tim Wu, https://www.amazon.com/Master-Switch-Rise-Information-Empires/dp/0307390993/ref=sr_1_1?s=books&ie=UTF8&qid=1532896729&sr=1-1&keywords=master+switch.

To follow the ongoing disputes about Google and abuse of privacy, Google and abuse of gateway power, or Google and abuse of platform envelopment, just Bing <<EU Google Judgments>> or <<EU Google Decisions>> and you can follow the action.

Chapter 10—Scenario Analysis and Managing Strategic Ambiguity: How to Remember Future Events, Before They Actually Occur!

Modern scenario analysis, of the form we have described here, originated at Royal Dutch Shell under the direction of Pierre Wack. The earliest publications on scenarios, and still the best, are his two groundbreaking articles. See "Scenarios: Uncharted Waters Ahead," *Harvard Business Review*, Vol. 63, No. 5, and "Scenarios: Shooting the Rapids," *Harvard Business Review*, Vol. 63, No. 6.

Wack's successors at Royal Dutch Shell, have continued his work and have continued the development of scenario analysis. See *Scenarios: The Art of Strategic Conversation*, by Kees van der Heijden, https://www.amazon.com/Scenarios-Conversation-Kees-van-Heijden/dp/0470023686/ref=sr_1_1?s=books&ie=UTF8&qid=1532898179&sr=1-1&keywords=The+Art+of+Strategic+Conversation%2C+by+Kees+van and *The Art of the Long View*, by Peter Schwartz, https://www.amazon.com/Art-Long-View-Planning-Uncertain/dp/0385267320/ref=pd_bxgy_14_img_2?_encoding=UTF8&pd_rd_i=0385267320&pd_rd_r=8XKTYA8WH5XNY6WHJZ0H&pd_rd_w=XJG5Y&pd_rd_wg=oyanJ&psc=1&refRID=8XKTYA8WH5XNY6WHJZ0H.

Paul Schoemaker's work is stylistically and philosophically most similar to my use of scenarios. See his "Scenario Planning: A Tool for Strategic Thinking," in *Sloan Management Review*, https://sloanreview.mit.edu/article/scenario-planning-a-tool-for-strategic-thinking/.

I have written previously about the use of scenarios to guide planning for information technology. See my article, "Using Scenario Analysis to Manage the Strategic Risks of Re-engineering," in *Sloan Management Review*, https://sloanreview.mit.edu/article/using-scenario-analysis-to-manage-the-strategic-risks-of-reengineering/.

Readers curious about why Chinese consumers might value western brands more than local Chinese products are invited to Google <<melamine scandal>>, <<clenbuterol scandal>>, or <<china tainted meat scandal>> to understand why Chinese consumers might prefer foreign brands.

Chapter 11—Examining the Wide Range of Business Models Currently in Use in Online Businesses: How to Understand a New Business Using Existing Framework

Chapter 12—Information Changes Everything: Implications for Society

Fake news is evolving so quickly, reactions to it are building so quickly, and Facebook is scrambling to develop a coherent response. It's hard to single out any single source on fake news and Brexit or fake news and the 2016 elections. Just search and look at the latest articles you find. This is the earliest example I could find of an attempt at a regulatory response, "*Fake News a Democratic Crisis for UK, MPs Warn*", https://www.bbc.com/news/technology-44967650.

Price discrimination has been well studied by serious economists. See, the Wikipedia article for a more complete taxonomy of forms of price discrimination and for numerous references, https://en.wikipedia.org/wiki/Price_discrimination. For a discussion of how this is already emerging online, see Ben Schiller's "First Degree Price Discrimination Using Big Data", benjaminshiller.com/images/First_Degree_PD_Using_Big_Data_Jan_18,_2014.pdf.

If you want to explore both Utopian and dysfunctional alternative views of our shared digital future, and why it is necessary to manage technology's impacts on society, see Jaron Lanier's *You Are Not a Gadget: A Manifesto*, https://www.amazon.com/You-Are-Gadget-Jaron-Lanier-ebook/dp/B002ZFXUBO/ref=sr_1_1?s=books&ie=UTF8&qid=1532900477&sr=1-1&keywords=you+are+not+a+gadget, *Who Owns the Future*, https://www.amazon.com/Who-Owns-Future-Jaron-Lanier-ebook/dp/B008J2AEY8/ref=sr_1_1?s=books&ie=UTF8&qid=1532900551&sr=1-1&keywords=who+owns+the+future, and https://www.amazon.com/Arguments-Deleting-Social-Media-Accounts-ebook/dp/B079DTVVG8/ref=sr_1_3?s=books&ie=UTF8&qid=1532900551&sr=1-3&keywords=who+owns+the+future.

"The Dark Side of the Sharing Economy ... and How to Lighten It", by Arvind Malhotra and Marshall Van Alstyne explores some of the issues we have discussed in the Chapter. See *Communications of the ACM*, November 2014, Vol. 57, No. 11, pp. 24–27. My own take on regulating platforms like Uber and Airbnb is available at "Regulating Online Platforms: Where, Not Whether, to Draw the Line", https://www.huffingtonpost.com/entry/regulating-online-platfor_b_10751960.html.

And if you want additional readings on the complexity of achieving universal health care in the presence of increasingly complete information, see my article, "Why Is Health Care so Complicated? An Information Economics Prof Navigates the Current Confusion", in the *Huffington Post*, https://www.huffingtonpost.com/entry/why-is-health-care-so-complicated-an-information-economics_us_58d43da2e4b0c0980ac0e44c.

Climate Change is complicated, but the importance of making a safe decision should be clear. For a non-technical analysis of the problem, see my article in the Huffington Post, "Pascal's Wager and Global Climate Change: Hedging Your Bet When the Cost of Error Is Too High", https://www.huffingtonpost.com/entry/pascals-wager-and-global-climate-change-hedging_us_59c944c3e4b0f2df5e83b066.

I didn't want to spend too much space inside the article attacking any firm. Readers curious about Google's abuse of gateway power to harm consumers by facilitating the import of illegal drugs can see the following DoJ press release: https://www.justice.gov/opa/pr/google-forfeits-500-million-generated-online-ads-prescription-drug-sales-canadian-online. Readers interested in understanding the EU's record-breaking (at the time) fine of Google for abuse of gateway power to harm competitors can see, https://www.nytimes.com/2017/06/27/technology/eu-google-fine.html. Readers who want to read the original text of the EU's press release concerning its (current) record-breaking fine for Google's abuse of platform power can see, http://europa.eu/rapid/press-release_IP-18-4581_en.htm. Readers interested in understanding Google's hacking Apple users' devices to get private information can see, https://www.businessinsider.com/google-tracking-apple-users-2012-2. Readers interested in understanding how Google tapped into WiFi systems all across the world can read the article in *The New York Times*, https://www.nytimes.com/2010/05/16/technology/16google.html, while readers interested in Google's fine for obstructing the WiFi investigation can see, https://www.nytimes.com/2013/03/13/technology/google-pays-fine-over-street-view-privacy-breach.html. Readers interested in my ongoing analyses of transgressions can see the sequence of six pieces I wrote for Huffington with titles starting with "Say it ain't so, Joe", detailing various abuses. Or you can always search for your own. When searching for Google misbehavior I find it better to search using Bing.

Chapter 13—Epilog: What Could Go Really, Really, Wrong?

To understand how our world looks now, and the major changes to international world order that are already occurring, I would recommend *World Order* by Henry Kissinger, available from Amazon at https://www. amazon.com/World-Order-Henry-Kissinger-ebook/dp/B00INIXVMK/ ref=sr_1_1?ie=UTF8&qid=1532803968&sr=8-1&keywords=henry+kissinger+world+order.

To really understand what China plans to achieve, I would read some of the articles about *Made in China 2025*. You can start with analyses from the *Council on Foreign Relations*, the *Washington Post*, or *Bloomberg*. Or you can search yourself and find more recent references than those available when I wrote the final chapter.

- https://www.cfr.org/blog/why-does-everyone-hate-made-china-2025
- https://www.washingtonpost.com/news/monkey-cage/wp/2018/05/03/ what-is-made-in-china-2025-and-why-is-it-a-threat-to-trumps-trade-goals/?noredirect=on&utm_term=.a10549b6d92d
- https://www.bloomberg.com/news/articles/2018-04-10/how-made-in-china-2025-frames-trump-s-trade-threats-quicktake.

Howard French's recent book, *Everything Under the Heavens: How the Past Helps Shape China's Push for Global Power*, provides an excellent summary of China's history, and of how that history provides an understanding of China's present ambitions, https://www.amazon.com/ Everything-Under-Heavens-Chinas-Global-ebook/dp/B01HA4JUKE/ ref=sr_1_1?s=books&ie=UTF8&qid=1532964986&sr=1-1&keywords= under+heaven+china.

And to understand just how alien future scenarios can feel, science fiction writes provide a much more complete and engaging description than I can. Start with Bruce Sterling's *Islands in the Net* and Neal Stephenson's *Snow Crash*, both available at Amazon.

- https://www.amazon.com/Islands-Net-Bruce-Sterling-ebook/dp/B00PD-DKVXK/ref=sr_1_1?ie=UTF8&qid=1532804505&sr=8-1&keywords=islands+in+the+net
- https://www.amazon.com/Islands-Net-Bruce-Sterling-ebook/dp/B00PD-DKVXK/ref=sr_1_1?ie=UTF8&qid=1532804505&sr=8-1&keywords=islands+in+the+net.

Index

A

AAdvantage 120

accelerator 165–168

access 8, 13, 15, 18, 20, 48, 55, 66, 98, 102, 106, 108, 113, 115, 116, 118, 120, 122, 127, 129, 133, 146, 147, 156, 158, 176, 183, 189, 191–193, 202, 207, 210, 215, 224, 230, 241

advertising 36, 59–61, 64, 66, 78, 79, 82, 84, 88, 108, 127, 129, 137, 143, 153, 191–195, 207, 208, 222, 226, 231

Affordable Care Act 217

aggregator 55, 213, 223, 227

agricultural revolution 194

AI vii

Airbnb 163, 192, 200, 202, 228, 232, 233

airlines 40, 42, 49, 50, 52–55, 73, 82, 99–101, 103, 108–113, 116, 119, 122, 126–129, 151, 152, 180

Akerlof, George 11, 22, 23, 246

Al Jazeera 196, 237

Allison, Graham 243

allocative efficiency 6, 223, 225

Alphabet 147

Amazon 3, 40, 67, 78, 87, 96, 97, 102, 103, 105, 128, 130, 131, 137, 186, 189, 194, 239, 241

American Airlines 49, 109, 112, 113, 120, 131

American Express 51, 117, 121

Amtrak 154

Anderson, Chris 248

Android 130, 132, 136, 137, 146, 148, 150, 157, 158, 160, 207, 208, 236

Anheuser Busch 67, 76

anonymity 231

antimonopoly 136

antitrust 103, 136, 241, 242

Apollo 42, 50, 100, 110–113, 119, 122, 126, 128, 130, 143, 147, 148, 151, 152, 154, 160

Apple 3, 98, 103, 130, 137, 146, 183, 184, 198, 231

Apple Pay 122

Art of Inquiry 43

astroturfing 78, 83

asymmetric regulation 17

© The Editor(s) (if applicable) and The Author(s), under exclusive licence to Springer Nature Switzerland AG 2019
E. K. Clemons, *New Patterns of Power and Profit*,
https://doi.org/10.1007/978-3-030-00443-9

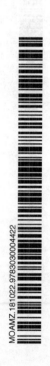